The New Majority

The New

Toward a Popular Progressiv

Yale University Press   New Haven and London

Edited by Stanley B. Greenberg and Theda Skocpol

Majority

Politics

Designed by Sonia L. Scanlon.
Set in Bulmer type by à la page, New Haven, Connecticut.
Printed in the United States of America by Royal Book,
Norwich, Connecticut.

Library of Congress Catalog Card Number 97-61147.

ISBN 0-300-07341-0

A catalogue record for this book is available from the
British Library.

The paper in this book meets the guidelines for perma-
nence and durability of the Committee on Production
Guidelines for Book Longevity of the Council on
Library Resources.

10   9   8   7   6   5   4   3   2   1

In memory of Robert F. Kennedy

Contents

Preface

In the winter of 1995, the two of us, Stan Greenberg and Theda Skocpol, were having lunch at a restaurant in Washington, D.C. We didn't know each other well then, and soon we were comparing our personal political histories: "Which candidate did you support in 1968?" "Robert Kennedy." "Me, too."

Not only did we discover that each of us had supported RFK rather than Eugene McCarthy, but, more important, we also discovered our mutual reliance on RFK as a kind of touchstone for what is best in the Democratic Party. Before his life was tragically cut short by assassination, we agreed, RFK had offered the best hope for an inclusive Democratic Party focused on the values and needs of working Americans. He was one of the few leaders prepared to show the way forward in the wake of the civil rights revolution. The year 1968 was a fateful turning point, an excruciating moment of lost opportunity for our party. Beloved by white Roman Catholics and African-Americans alike, RFK had started down a path that was more promising than those actually taken by Democrats from the late 1960s through the 1980s.

Although we had both earned our doctoral degrees at Harvard University some twenty-five years before, we had not met back then. We eventually learned about each other through our writings, but we did not actually meet until November 1993, when we attended a dinner discussion at the White House. Now, a year and a half later, we were meeting over lunch to dissect what had happened to the Clinton health care plan. Theda was gathering material for a book about the politics of the failed health security effort of 1993–94; Stan had done polling for and given political advice to the White House during that time. We argued about White House strategy and the role of public opinion and polling, about which we never did entirely agree. The lunchtime conversation then drifted to the central preoccupation of progressives in the wake of the sweeping Republican congressional victories of the fall of 1994: What had happened to the Democratic Party? And what would it take to build a new majority?

The New Majority project began with these lunchtime questions. We decided to pull together a group of publicly minded intellectuals and political strategists dedicated to both analyzing the challenges that Democrats needed to address and also articulating a moral vision and practical politics for building a new popular majority. Conservative Republicans had forged a new strategy after their disastrous defeat in 1964. Progressive Democrats could do the same thing three decades later. We drew up a preliminary list of names and agreed to make some calls. Every person we contacted responded warmly—even those who had supported McCarthy in 1968. It was time, everyone seemed to know, for new thinking.

Over the next year and a half, from six to twelve people met every month or so for wide-ranging discussions. People did this for love, not money, fitting three-hour meetings held in Washington, New York, or Boston into extraordinarily busy schedules. In addition to the two of us, the working group of the New Majority eventually included Bob Borosage, Alan Brinkley, Marc Caplan, Michael Dawson, Jeff Faux, Roger Hickey, Ira Katznelson, Bob Kuttner, John Mollenkopf, Miles Rapoport, Paul Starr, Ruy Teixeira, Margaret Weir, and William Julius Wilson.

We had spirited, even heated, discussions. Sometimes we surprised ourselves about how much we shared; sometimes we despaired about issues that we could not talk through to a happy conclusion. But step-by-step, we came to a shared belief that this was a period of opportunity for progressives. We did not delude ourselves about the immediate political situation, which is anything but a happy one for progressive Democrats. But what distinguished this band of scholars and activists was a determination to understand the larger changes that were unfolding and to look ahead and explore the political openings. We came to a shared sense of possibility.

The group decided to produce a book that would first be debated and shaped by a New Majority conference, an event that would assemble a broader array of authors and discussants to help chart a popular progressive course for the future. We were determined to produce, not a collection for academics only, but a manifesto that would spark conversations, among widening circles of activists and fellow citizens, about the future of the Democratic Party.

Tina Weiner and John Covell at Yale University Press had enough faith in our undertaking to work with us and arrange an advance to assist us in funding the New Majority conference, which was planned for Airlie House in Virginia on January 10–12, 1997. Robert Borosage and Roger Hickey of the Campaign for America's Future helped us to organize the conference, whose timing was intended to seize a moment. Through November 1996, we knew, people would be preoccupied with fighting the election and assessing the new balance of forces between the parties. But we expected that a good time for stocktaking and longer-term thinking would come around the time of the second inauguration of William Jefferson Clinton. As it happened, our hunch turned out to be correct. The 1996 election rekindled hope among Democrats. But it left plenty to think about and to build upon. And the more than thirty civically engaged scholars, activists, unionists, and political strategists who gathered at Airlie House were ready for several days of intense discussion and debate about the future. Amy Lubchansky of Greenberg Quinlan Research did remarkable work, getting everyone there, papers in hand.

The usual course of events following a conference is a several-year delay before a scattershot miscellany of articles finally appears. But the New Majority authors committed themselves to an unusually disciplined course. Within two months of the January 1997 conference, essays were revised and edited for individual clarity and collective coherence. Because all the authors cared enough to work quickly on passionate statements for a broad readership, this book came together in a little over six months.

We are very grateful to our New Majority colleagues—those who participated in the group discussions of 1995 and 1996, those who debated ideas at the Airlie House conference, and, of course, those who contributed essays to this book. We all look forward to working with many other progressives across the country to further debate the ideas, values, policies, and political strategies needed to build a new Democratic popular majority in America. A New Majority must be built, not for the sake of political victory alone, but for making America a place of opportunity, security, and justice for all working families in the new century. Realizing this goal will require clear thinking and concrete action, and we are reenergized for the work ahead.

—Stanley B. Greenberg and Theda Skocpol

A Politics for Our Time

Theda Skocpol and

Stanley B. Greenberg

D emocrats can build a new majority in national politics by championing the needs and values of American families striving for a better life in the face of unsettling changes. While daily headlines may trumpet the partisan bickering in Washington and the public cynicism everywhere else, most people yearn for a responsive government that will take their side and help them cope with unprecedented transformations in the economy and in the lives of families. People want to tame and channel changes that may threaten the family, exacerbate racial conflicts, and separate the rich from all others. Most Americans hope for a stronger national community that supports working families, furthering security and opportunity for all.

But American institutions are faltering in the face of today's challenges. Leaders have failed to tell a convincing story about the economic and social changes of our time, and politicians have not explained how Americans can work together for a better future. They have mastered the rhetoric of the family but pursue policies that leave real families ever more on their own. That is why the Democratic Party has a historic opportunity to lead the way toward a renewal of the nation's social compact and a revitalization of our democracy—but only if Democrats determinedly choose to take the side of regular people on the job, at home, and in the community.

This book argues for such a popular progressive politics. We urge the Democratic Party, our party, to move beyond outmoded debates among factions to embrace a new synthesis of cultural common sense with effective measures to support and empower regular citizens in workplaces, families, and shared social institutions. By taking this course, Democrats can become the moral voice of all American families coping with times of challenge and change.

Beyond Failure and Stalemate

A new progressive politics? Let's face it, many of the best minds consider this an implausible scenario at best. The Democrats in Congress fell short in 1996, and the party's reelected president suppresses progressive impulses with a public discourse about little more than balancing the federal budget. We see the immediate difficulties but are not blinded by them, any more than conservative Republicans were blinded in the 1960s. With farsighted persistence, they moved forward to transform their own party and then the country. Now it is time for Democrats to renew themselves, because this is a period of opportunity for a popularly oriented progressive politics.

We understand why people on our side of the political spectrum are cautious. In 1993 President Bill Clinton took office promising a "new beginning." The centerpiece domestic initiative of his first term was a comprehensive health security proposal, dedicated to including all Americans in "health care that is always there, health care that can never be taken away." A victory for this effort might well have renewed popular support for a progressive Democratic Party. But Clinton's proposal was awkwardly designed and fell victim to divisions among Democrats and concerted attacks from the right (Skocpol 1996a). In late 1994, health reform went down to crushing defeat in Congress, amidst rising public disillusionment with both Democrats and the federal government, which they appeared to control. In November 1994, many voters who previously supported Democrats stayed home, and a conservative surge swept away many Democratic officeholders. Republicans won elections in dozens of states and gained control of the House of Representatives for the first time in four decades.

Many of the newly triumphant Republicans were conservatives fiercely hostile to government above the local level (Balz and Brownstein 1996). As he took up the gavel as Speaker of the House, the militant Newt Gingrich of Georgia pronounced an end to the New Deal, the Great Society, and the "liberal Democratic welfare state." He promised to inaugurate a conservative "opportunity society," in which individual Americans would be expected to get ahead on their own, each person doing his or her best to ride waves of technological innovation and globally driven economic transformation (Gingrich 1984, 1995).

At first Democrats were visibly stunned. And progressives only slowly regained their confidence. The titles of the first books designed to rally the faithful against the right-wing onslaught were strikingly equivocal. *They Only Look Dead* proclaimed E. J. Dionne (1996), in a book predicting a progressive revival. *The Party's Not Over,* echoed Jeff Faux (1996), in his call for a fighting Democratic Party led by labor-oriented populists. Although both of these books were clarion calls for renewal, their titles indicated less than full confidence that a bright progressive future could actually be expected.

Of course, there have been few recent signs of intellectual ferment on the right, either. Back in 1993 and 1994, right-wing manifestos proliferated, but of late the best-seller shelves have held few new works by confident conservatives. Indeed, there have been few political titles of any kind. The exceptions have been memoirs such as those by two retired television anchormen, Walter Cronkite and David Brinkley. The impression one gets in the bookstores is that America's best political days are behind it.

The 1996 election seemed to confirm the national frustration with politics. There was no full Democratic rebound and not much national political clarification, either—not during the campaign, and not after the election. Despite sustained efforts by environmentalists, pro-choice groups, and the newly militant American Federation of Labor and Congress of Industrial Organizations (AFL-CIO), Democrats fell short of ousting most of the Republicans who won in 1994. To be sure, Gingrich's conservative "revolution" met its Thermidor, as millions of voters repudiated right-wing attacks on Medicare, Medicaid, federal education programs, and national environmental safeguards (Teixeira 1996). But fewer citizens turned up at the polls than in any election since 1924. The Democratic president, Bill Clinton, won reelection to a second term but with less than a majority of the votes cast, even though the country was experiencing a strong national economic recovery.

On the way to his incomplete victory, President Clinton (1996) pronounced an end to "the era of big government," and immediately after the election he seemed to distance himself more than ever from the Democratic Party. Liberals were not appointed to any leading spots in the second Clinton administration. Along with chastened Republican congressional leaders, the president made gestures in the direction of a "bipartisan" elite agenda—embracing federal budget balancing and cuts in the very social programs, such as Medicare, whose defense by Democrats had helped to propel the president's reelection. Both the Clinton administration and Republican leader Newt Gingrich soon found themselves mired in ethics scandals and disputes about the burgeoning role of big money in U.S. politics. The bipartisan budget compromises meant to rescue the reputations of both parties were attacked as empty by both the left and the right. Neither the second-term Democratic president nor the reelected Republican Congress has offered any strong diagnosis of national problems or any bold prescriptions for moving the nation forward.

Rather than ushering in a new progressive era, the current period seems to reflect the exhaustion of political forces that have battled to an inclusive and ugly draw. But Democrats and progressives should take a second look and recognize that this bipartisan embrace is also a moment of palpable opportunity for a new popularly oriented politics.

During the decade of the 1990s, we have witnessed a shift of the electoral landscape. Democrats have reestablished their ability to have a conversation with millions of voters in working middle-class families. At the same time, these working Americans are increasingly concerned about being alone before the forces of change and about issues that require a response from sensible democratic government. They are more and more worried about right-wing assaults on regulations and social spending, skeptical about elite pressures to dismantle "entitlements" that are crucial supports for everyone's retirement security, and disappointed by those Democrats who can't think beyond balanced budgets and the priorities of privileged contributors. Among most of the American people, a set of concerns amenable to a popular progressive politics is taking shape.

The Reagan Democrats Are Listening Again

Taken together, the elections of 1992 and 1996 marked the last gasp of Reagan Republicanism (even though conservative Republicans and many conservative Democrats may be the last to notice its expiration). The threat and achievement of Reagan Republicanism came from its capacity to win over a majority of working-class voters. After the late 1960s and especially during the 1980s, working middle-class voters—those without college degrees in families earning $30,000 to $50,000 a year—became an integral part of the Republican national majority, particularly in presidential contests (Greenberg 1996c). But in the two presidential elections of the 1990s, Democrat Bill Clinton has won the attention and support of this crucial segment of the electorate, especially its female members.

In 1996, for the first time since Ronald Reagan insinuated his conservative Republican message into the lives of working families, a Democratic presidential candidate contested the votes of married women and married mothers. Added to longstanding Democratic majorities among single women and households headed by one parent, this development produced a gigantic women's vote in favor of Bill Clinton. In addition, like his Republican predecessor, who created a "Reagan generation" in the younger reaches of the electorate, Clinton may have created a "Clinton generation" newly oriented to the Democrats. Voters under thirty are now the age cohort most likely to vote Democratic. This development opens many possibilities for the future.

The Clinton legacy does not include many new progressive initiatives. But along with congressional Democrats, the president did stall the Republican attack on the social insurance and education programs on which so many people depend. And he has at least opened up a new conversation about the pressures on American families. Our party is now getting a hearing from millions of working Americans who were until recently skeptical or downright dismissive of Democrats as they thought they knew them. Whatever the limits of Clinton's stands on particular policy issues, an overall transformation in the relationship between Democrats and working middle-class Americans may be his most propitious legacy for a future popular progressive politics.

Through two successive presidential campaigns, Bill Clinton has skillfully articulated popular themes. He has called for broad economic growth, more access to health care, and the transformation of welfare programs into supports for work and responsible parenthood. He has championed the causes of punishing and preventing crime, reforming schools and expanding educational opportunity, trimming taxes on the working middle class, and strengthening the hands of parents and the civic capacities of communities. Voters have noticed—and approved. They have not seen very much concrete change, except the stabilization of the economy and job growth, but they have taken note of the new Democratic priorities. By articulating these themes so successfully, Clinton has inspired many other Democrats to offer similar messages.

Together, Clinton and other Democrats have at least provisionally laid to rest the specter of a party obsessed with elitist cultural liberalism or aid to the very poor alone. They have helped the Democratic Party speak for and to mainstream America. This makes it possible for Democrats to do again, and more inclusively this time, what the party partially accomplished during the New Deal era: uniting middle-class and less-privileged working families in a broad, winning electoral alliance. This is what we mean by popular progressive politics.

The Combined Economic and Family Squeeze

Our elections now highlight public worries about economic and family changes that are remaking American life at the end of the twentieth century. The U.S. economy in the first decades after World War II was an engine of shared prosperity, a tide that lifted middle class and poor alike, ensuring some measure of opportunity, rising wages, and security to most blue- and white-collar families (Danziger and Gottschalk 1995). But since 1973, each wave of national economic expansion has brought heightened inequality and spreading insecurity for most working people. Although a privileged minority at the top is flourishing as never before, most working Americans—especially the three-quarters of employees who lack four-year college degrees— find themselves working longer hours without getting significant raises. Families cannot keep up with the bills; people worry about what the future may bring—when earners age, sickness strikes, and children need to obtain higher education to have any prospect of success and security in tomorrow's world.

As employers cut back or eliminate social benefits for employees, and as more and more Americans work for small businesses that do not offer such benefits, more people also worry about employment security and holding on to pensions and health care coverage that are vital to them and their families.

At the same time, Americans hear opinion leaders telling them that their hard-won public social protections, Social Security and Medicare, may soon be dismantled, too. Millions of working Americans feel that they are treading water on their own, abandoned by employers and political leaders who no longer adhere to a shared social contract (Greenberg 1996b).

While the American economy leaves more and more people at risk, a family squeeze is happening along with the economic squeeze. Marriages and child-rearing families are more fragile and face increasing stresses (Bronfrenbrenner et al. 1996, chap. 4; Rubin 1994; Hewlett 1991). Nowadays, fathers and mothers are less likely to get married or to stay married if they do wed. Nearly one-half of all American kids grow up with just one parent during all or some of their childhoods. For millions of men and women, the struggle to bridge duties at home and at work is harder—and more lonely—than ever before. Single parents, mostly mothers, must care for kids without a daily partner while, in most cases, holding down inadequately paid jobs with few, if any, pension or health benefits.

Families with two married parents usually do better than single-parent families, both economically and in terms of the well-being of children (McLanahan and Sandefur 1994). Yet most two-parent families must juggle parental duties against the demands of two or three jobs. Working parents feel pressed to come up with the new reserves of time and energy that they need to educate children for an ever more demanding economic future, while guiding them through the shoals of a culture dominated by messages of libertine commercialism. Whether families have one or two parents, they often have to worry about inadequate schools and unsafe neighborhoods. Americans today, as James Garbarino (1995) has aptly put it, face the challenge of "raising children in a socially toxic environment," because economic and social conditions alike make effective parenting daunting.

The challenge for progressives today is to address simultaneous changes in the economy and in families that leave people struggling on their own. People need their families to help manage the economic and cultural changes that swirl around them, but many families are in trouble. During the 1996 campaign, no single party or candidate presented a full overview of the real-life pressures that America's families are facing. But various people did bring fragments of the picture into focus. Newspapers dramatized corporate downsizing and the profound insecurities that it has brought to many employees and their families. The insurgent populist Republican primary candidate, Pat Buchanan, voiced worker resentments about insecurity and declining living standards in a time of economic globalization. Implausibly, as it turned out, even Republican presidential candidate Bob Dole tried to dramatize the economic squeeze on the working middle class. Dole blamed taxes, while other more credible voices—such as that of John Sweeney (1996), the bold new leader of the AFL-CIO—proclaimed that "America needs a raise."

Seeking reelection, Bill Clinton said a little bit of everything. But he spoke with special eloquence about the demands of work and education in an era of technological and global economic transformations on the scale of the industrial revolution. Clinton also dramatized cultural and economic stresses on families and championed practical support for parents. By articulating a "Families First" agenda, the Democratic Congressional Campaign (1996) also took up the cause of opportunity and social supports for working families.

Of late, then, many voices have contributed to an economically populist and family-oriented public debate, articulating a new state of mind that, we believe, popularly oriented Democrats are uniquely positioned to champion. Most Americans in our time are struggling to make a better life in a rapidly changing economy and society. They respond to a politics about security for families and opportunity and social responsibility for individuals. They are resentful of a politics that is cozy with the glamorous and most privileged and indifferent to the new uncertainties facing everyday families. In short, they respond to politicians who address the challenges that regular people face and who suggest substantial ways to improve life for working Americans in the workplace, the home, and the community.

Conservative Bankruptcy, Democratic Opportunity

The "conservative revolution" has been unable to deal with the real-world economic and family squeeze most Americans now face. With formidable resources of moral certitude, big money, and grass-roots organization among evangelical Christians, gun owners, and small-business people, conservative Republicans are not about to go away. They will remain a serious political threat to Democrats and progressives. But developments in 1995 and 1996 demonstrated the hollowness of much of contemporary conservatism, which proclaims its concern for families and communities yet sponsors unconstrained economic forces and extreme policies that would in fact further undermine the integrity of actual families and groups in civil society.

In 1994, Newt Gingrich and his insurgent Republican allies seized the Congress of the United States, promising to dismantle much of the federal government and throw responsibility back to localities and the individual. For the right-wing Republicans determined to "renew American civilization," aloneness is a kind of virtue, since it unfetters market forces and puts the spotlight on liberated individuals who could—and should—make their own way, sink or swim. But while an attack on government in the name of individual freedom may have been useful as a battering ram against entrenched congressional Democrats who had failed to meet popular expectations during 1993 and 1994, such knee-jerk antigovernmentalism became a heavy burden when Republicans actually took legislative charge. In a reckless quest to slash taxes and the federal budget all at once, the Gingrich Republicans took indiscriminate aim at "the welfare state," planning huge cuts in Medicare, school lunches, educational loans, and environmental protections as well as cuts and restructurings in programs for the poor.

By late 1995, the Republican revolutionaries discovered that most Americans don't really hate many parts of big government. On the contrary, people support broad public measures that enhance opportunity and security for ordinary working families. Republican congressional candidates survived, barely, in 1996—but only because they called off their ideological assault in the waning months of the 104th Congress. Just before it had to face the voters, the Republican Congress actually enacted new social protections, such as the Kennedy-Kassebaum legislation to make employer-provided health insurance somewhat more portable, and new economic regulations, such as the increase in the national minimum wage. Republicans sensed, however reluctantly, that people don't really want to be all alone, abandoned by their government, in the face of today's simultaneous economic and family squeeze. Those committed to undoing these social supports and regulations and compounding life's uncertainties are increasingly viewed as part of the problem.

Recent developments have, in short, opened the door for a reinvigorated Democratic Party. But the Democratic Party will be able to rebuild its moral authority and electoral clout only if its thinkers and activists devise a new popular progressive project, one that respects and learns from all the political trends of recent years.

To deepen support among working American families now that the Reagan Democrats are listening again, the party must speak to the full range of economic, cultural, and family problems of our time, moving beyond any mechanical opposition of "values" to "economics" (as in B. Wattenberg 1996b). Democrats must find ways to bring the working middle class and the working poor together, healing racial divisions by defining new common ground across white, African-American, Latino, and Asian-American working families—all of whom face many shared dilemmas in the present era.

The Democratic Party must also move beyond fruitless wars over big government vaguely defined. Merely preserving existing federal programs cannot be the mission of reinvigorated Democrats; the focus must be on doing what really works for families and communities. But neither can the party usefully engage in a reflexive antigovernmentalism that always seeks to substitute market competition and unrealistic individual choices for economic regulation and shared public protections. A winning popular progressive strategy will learn from the existing Democratic right and left alike, while at the same time going well beyond what any existing faction has as yet said or done.

New Democrats and Working Families

Democrats cannot merely swallow the policy nostrums proffered by today's Democratic Leadership Council (DLC) and its associated think tank, the Progressive Policy Institute (PPI) (W. Marshall 1997). As we see it, the DLC and the PPI are veering off course these days, refusing to take new steps to build on the responsiveness toward the everyday concerns of working and middle-class Americans that many New Democrats originally championed.

When the New Democrat movement was launched in the 1980s, it argued, with considerable justification, that the party was not steadily in touch with the day-to-day lives of many working Americans—especially not with their worries about crime and deteriorating schools and neighborhoods and their desire to reinforce values of work and parental responsibility. Pay attention to issues of family and community integrity, New Democrats urged party candidates—first those running for the presidency, and then many seeking election to Congress. By now, most Democrats have taken this advice to heart. Significant differences may indeed remain among Democrats over *how* to do many of these things—including how best to move people from welfare to work and how to improve the public schools that are substandard. But virtually all Democrats now stress strong measures to contain crime (which, after all, hurts poor families more than any others). Most Democrats call for work rather than welfare, and most want to improve educational quality as well as further educational opportunity. The original New Democrats have gotten their message across.

Given this accomplishment, how ironic it is that leaders of the 1990s Democratic Leadership Council are distancing themselves from the very Democratic Party that they helped to transform. Today's DLC is moving on to champion a so-called centrist and bipartisan agenda, much of which fails to address—and some of which actually subverts—basic popular concerns. After the 1996 election, DLC leaders seemed to go out of their way to urge Clinton not to move forward in partnership with his own party. What is more, the DLC has chosen to push privatizing "entitlement reforms" of Social Security and Medicare (Marshall 1997 chaps. 4–5), changes that resonate much more with the ideas of Wall Street than with the needs and values of average Americans. After their early success in helping Democrats to reopen a full dialogue with American families, the DLC has grown uncomfortable with a politics centered on the lives and values of ordinary citizens.

Most Americans, for example, see Social Security as an efficient, reliable, shared source of retirement support for people who have put in lifetimes of work as good employees, caregivers, and citizens. Americans also value Social Security as a welcome help to working adults who have to take on caring for their elderly parents at the same time that they are raising children. But the DLC has recently announced that Social Security is simply "too expensive" for the nation to sustain, and it proposes to replace this keystone of America's social contract with an administratively cumbersome system of partially privatized individual investment accounts to be managed by Wall Street brokers (Shapiro 1997). Under this scheme, decent retirement support for most Americans would become much more uncertain over time. The rationale for the DLC decision to abandon a unified Social Security system with guaranteed benefits—one of the finest achievements of the modern Democratic Party—seems to be a larger ideological commitment to replacing big government with market incentives and individual choices. Social Security can be adjusted for the future in ways that maintain its socially solidary nature, but the DLC reflexively favors a marketizing course—even if that course would exacerbate social divisions, make people less secure, require much more regulatory complexity, and grant a vast new tax-financed subsidy to private investment managers. A similarly rigid DLC commitment to market solutions carries over into almost every area of public policy, from health care and education to Social Security.

Today's New Democrats are also insufficiently sensitive to the economic stresses faced by young working families. To be sure, New Democrats continue to highlight many concerns about family integrity and parental responsibility. But too often they spotlight only the extreme circumstances of (for example) teenage mothers or very poor families on welfare or delinquent children. Even when the dilemmas of average families are movingly described (as, for example, in Galston 1997), what follows is a laundry list of policy proposals that are largely symbolic or are focused on extreme situations, adding up to little that would improve the daily lives of most families.

At the root of this turn away from everyday working families may be a DLC vision of the current American economy that notices only the upside of current trends, celebrating developments relevant mostly for privileged suburbanites who normally vote Republican. Thus the 1996 DLC "New Progressive Declaration" (reprinted in W. Marshall 1997) declares that the American economy is experiencing a worldwide transition from the industrial age to an information age. Ignoring the dislocations and rising inequalities that have accompanied economic growth since the 1970s and downplaying the insecurities that recent economic changes have brought for many American workers and families, the "Declaration" celebrates businesspeople who are "pioneers" in building "new knowledge industries" and workers who are "exchanging the mind-numbing drudgery of manual labor for jobs that allow them to think, create, and share in decisions." But this description hardly speaks to the experience of most working men and women in the late twentieth-century United States.

The Incomplete Stories of the Left

If those speaking out programmatically on the center-right of the Democratic Party offer a story inadequate to the task of building a new popular majority, then what about thinkers and activists on the party's left? Until recently,

Democratic Party left liberals have been most visibly an assortment of advocacy groups, including pro-choice feminists, environmentalists, and spokespersons for the rights of minorities self-consciously fighting historic discrimination. Much of the organizational and moral vitality of the Democratic Party since the 1960s has resided in such advocacy groups, and the causes that they espouse remain important. We cannot imagine a Democratic Party that abandons environmental protection, even if new ways must constantly be devised to meld concerns for clean and pleasant natural surroundings with the simultaneous need to promote jobs and economic growth. Democrats must also remain a socially inclusive and tolerant party—the major party that champions equal rights for women and fights for full inclusion and justice for African-Americans and other groups whose members have suffered discrimination. Most Americans today strongly value environmental protection, social inclusion, and opportunity for all. Americans also want tolerance of diversity, even as they seek a reaffirmation of shared cultural norms about individual and social responsibility. Democrats have benefited from being the party of environmental sanity and social inclusion, and the party must continue to champion these causes, especially in the face of Republican attempts to roll back past gains and undercut future progress.

But Democrats cannot only be, either organizationally or programmatically, the mere sum of the advocacy and cause groups that surround the party. In practice, a politics dominated by advocacy groups left the Democratic Party marginalized electorally—popular with the very most-educated and the least well-off, but less appealing to many of the working families that we are supposed to represent. There must be more of an overarching mission, vision, and strategy—a Democratic story and a partywide undertaking that speak to the cultural and material concerns of everyday working families.

In the past few years, economic populists on the party's left have stepped forward to offer one possible formula for such an overarching "story" (to use the word favored by Faux 1996). The newly assertive economic populists include the AFL-CIO under the leadership of John J. Sweeney (1996), the researchers and analysts of the Economic Policy Institute, and the Campaign for America's Future (CAF), a new advocacy group launched in the summer of 1996 as an economic populist counterweight to the Democratic Leadership Council.

Labor-oriented populists offer a biting analysis of the new economic conditions and uncertainties faced by most working people. Most employees in the United States today, argues the CAF, are trapped in an "age of anxiety," because of developments in an internationalizing economy dominated by corporations who are squeezing their employees harder and harder. "Inequality has risen to heights not seen since before the Great Depression. CEO salaries have soared, while wages have fallen. . . . America, which once grew together, is now growing apart" (CAF 1996). Economic populists call upon Democrats to differentiate themselves from Republicans with appeals to the most hard-pressed workers. At the level of specifics, they urge Democrats to focus primarily on promoting unionization, achieving workplace reforms, curbing corporate power, and regulating international trade in order to protect wages and benefits for American workers.

Economic populists and the revitalized union movement have done much to push Democrats toward an encompassing analysis and message, and, frankly, their analysis is a lot closer to the mark than the rosy picture of the U.S. economy painted by some on the party's center-right. While Democrats must welcome technological changes and new economic opportunities, the party must also remain sensitive to the worries of employees and families who are barely holding their own or are actually falling behind in today's unforgiving market economy. Democrats need to speak for people of ordinary luck, not just for the few who happen to be the luckiest in an increasingly winner-take-all system (Frank and Cook 1995). Economic populists are right to shine the spotlight on those who would secure their own privileges by increasing the odds for everyone else. Economic populists are right to remind the Democratic Party of its historic commitment to regular working people.

But all this said, we cannot ignore the shortfalls of a one-sided economistic approach focused on only some segments of the workforce. Tailoring messages very specifically to the concerns of pro-union blue-collar voters and employees of large, transnational corporations cannot suffice in an era when unionized workers account for only 11 percent of the private-sector workforce and more and more people are employed in small businesses or nonprofits. Only one in five Americans are employed in larger businesses; in fact, only one-third are employed in private-sector firms of any size.

Some labor-oriented populists want to center a new Democratic Party strategy on calls for regulating international trade, taming corporate power, and improving the ability of unions to bargain for better wages and benefits.

Such concerns must be part of a renewed popular politics. But to make them the main story leaves out other important issues and constituencies. What will a waitress trying to raise kids while working at a minimum-wage job (with no benefits) make of a narrowly labor-populist message? The problems that she faces cannot transparently be traced to international trade or corporate power. What about a small businessman who wants health and pension protections for himself and his employees but who just cannot afford to provide them? And what about a married mother worried about her husband's job security and about the safety and education of her children? Democrats must speak with—and for—all of these people.

A restricted focus on large-scale corporate and workplace practices misses families, communities, and social institutions beyond work as the places where most people organize and manage their lives. Working families care deeply about achieving a better quality of life in not just their jobs but in many other areas, and they define security more broadly than in terms of wages alone.

An excessively workplace-centered populism risks discarding the considerable credibility that Democrats have won on such issues as fighting crime, supporting parental responsibility, promoting better schools and safer neighborhoods, and aiding working parents. These are critical considerations for millions of voters and especially working wives and mothers, now a key party constituency. Popular progressives need to speak to people's concerns at home and in the community as well as at work. A new popularized politics must incorporate all the values and concerns that matter to women and men in the large majority of families striving to build decent lives in a period of historic change.

A Popular Politics for Our Time
The contributors to this volume believe that this is a special moment of opportunity. Together, we outline a multifaceted program for Democratic Party renewal. Some of us are labor-oriented populists, and all of us focus on the needs of working Americans of regular luck and ordinary prospects. We see no future for a party competing more and more narrowly for the votes of upscale suburbanites, while grasping at the monied contributions of the well-to-do. We see no future in a public debate reduced to how best to balance the federal budget. That is the road to atrophy, steady decline, and insignificance.

But Democrats need not go down that road. We are confident that an expansive, truly democratic vision can open the way to a new majority.

As we heed the populist call to stand with the majority of working Americans, we also affirm longstanding New Democrat concerns about family integrity, improving schools, and fighting crime. And we accept the message so well articulated by moderate Democrats like Bill Bradley (1995): civil society must be central to democratic renewal. Along with government at all levels, communities, religious institutions, and businesses must be engaged as partners in a larger quest for the good society.

The three parts of this volume take up the challenge of spelling out both the vision and the politics of a popular progressive renewal for Democrats. Our project takes account of the obstacles that people encounter today and suggests how Americans can harness our democracy and our government to help everyone move forward together toward a better future.

The essays in part 1 argue the United States needs a renewed social contract. Contrary to what conservatives in both political parties are saying, all of us believe that America's working families cannot be left on their own in mutual isolation to cope with the new insecurities of our time. As a nation we have important work to do if people of ordinary means and luck are to prosper and become fully participating citizens. Economic growth must be regulated and channeled, and powerful profit-seeking actors must be required to bargain fairly with America's workers, families, and communities. On the job, Americans must have more security, better prospects, and decent wages and benefits. At home and in our communities and social institutions, Americans need new measures to help ever more fragile families raise good and healthy children, care for aging grandparents, and participate in the life of the larger community.

Fortunately, there is no reason that American citizens should be abandoned to their isolated fates in an unforgiving economy or a libertine culture. A renewed social contract would be good for the economy, good for civil society, and good for people of all backgrounds. Such a renewal would also be in keeping with the best American democratic traditions. As the contributors to part 1 show, the United States has a long history of using government actively—to promote economic growth, social justice, a strong civic community, and opportunity and security for individuals and families.

The finest achievements of the New Deal, such as Social Security, must be adjusted for the future, not dismantled. Social insurance is more important than ever in an information-age economy, where workers need to be adaptable and families more secure. Progressives also know that Social Security and other national social programs are not merely instruments of economic growth and individual material well-being; such programs embody a sense of mutual obligation among citizens and between individuals and the community. Preserving and promoting broadly shared social programs is therefore a civic imperative as much as a way to further economic justice and efficiency.

Within America's renewed social contract, new ways must be found to launch public investments in our cities, our civic infrastructure, and our people, adding new chapters to the long American story whose earlier chapters included the creation of widespread public schools, investments in family farms and national transportation systems, and the opening of popular access to higher education and home ownership through the GI Bill of 1944.

Throughout our history, millions of African-Americans and other excluded groups have been barred from getting ahead and participating as full citizens. They have also experienced terrible economic and family insecurities that were not completely different from but were more severe than those faced by other Americans. Today, we must continue affirmative undertakings to extend full opportunity and extra social support to the historically excluded. At the same time, progressive Democrats need to rededicate ourselves to the inclusive social vision of the most farsighted leaders of the Civil Rights era—Martin Luther King, Jr., Robert F. Kennedy, Bayard Rustin, and Walter Reuther. We need to move beyond a politics of poverty programs and endless fights over shrinking welfare subsidies, championing affirmative opportunity for all working Americans and social supports for families in every racial and ethnic group.

Popular progressives, in short, offer bold, democratic answers to the challenges and dilemmas that America's families face today. Yet it is not sufficient to outline how we might ideally lead the nation toward a better future. Today's public stasis reflects a failure of democratic politics as well as a thinness of vision. As the essays in part 2 spell out, a popular progressive strategy for America means marrying the vision of a renewed social contract with a revitalized civic life and new ways of doing politics. We must rebuild the infrastructure of popular progressive politics and join with all of our fellow citizens in the quest to realize a full and vibrant citizenship.

Twentieth-century Americans have lost sight of the full civic possibilities of democratic politics. Modern liberals have certainly been correct to say that there can be no full democracy unless every person has a chance to reach for the American dream, unless every family enjoys at least a modicum of economic security. The modern Democratic Party has rightly used the powers of government to regulate the economy, promote economic growth, and further social justice. And it must do so again in our time, grappling with new extremes of wealth and poverty and seeking to buffer all working people in a time of rapid technological change and intensified global competition. But a renewed popular Democratic politics cannot be only about helping individuals cope with economic and social change.

Our politics must reaffirm the primacy of a fully connected and participatory civic community. By civic community, we most emphatically do not mean self-enclosed local enclaves, antiseptically sealed off from one another and hostile to government. We mean real groups, each in a particular place and setting, that are also connected to one another at the national, state, and regional levels. To foster a truly inclusive national community, we should not hesitate to deploy the proper powers of government—to fashion partnerships with businesses and other institutions and further a shared social order to which all contribute and in which all are valued. And to foster a new and sustained infrastructure for politics in touch with people, we must directly engage our fellow citizens in religious congregations, family centers, civic groups, and union halls.

Popular progressives must also renew the Democratic Party as an institution, turning it into much more than a label and a set of fund-raising activities. As New Right Republicans have done over the past generation, popular Democrats must sink extensive new roots into local and popular life. Much of American civic life has ever been—and always should remain—outside of any particular political party or partisan effort. But there is no reason at all that a party—especially our party, the Democratic Party—cannot be a civic institution, too.

Commitment to the Democratic Party needs to become a cause, one to which many people will give time and effort and argument and passion (while, to be sure, still writing the occasional check). To realize this possibility means considering ways to revitalize the party as a network of local and state organizations. It means giving the party social reality in neighborhoods, state capitals, workplaces, and social centers so that loyalists can come together regularly to debate platforms, choose priorities, build coalitions, and nominate leaders. The Democratic Party, in short, must become a party of as well as for the people.

A revitalized Democratic Party can inspire a new majority and win elections at all levels. As the essays in part 3 explain, the Democratic Party today enjoys important new opportunities to lead and win. Americans are listening to Democrats again—blue-collar as well as white-collar employees, black and Latino families as well as Asian-Americans and whites, married as well as single women, and younger as well as older Americans. Even those, including many white southerners, who are not currently voting for Democrats can be reached by fresh appeals, if Democratic candidates speak to fundamental concerns that bridge the racial divide.

Building a new majority is not a matter of awaiting some inexorable demographic destiny, still less of adding up slivers of the electorate. Throughout American history, no party has come to the fore in either of these ways. A rising party speaks to the dilemmas of its age, offering a moral and practical vision for the entire nation. Today, popular progressive Democrats are the ones with a compelling new vision for America.

The shared problems and challenges facing working Americans and their families are at the heart and soul of the new progressive story. The United States is at a crossroads: along one way lies spreading insecurity, burgeoning inequality, broken families, and civic decline; along another way lies a renewed social contract, racial healing, and a revitalized democracy. Democrats can lead the nation along the better path, but only if the party rediscovers its historic mission to speak for, and with, all working families.

No longer, we say, should Democrats allow conservatives and Republicans to be the only ones offering a story about where America finds itself and how the country can move forward. The conservative story—a story about unfettered markets and individuals on their own—has already begun to sound unreal and hollow. But an exhausted conservatism will not be replaced by mere interest group advocacy, still less by a politics of telegenic gestures.

National atrophy could come as readily through stalemate and cynical exhaustion as at the hands of misguided antigovernment militants.

Weary of government bashers and out-of-touch elites, the vast majority of Americans are ready for a new civic vision. People will respond to a revitalized Democratic Party that is both culturally sensible and politically bold. Democrats must speak to the values and concerns of daily life. And they must be bold enough to renew and use the powers of democratic government, making a genuine difference for the better in the lives of all American families and communities.

If the Democrats choose to go forward along this way, then millions of Americans will surely choose to travel with them. The new majority of our day is ready not only to hear but also to help tell the popular progressive story.

part one

A Renewed Social Contract

You Are Not Alone

Jeff Faux

Expanding economic opportunity is at the core of most Americans' conception of the good society. People all over the world want a better material life, yet a rising standard of living is especially valued by, and necessary to, a multi-cultural and mobile people like ourselves. We vary by ethnicity and religion, but we are united by our faith in the American dream—the hope that, through hard work, we can do better for us and our families.

Economic opportunity is not the only value that makes up the American dream and thereby energizes national politics. But in a highly commercialized, market-oriented culture, it is the prism through which many important social concerns—from family instability to crime—are viewed. It is therefore obvious that a revitalized progressive politics should promote a decent life and rising opportunities for all Americans.

Whose Opportunity?

It is less obvious to whom these opportunities belong. Today, the dominant story of how the economy should work reflects Ronald Reagan's definition of economic opportunity: the freedom to get rich—richer than others. This definition reflects Reagan's story that wealth is created almost exclusively through the efforts of competing individuals, primarily investors. Therefore, as long as markets are unregulated, a polarized distribution of income, wealth, and power is "fair"—those with *extraordinary* luck, talent, and perseverance are being rewarded according to their contribution. Winners are those who have proven their economic virtue, and they deserve to take all—or as much as they can get.

During the half century before the Reagan years, American politics reflected another definition of economic opportunity, even when Republicans controlled the White House. It defined opportunity as the chance for people of *ordinary* luck, talent, and perseverance—who by definition make up the majority of any society—to support a family, educate their children, and achieve a dignified old age. The social contract in place after World War II implied that widespread opportunity to achieve economic security— pooling risks to provide a modest amount of freedom from the brutal competition of all against all—was as important as the freedom to buy low and sell high.

That social contract was a great success. For the quarter century following World War II, Americans got richer faster and *together,* reinforcing the notion that our common citizenship contained claims on the American dream. Income rose more rapidly than it had in the past, and its distribution became more equal. Between 1947 and 1973, real family income rose 2.6 percent per year. Over that same period, the ratio of the income of the top 5 percent of families to the lowest 20 percent of families slipped from 14 to 1 to 11 to 1 (Mishel, Bernstein, and Schmitt 1997). Traditional barriers to upward mobility broke down as the working class began to consume like the prewar upper middle class, acquiring cars, homes of their own, even college educations for their children. Moreover, by the 1960s, ordinary white Americans had gained enough confidence in their continued upward mobility to give their political support—however grudgingly—to efforts to bring black Americans into this new promise of prosperity.

In the early 1970s, the economic underpinnings of the social contract began to crumble. The *average* earnings of all American workers stagnated, while the earnings of three-quarters of them fell. By 1979, the *median* real wage of the typical American worker (the worker exactly in the middle of the earnings distribution) was slightly below its 1973 level. Family incomes and living standards were propped up by wives going out to work and a dramatic expansion of consumer debt.

Since 1979, the median real wage of Americans has plunged 10 percent. Both college and non–college graduates have been hit, but the latter—representing three-quarters of the labor force—have been hit hardest. For example, a male high school graduate with five years' work experience lost almost 30 percent. One measure of the downward shift in the economic trajectory is this: had the pre-1973 trend continued, a young male high school graduate today would be making an annual income of $33,000, as opposed to his current income of $13,000.

By the mid-1990s, all of the gains in income and wealth equality of the postwar years had been wiped out, calling into question the social contract that ensured opportunity for those of ordinary luck. The ratio of the average income of families in the top 5 percent to those in the bottom 20 percent had risen to 19 to 1. In 1974, the average chief executive officer of a major American firm was paid 34 times the earnings of the average worker. Twenty years later, he was making 179 times the pay of the average worker. Before 1973, we grew together; now we grow apart.

The erosion of income is both the reality and a symbol of the general deterioration of security and opportunity for the working majority. Health care and pension coverage for the typical family has shrunk, full-time permanent jobs are disappearing, and families are putting in longer working hours. As the slowdown in economic growth reduced tax revenues, the public sector's ability to respond to the squeeze on working families has been undercut. Finally, the staggering loss of access to reasonably well-paid jobs for the non–college educated has knocked the rungs out of the ladder of upward mobility, the traditional route through which minorities and immigrants have been integrated into American society. As a result, economic competition among middle- and lower-income workers has intensified, heightening racial and ethnic tensions. And it has fanned the embers of nativist politics while dampening those of the American dream.

Most serious observers of the economy would agree that a number of basic trends slowed growth and widened the income gap. A well-regarded study by Harvard economists Richard Freeman and Lawrence Katz (1994) allocated the causes as follows.

Technological change	7–25 percent
Deindustrialization	25–33 percent
Deunionization	20 percent
Low-wage imports and immigration	15–25 percent
Trade deficit	15 percent

Experts may argue over the relative importance of these and other trends, but we do not have to settle these disputes to understand their implications. First, all of these factors have increased competition among workers in both domestic and foreign markets, undercutting wages and living standards. Second, the market pressures are ongoing, as new production capacity and as new technology come on line somewhere in the world every day. Given the higher wage levels at which Americans start, the worldwide pressure to cut labor costs, and the demands of a footloose capital market to maximize short-run profits, we can expect on our current course that the long-term erosion in real incomes for the majority of working families will continue for the foreseeable future. In its wake, we can also expect increased social stress, widening political cynicism, and a weakening of the national unity that has been tied together by faith in the American dream.

The Political Debate

What has happened to the great majority of Americans in this new period should be the main subject of our politics today. But for most mainstream politicians, seriously pursuing this subject risks discomforting those who enjoy the increasingly skewed distribution of wealth and power—and who tend to contribute generously to campaigns, control the major media, and provide lobbying contracts and seats on corporate boards for former public officials. Our most visible political leaders are therefore working hard to contain and sugarcoat the bad news. Republicans and Democrats, despite their differences, have seized on the idea that the financial squeeze on the middle class represents a transition to better times—a shift to an information age, which will eventually bring great societal benefits on the order of the historic shift from agriculture to industry.

According to this story, successfully competing in the new age requires that people become more skilled and educated and that companies become both more flexible—leaner if not meaner—and liberated from government restrictions. Adaptation requires workers and firms to sacrifice for the future and the public sector to shrink its spending in order to free up capital to private firms. If we follow this agenda, we will at some unspecified time in the future reach the other side of our economic Jordan—to a promised land of prosperity and technological wonder.

The principal teller of the Republican version is Newt Gingrich. "The price of labor is set in South China," Gingrich tells us, "because that is the largest center of work force [*sic*] on the planet. So if you want to live seven times as well as somebody in Canton, you're going to have to be seven times more productive." Gingrich's message to the typical American is this: *you are on your own,* competing as an individual against 6 billion people, most of whom earn much less than you do. Your salvation lies in being technically better and more entrepreneurial than your competition—next door as well as in China. But the government is dragging you down with taxes and burdening businesses that otherwise may want to hire you with too much regulation. It follows that government should get off your back—return your tax money so you can invest in yourself.

There are several obvious problems with Gingrich's formula. One is that the last two decades of declining real wages have already seen a reduction of government influence in the economy. Regulation has been reduced dramatically, federal taxes on business have been halved, and large sections of the public sector have been privatized. Indeed, the United States has the smallest public sector of the major industrial nations. Moreover, the drop in real wages has occurred *before* taxes; at issue is not what the government is taking out of your paycheck but what the employer is not putting in.

Speaking for the Democratic mainstream, Bill Clinton uses the image of a bridge to symbolize a fundamentally benign transition to a prosperous new age. Like Gingrich, Clinton lectures Americans that the answer to their financial anxieties is to be more productive by becoming more skilled. "The world we face today," says the president, "is a world where what you earn depends on what you learn." But unlike Gingrich, Clinton sees a role for government in providing access to the education and training with which Americans will then compete with workers in South China.

The president's formulation is more sympathetic than Gingrich's, but it also fails to address the reality facing Americans. As noted, lack of education and skills is at best only part of the problem. Technology is always changing, and working people always need new skills and education to keep up. But there is little evidence that a "skills gap" is the heart of the problem. In fact, employee productivity has continued to rise. The problem is that the gains are not being shared, which reflects the weakened bargaining position of most of the workforce. Globalization has slowed down the growth of the overall U.S. economy, but it has also been an excuse for the economic elite to tear up the social contract.

Thus, while the corporate profit rate rose to a thirty-year high by 1996, American corporations, freed from previous political constraints, used the threat of subcontracting both in the United States and to low-wage foreign countries to force wage and benefit concessions from employees and to push the limits of what is socially acceptable. The indifference of top management to employees—from Christmas Eve layoffs to reneging on promises of pensions and health benefits—is now accepted as normal in the American labor market. Not surprisingly, employees report that they feel less loyalty to their employers than they used to.

An example of what now passes for normal is the reappearance of the commercial use of prison labor, despite its prohibition by international conventions. Prisoners now provide data entry for Chevron, Bank of America, and Macy's; make telephone reservations for TWA; and stock shelves for Toys-R-Us. A November 1995 report from the Department of Justice tells businesses that "readily available and dependable" prisoners represent a "cost-effective alternative to work forces found in Mexico, the Caribbean Basin, Southeast Asia, etc." Says one industry executive, "We can put a Made-in-the-U.S.A. label on our product" (Sexton 1995).

But even if one believes that the downward wage pressure produced by the gap between South China and Seattle can be overcome simply by having Americans acquire more education and training, the president cannot deliver on his promise of government help. Clinton and the Democrats remain caught in Reagan's trap. Having yielded to the Republican post-Reagan demand for a balanced budget and conservative spending priorities, Clinton's government simply does not have the money for the necessary investment. The cost of providing enough job training to bring the wage differential between high school and college graduates to where it was in 1979 has been estimated at about $170 billion. The U.S. government now spends about

$8 billion and has no plans to increase it. Clinton has proposed a modest package of tax cuts, spending, and "voluntary" national standards to support education. But it is nowhere near what would be necessary to counteract intensified wage competition—if indeed it were possible at all (Faux 1996).

Thus, despite the president's ideological differences with Gingrich, his practical message to the American people is similar to Gingrich's: you are on your own.

The message has not been lost on the electorate. If our success in adjusting to this new world is up to us individually, politics becomes less relevant to our lives, and the notions of solidarity and community of interests with our fellow citizens ring hollow. In the face of a bipartisan effort to lower expectations of what government can do about voters' considerable economic anxiety, voters are increasingly indifferent to the fate of one candidate or party over another.

The Gingrich-Clinton vision of a working life of many different careers, where one's labor is a commodity whose price is subject to an ever more competitive world market, is exhilarating for the well-educated and confident people that Robert Reich has called "symbolic analysts." But the prospect of spending one's life on a perpetual treadmill of retraining, in constant fear of becoming obsolete and out on the street, is not most people's idea of the American dream.

As the expectations of what government can do have been lowered, the political debate has narrowed from a vision of government as an instrument of economic development to an obsession with public-sector accounting. Thus the broad goal of reducing poverty has been transformed to the narrow goal of reducing the government's welfare rolls. The goal of constructing a comprehensive, cost-effective health system for the nation has shrunk to the goal of cutting the government's Medicare and Medicaid costs.

Market economies are always in transition, but no one knows where they are going. The glib story that a combination of unconstrained markets, public austerity, and individual self-improvement will eventually put American workers back on the path of prosperity is eerily reminiscent of the conventional wisdom of the 1930s: the notion that the world had to rely on market forces to "restructure" its way out of the Depression. The economist Alvin Hansen—later to defect to the Keynesian position that government could jump-start growth—expressed the consensus in 1932 when he wrote: "We shall come out of it only through hard work and readjustments that are painful. There is no other alternative" (Garraty 1986).

But, of course, the world did not wait for a market-driven transition. Before the forces of supply and demand could drive incomes and prices low enough to spark a revival of investment (if indeed they could have at all), the worldwide political reaction to economic pain set in motion the most destructive war in history. The economic problems of the 1930s were solved not by market forces but by its opposite—expanded government deficits to finance World War II.

Redrafting the Social Contract

To steer the nation clear of that fate and to prevail as a political force itself, the mainstream left of American politics must address this question: in the post–Cold War global and high-technology marketplace, what is the *economic* definition of being an American? Are you alone in a struggle to compete with 6 billion people for a share of the globe's wealth and economic security? Is your family alone as it seeks to raise its living standards and realize the promise of the American dream? If not, what are the mutual obligations between you and your country?

The answer should begin by challenging the facile and hopeless assertion that global forces, technology, and competition have rendered the people of the United States helpless to do anything but adjust individually to the decisions of an unregulated market. It should challenge the idea that only firms, individuals, and tiny units of government can engage in economic competition. It must reject the romantic localism of both right and left, which contends that national policies are irrelevant and that American cities and towns themselves can prosper independent of one another. On the contrary, the nation-state remains the central instrument available to address the widening decline in living standards and the growing levels of economic anxiety generated by the unregulated market. How and in what form this instrument should be deployed is the substance of political debate.

The U.S. economy has the resources, the entrepreneurial culture, and the technical prowess to support a rising standard of living for all of its citizens who are willing and able to get up and go to work every morning—and to support the small number who can't because of age or disability. The world has changed substantially since the golden years of the post–World

War II era, and we no longer have the extraordinary power we once had. But we remain more in control of our economic destiny than any other nation in the world. Almost 90 percent of the goods and services consumed in America are produced here. Moreover, our bargaining power with the rest of the world, while diminished, remains strong. The ability of the U.S. government—the United Nations' chief bad debtor—to unilaterally force out the secretary-general of the United Nations against the wishes of almost the entire membership is one small example of our leverage. Our influence is partly a function of our military hegemony, but more important, in this post–Cold War era, it is also a function of the fact that almost everyone in the world still wants access to the U.S. market.

Our economic drift is a function more of political paralysis than of a reduction in our capacity to create wealth. It is a paralysis born of our failure to acknowledge that the ability of the American people to prosper in the global economy requires a stronger, not weaker, public sector.

The basis for rebuilding the new social contract in this period is citizenship. Because you are an American, you are not alone in the competition for economic opportunity. By virtue of being an American—not by virtue of your race, your gender, *or your talent*—you have certain basic rights and obligations.

You have a right to a job and a minimum level of earnings, *and* you have an obligation to work.

You have a right to enjoy the investments that previous generations have made in your productivity, *and* you have an obligation to invest part of your income to care for the elderly and foster the productive capacities of future generations.

You have the right to create a business enterprise, *and* you have the obligation to help support the community in which it prospers.

You have a right to protection against certain risks (unemployment, ill health, diminished earnings in old age), *and* you have an obligation to pool resources with your fellow citizens to meet those risks through social insurance.

You have the right to collectively bargain with your employer, *and* you have the obligation to cooperate in creating more productive workplaces.

You have the right to consume the products of the global economy, *and* you have the obligation to insist that they be produced in a way that does not violate the rights of other workers.

Making the New Social Contract Work

A social contract is as much a matter of people's attitudes as it is one of public policies. It is based on a shared identity, reciprocity, and sense of community. But to move from the abstract to the real, these ideas need to be buttressed by appropriate public policies. They send a signal about what the individual in practice can expect from his or her relationship with society.

The following set of policies give economic definition to American citizenship.

A Job for All Who Want One. A society rightly expects those who can work to do so, and it has no obligation to support those who refuse. But it cannot demand a work ethic of its population if its monetary and fiscal policies ensure that there will always be fewer jobs than people who want to work. What's more, a return to the notion of a job for every willing worker is the only way for progressives to shift the subject of domestic policy debate away from the obsession with welfare, a battleground upon which they cannot win, to the more advantageous territory of job creation—where the main debate is about how the majority of people can contribute and prosper in this era of change.

The goal of full employment is, by definition, a challenge to the current Wall Street–driven monetary policy, in which the Federal Reserve maintains high real interest rates precisely in order to keep labor markets from tightening. This is a values issue. The Fed protects the value of financial assets over the value of jobs by consistently overestimating the level of unemployment necessary to retain price stability. No one knows what the right level is, but we do know that the opinion of the financial punditry on this question has been consistently wrong.

One early task of a relevant progressive politics would be a demand that the Federal Reserve live up to its mandate to pursue both high employment and price stability by probing much more forcefully the limits of the economy's capacity to produce without inflation. For now, this is a discussion among elites. But Americans are more likely to participate in a national debate over what it takes to achieve full employment than in the current dispiriting argument over how many people must be denied work in order to make the bond market comfortable.

Investing in America. Public investment shapes the future. America's history has been studded with society-shaping ventures financed by government and implemented by business. Early in the republic's life we built canals and highways and provided land for towns and schools in the territories. Government financed the first assembly lines and subsidized the railroads to settle the West. Its investments created the suburbs after World War II and explored space. Government leadership developed the jet engine, the computer, the Internet. Each of these investment programs created jobs and businesses in the short term. In the long run, they spun off technological advances that became what economist Robert Heilbroner calls economic "klondikes"—massive veins of private investment opportunities that have been the building blocks of American prosperity.

By any measure, America has fallen behind its major competitors in investment in infrastructure, education and training, and civilian research and development. In these areas we now spend less than half of what we spent a quarter century ago. Economists may argue about what estimates are the most accurate, but we know that the relation between public investment and long-term growth is positive and strong.

Moreover, there are clear opportunities to mine new klondikes—beginning with a commitment to making the shift to renewable energy a national investment priority.

In addition to being essential for sustainable economic health, the expansion of public investment also provides powerful economic support for the great moral task of post–Cold War America: *rebuilding the inner cities—* and the lives of the people trapped in their slums. An effective urban strategy involves restructuring urban transportation, water and sewer lines, housing, parks, and communications as well as training, education, and other programs necessary to support such investments. A commitment to redevelop the inner cities also represents the best way to bridge the growing racial divide in America. It is the only strategy that could bring the large numbers of unemployed urban minority males back into the workforce.

The vision of this effort should not focus on the provision of work for the poor, with its political taint of make-work. Certainly, it should not be tied to welfare. The vision should emphasize the need to revive an important part of America in order to add to national wealth and productivity.

The immediate objection is that there is no money for such investments because we must balance the budget by the year 2002 and beyond.

This obsession with a permanently balanced budget is economic nonsense. Among other things, it would turn recessions into depressions by preventing the federal government from keeping a floor under purchasing power during economic downturns. It would also prohibit the federal government from borrowing money for investment. As with a business or a household, the correct measure of fiscal responsibility is a stable or falling ratio of debt to income, or in this nation's case, gross domestic product (GDP). As long as that ratio is not rising (and it is not rising today), there is no economic reason not to expand public investments, especially at a time when they are so desperately needed in order to provide our children with the tools that they will need to compete in the world. Recognizing this, we could right now establish a capital budget, separating long-term investments from the short-term operating expenses of the federal government, and support a permanent new infusion of 1.5 to 2 percent of GDP for investment purposes.

But even if we accept the political constraints of a five-year balanced budget, there is room for shifting more revenues to public investment. A few examples make the point.

- Military-associated CIA spending is far beyond what we need for defending ourselves and our allies in the post–Cold War era; we could cut it by $50 billion a year and still be the world's greatest military power.
- A tiny tax on financial speculation could generate $40 billion per year, all of it earmarked for education.
- Still another $50 billion could be saved by cutting a variety of corporate tax breaks and subsidies to corporations that do nothing to enhance productivity or competitiveness.
- A small energy tax collected over a thirty-year period could leverage large amounts of capital for major public infrastructure investments.

Empowering Workers. Another first step in rebalancing the social contract on the job is to remove the legal obstacles to joining a labor union. We need to restore economic meaning to the rights of citizens to assemble.

The decline in the unionized labor force has been a major factor in the loss of employee bargaining power. Despite the negative images of labor unions in corporate-controlled media, people who work for a living understand the benefits of collective bargaining. A survey of private-sector workers in 1994 reported that, while only 14 percent of those sampled belonged to a union, 40 percent wished they did. Moreover, nearly two-thirds (63 percent) of workers "would like more influence at work," including a majority (53 percent) who believe that group representation—a union without the name—would result in at least somewhat more influence.

Expanding unionization can also be an important asset in the effort to increase the efficiency of American production. As former secretary of labor Ray Marshall has noted: "It is not at all inconsistent for workers and their leaders to cooperate with management to increase performance and to bargain with management over the distribution of a company's gains" (Marshall 1996, p. 112).

Most workers are not organized and will not be for the foreseeable future. A progressive politics must therefore speak to the lack of bargaining power among the unorganized majority as well.

Progressives should promote, for example, a formula that would automatically link the minimum wage to one-half of the average wage of all nonsupervisory workers. Another policy priority is to mandate that employers pay prorated benefits to part-time and temporary employees.

Still another longer-term objective should be a shorter workweek, that is, requiring overtime pay for work performed by nonsupervisory employees in excess of thirty-five hours a week. The standard workweek has not been changed since the 1930s. A shorter workweek should be proposed not as a job-sharing policy but as a long-overdue sharing of the benefits of rising productivity with stressed-out working families.

Social Insurance and the Safety Net. Increasingly disorganized labor markets require a strengthening and extension of public social insurance, not a weakening, as posited by the conservatives. Working Americans and their families can adapt to the challenges of a more globally competitive era only if they can count on basic social protections.

Despite Bill Clinton's health care debacle of 1994, health care security remains high on the list of America's needs. A September 1996 Harris poll reports that 69 percent of Americans think that Clinton in his second term should "propose major health care reforms" (Harris Poll 1996).

Taming overall health care costs is in turn the key to controlling the budget deficit. The entire projected rise in the deficit over the foreseeable future is made up of rising costs in government health care programs. This is not because government programs are less efficient (compared with the operation of private health insurance plans, the administrative costs for Medicare are proportionally much less). It is because they serve a less healthy population—the elderly and the poor. Addressing this problem in the narrow confines of the specific public programs can lead only to a reduction in the quality of care, higher costs for those who can least afford it, or both. This is a problem of the American community as a whole, and the only way to finally address it is to spread the risk in a national health insurance pool.

Like health care, pension coverage has steadily declined over the last decade and a half. Today, only 45 percent of all private-sector workers have employer-provided pension coverage. Progressives should work to make pension systems portable, by giving new employees the right to transfer their pension assets to new employers.

Progressives should also stand firm in defense of the integrity of the present Social Security system. There is a reasonable argument that the system should cautiously invest some of its proceeds in the stock market. But Wall Street firms have been financing a campaign to shift Social Security taxes to individual retirement accounts, which would of course be invested with Wall Street firms. The campaign has created the false impression that the retirement of the baby boomers will bankrupt the system. Baby-boomer retirement is a problem, but not a crisis, and it can be solved with modest adjustments in taxes or benefits. The defense of a sound retirement system is a central task in the renewal of the social contract.

Tax Reform. Over the long term, the tax system itself must be overhauled and streamlined. The system's complexity and loopholes offer too much temptation for manipulation, distort economic decisions for little compensating social value, and end up favoring those who can afford the best accountants, lawyers, and lobbyists. Since the reform of the federal income tax in 1986, the system is not nearly as complex as it used to be. (Some 40 percent of taxpayers filing hard-copy tax returns use the short form.) But it remains a source of suspicion and distrust of government.

The simplest solution is a single federal tax rate schedule for all income regardless of its source. Individual and corporate income taxes, payroll taxes, gift and estate taxes, and so forth would be combined into one system, which could then be taxed at a progressive rate. Taxes would be applied at the level of the individual, eliminating the double taxation of corporate dividends. Social Security and Medicare would be financed out of a progressive general tax rather than the highly regressive payroll tax. Corporate welfare in the form of tax breaks would be eliminated. Reform should explicitly include the taxation of state tax subsidies resulting from the destructive competition among states for private investment, which now reduces the nation's overall tax base with little economic gain.

Campaign Finance Reform. A fundamental reform of campaign finance is critical to any progressive project. Despite expanded fund-raising by labor, women's, and environmental groups on the left and the Christian Coalition on the right, money from corporations and the wealthy dominates politics. A new progressive politics needs to be identified with a radical, credible, and populist crusade to reduce the influence of money on elections. The argument should be directly linked to the economic story of the growing inequality of wealth and power. Government sits idle as ordinary Americans languish, in part because monied interests are buying a different role for government.

Washington insiders claim that big contributors get nothing for their money but the chance to have high-toned policy chats with the beneficiaries, but that doesn't pass the laugh test around America's kitchen tables. A national and state-by-state campaign for a constitutional amendment to place hard limits on spending and contributions could help to provide a comprehensive, economic class-based, organizing vehicle for a new majority.

Global Policies with a National Purpose

Secretary of State Warren Christopher remarked in July 1996 what few policymakers will publicly admit: "We have passed the point where we can sustain prosperity on sales just within the United States" (Erlanger and Sanger 1996, p. A1). The shift of policy focus from the domestic to the international arena has enormous importance: if the source of growth is foreign markets, policies to directly increase domestic incomes are less important. Indeed, keeping competitive—that is, keeping labor costs low—now rivals the maintenance of domestic purchasing power as the primary goal. The long-term decline in wages is an important part of how the United States and American corporations try to compete in the world.

An expansion of trade per se is neither good nor bad for the economic well-being of the average American. What matters is the degree to which it supports the more important goal: the broadly based internal economic development of the American economy.

Currently, it does not; after more than a decade of intense effort at trade expansion, we have a worsening of the trade deficit. Since 1979, the deficit has cost the United States 2.5 million jobs, with imports from low-wage areas of the world being a major cause of the disappearance of jobs offering decent pay for the minority poor. The trade deficit understates the impact of the global economy on U.S. incomes. It does not fully reflect investments shifted elsewhere, nor does it reflect the effect that employers' increasingly credible threats to move overseas has had on wages.

A sensible international economic policy should include a number of elements. First, the highest priority should be given to setting and enforcing international labor and environmental standards. This is the key to an international system that raises purchasing power in all countries, and it should be the essential condition for American participation in trade with anyone.

Second, U.S. trade negotiators must recognize a distinction between the interests of U.S. companies, who can produce anywhere, and the interests of U.S. employees and indeed U.S. citizens. The many advisory and quasi-government committees and councils that help to determine government policy on trade are now completely dominated by multinational business. They should be opened up to labor and public-interest representatives.

Third, we need to build a more sensible relationship with Mexico, whose economic troubles spill over our borders every night. The only permanent solution to our unstable southern boundary is a prosperous Mexican economy. The current course, which has lowered the average real wage in Mexico by 40 percent in the past two years, is suicidal. Austerity will not work on either side of the border. Mexico has two central problems: its debt and its oligarchy. The answer is for the United States and Canada to offer Mexico debt relief conditioned upon true democratic reform: truly free elections, enforceable labor and environmental protections, and an end to official lawlessness.

Finally, we need assertive American leadership to construct rules for a global marketplace whose instability is threatening working families of most of the world's nations. Just as national markets need restraints, so do international ones. Eventually, a truly international economy will need the international equivalent of a Securities and Exchange Commission, a Federal Reserve, and a mechanism for coordinating national fiscal policies. The message from America to the world should be that the global economy makes sense only if it raises the global quality of life.

Is All This Possible?

It is easy to dismiss the agenda that I have outlined as unrealistic in the current political environment. But efforts to build a new progressive majority must aspire to change that environment. The process of change begins by setting out a clear agenda in order to start a conversation—a conversation that can gradually widen and, if successful, help to inspire a political majority. The threshold question is, Do these major themes have sufficient appeal to start a conversation that many Americans will want to join? There is sufficient reason to think that they do.

The vast majority of U.S. families are not winners in today's economy, and they know it. A *New York Times* (1996) poll last winter reported that the share of the electorate that identifies itself as "working class" now outnumbers those who consider themselves "middle class," 55 to 36 percent. If the self-identified "poor" are added to the working class, the share comes to 61 percent of the electorate.

The 1996 election was another straw in the wind. Clinton began his campaign under the assertion that "the era of big government is over," yet his comeback from the post-1994 political grave was primarily based on his defense of Medicare, Medicaid, federal aid to education, and federal protection of the environment. By the fall of 1996, Republicans were professing their devotion to Medicare and proclaiming support for a rise in the federal minimum wage. If these aren't Big Government programs, what are?

The reemergence of a sense of economic class can be seen among young people, who, despite their better education, are doing and expect to do worse than their parents. Conventional wisdom assures us that young people are apathetic about politics. But this may well be a generation gap. With the student activism of the 1960s as their reference point, aging baby-boomer pundits tell us that the baby busters are too worried about their own job security to pursue social justice for others. But that defines political activism as altruism. Concern about their own future may make today's youth responsive to proposals for broad-based economic, as opposed to social, change. Moreover, as the welfare system collapses and the limits of affirmative action become more apparent, there is reason to expect that women and minorities will be defining themselves more in class terms, rather than in strictly race or gender terms.

Today's voters are not likely to respond to simple populist fables of fat-cat villains and noble poor people. But there is evidence that those who still bother to vote understand the link between politics and economics. In the last three elections—no matter which way they went—economic issues were the voters' biggest concern. In 1996, those who worried most about economic issues voted for Clinton, whereas those who worried most about welfare voted for Dole.

It is hard to see another way toward a new social contract. In the face of the growing gap in wealth and power between the working majority and a self-assured elite, only the hopelessly naive can believe that a stable bargain can be fashioned with private charity as a substitute for social democracy. Power has shifted today so significantly toward those at the top of the income and wealth pyramid that there is simply no incentive for elite representatives in either party to negotiate. What is to be done? The answer is to mobilize the majority of Americans who are struggling in this new economy and to thereby bring the elites back to the bargaining table. For most Americans, the Gingrich-Clinton bargain for the future is just not a good enough offer.

There are potential allies in the business community for a new social contract, for a politics that stresses the interests of those who produce goods and services to be sold primarily in America, as opposed to those who make a living trading securities or pursuing cheap labor in the global marketplace. American labor and United States–centered capital have the same interest in promoting broad-based domestic growth and security. Thus, for example, both the AFL-CIO and the National Association of Manufacturers are major critics of Federal Reserve policies that keep real interest rates high.

Some will allege that it is "old liberal" politics to emphasize economic issues and class identity as a strategy for widening the political space for an activist federal government. But this begs the question. There are no entirely new departures in politics. Much of American politics is, was, and will continue to be over "who gets what." Although it is true that a vigorous economic program to support a renewed social contract draws some of its inspiration from Franklin Roosevelt and his fellow New Dealers, there is no reason that progressives today should concede newness to a politics of passive government and laissez-faire markets inspired by Calvin Coolidge.

The Economy, the Community,
and the Public Sector

Alan Brinkley

One of the most conspicuous casualties of the past twenty-five years of national anxiety has been the idea that the federal government has any useful role to play in promoting economic growth and social progress. A broad coalition of Americans once had considerable faith in the power of public investment to assist economic expansion and improve the quality of citizens' lives. The absence of that faith today is a major impediment to creating a new progressive majority. Restoring it should rank high on a new progressive agenda.

Republicans have been arguing for years that virtually all public spending (other than military expenditures) is in effect wasteful pork and that private investment—subject to as little regulation and taxation as possible—is the only effective way to make the economy expand. In the past several years, increasing numbers of Democrats have begun to echo these claims or have at least ceased to refute them with any energy. Both political parties now seem simultaneously committed to the deflationary goal of balancing the budget and, although in different ways, to a cluster of tax cuts designed to promote growth by facilitating private choice. The case for public contributions to economic growth has all but vanished from public life.

And yet even a momentary glance at the present predicaments of the American economy makes clear that public investment is critical to almost all our long-term economic hopes. Our transportation system is desperately in need of refurbishment, and there is no reasonable possibility of private investment flowing into the rebuilding of roads, bridges, and rail lines or into the construction of new airports and highways. Our public school systems are deteriorating, and the chimera of "school choice"—whatever its virtues— offers no solution to the crumbling public school infrastructure and the languishing pay scales for public school teachers. With the end of the Cold War, public investment in scientific and technological research—once driven in large part by military spending—has declined dramatically; it will decline still more as the drive to a balanced budget further constricts federal and eventually state and local discretionary spending. Universities, cultural institutions, hospitals, and laboratories are all straining to maintain services as public support dwindles. So are public parks, beaches, pools, and playgrounds, which are critical to the health (and stability) of many communities.

At perhaps no time in our modern history has the paradox that John Kenneth Galbraith identified forty years ago in *The Affluent Society* (1958) been clearer or more menacing: the simultaneous growth of private wealth and public squalor. As Galbraith predicted then, the public squalor represents not simply a diminution in the quality of life of people dependent on public services, disturbing as that is by itself. Public squalor is also a threat to the nation's long-term ability to sustain a healthy, productive, and growing economy—and to its ability to sustain any sense of public community capable of holding our increasingly heterogeneous society together.

A History of Public Engagement

The need for and value of public investment may seem self-evident to some. But to many others, the idea of public investment has become a powerful symbol of government waste, inefficiency, and incompetence. All the rational arguments in its favor have little effect against the overwhelming popular animus—actively fanned by political figures in both parties—toward any public expenditures, however vital they may be, and toward the bureaucracies that would have to administer them. One of the best ways to confront that animus is to reacquaint the American electorate with the many ways in which the government has been indispensable to the development of our economy— and to the ways in which it can, and must, be again.

The long record of government involvement in economic growth is so familiar to scholars that within the academy there is hardly any debate about its historical importance. But that same story seems to have penetrated popular discourse hardly at all. Almost nowhere in contemporary discussions of public investment is there mention, for example, of the way in which the government of the early Republic opened up the western lands of the United States and distributed them efficiently and cheaply to white citizens (while moving equally decisively and much more brutally to clear the Indian tribes out of the way). Seldom is there any mention of the extent to which the government subsidized construction of roads, highways, and canals to facilitate the economic life of the new lands. Nor is there much awareness of the central role of government in the construction of the railroads, the major avenues of American industrial growth until the mid–twentieth century. Both federal and state governments provided massive subsidies in land and dollars as well as continuous political support for the railroad corporations as they battled private citizens and local institutions.

Private-sector ideologues have effectively obscured other late nineteenth- and early twentieth-century government contributions to economic growth as well: the construction of the Panama Canal; the subsidies (in both land and dollars) to state colleges and universities; the enormous boost that highway building gave to the two largest industries of the 1920s, construction and automobiles. The rapid industrialization of the United States would have been impossible without the energy, ambition, and talent of thousands of entrepreneurs, many of whom rose to power and wealth from modest circumstances, and without the labor and skills of millions of workers. But it would have been impossible as well without the active support and often lavish subsidies that the industrial economy received from government.

The New Deal as Public Investment

Perhaps the most notable example of government's contribution to economic development came during the New Deal, which may have failed to end the Great Depression but which, in the process of trying to do so, laid the groundwork for much of the nation's postwar expansion. Indeed, one of the New Deal's most important legacies is also one of its least remembered: its far-reaching programs of public investment, which reshaped the nation's economic landscape. To many New Dealers, the most important achievement of the Roosevelt years was not the creation of Social Security, not the passage of the Wagner Act, not such job-creating relief programs as the WPA and the CCC, not even the legitimation of Keynesianism. It was the federal government's recognition that public investment could be a powerful engine of economic development and the New Deal's success in promoting, in particular, the economic development of the South and the West. The historian Jordan Schwarz (1993) summarized this legacy: "The New Dealers sought to create long-term markets by building an infrastructure in undeveloped regions of America. [They] believed that national economic growth was stifled by the monopolization of capital and manufacturing in the Northeast quadrant of the country—making the South and the West undeveloped countries. They concluded that relief and recovery were stopgap solutions to the problems of unemployment and stagnation; poverty required development through hitherto unimagined quantities of public investment."

The New Deal experiments in what Schwarz calls "state capitalism" were the culmination of a generation of efforts by powerful representatives of the South and the West, who sought for over a decade to harness the government to their dreams of regional development before finally succeeding in the early 1930s. Chief among them for a time was William Gibbs McAdoo— Woodrow Wilson's secretary of the Treasury (and son-in-law), the celebrated railroad "czar" during World War I, and perhaps the preeminent Democrat of the early and mid-1920s. McAdoo's posthumous reputation has been clouded by his unsuccessful presidential campaign in 1924, during which he refused to repudiate the support of the Ku Klux Klan. But whatever his political mistakes, McAdoo was a formidable, even visionary, figure. A native of Tennessee who spent many successful years on Wall Street, he came early to understand how badly his region suffered from limited access to capital. He envisioned a new economic order in which the federal government would do what the northeastern financial community had consistently failed to do: assist in the economic development of the South and the West through public investment.

The New Deal translated much of McAdoo's vision into reality. It spent billions in government funds on great public projects that helped not only to alleviate the immediate problems of unemployment and economic stagnation but also to make permanent contributions to the nation's economic development. It built dams, bridges, highways, harbors, schools, and hospitals. It controlled flooding and erosion in the Tennessee Valley and elsewhere. It created vast systems of public power, which made electricity affordable to millions of Americans for the first time. It funded the electrification of hundreds of thousands of remote rural areas.

Many of these projects were of disproportionate benefit to the South and West—and by design. The investment-oriented New Dealers understood that the nation's future depended on creating flourishing new markets in these undeveloped regions, that cultivating the economic potential of what would later be called the Sunbelt could be America's economic alternative to colonialism. Jesse Jones, the calculating Texas banker who headed the Reconstruction Finance Corporation (RFC) from its inception in 1932 and continued to control the government's principal investment bank until the end of World War II, was a particularly important part of this group. His commitment to public investment is especially notable because he was, in almost all other respects, a cautious, even parsimonious conservative with a skeptical view of government. But Jones had made his career by attracting federal funds to his native Houston for projects that had greatly increased both the city's economic prospects and his own fortune. And as head of the RFC, he understood the importance of what his agency could do. If his lending policies favored healthy, established firms over struggling ones, they nevertheless contributed in vital ways to the great public projects that changed the face of the South and West.

Other Texans—among them Sam Rayburn and Lyndon Johnson—were similarly committed to the New Deal projects that were helping to develop their region. They disliked and mistrusted Jones, and they tried at times to challenge what they considered his restrictive and elitist lending policies. But they shared much of his vision of an economically expanding Southwest assisted by federal funds, and they used their considerable political skills to ensure that Texas received from Washington what it had never acquired from Wall Street: the capital it needed to become an economic powerhouse.

The New Deal departed from earlier traditions of public investment both in the extent of its commitment and in the broad scope of its concerns. Haltingly and tentatively, it began to put the resources of the government behind efforts not just to promote growth but to improve the fabric of society.

The bulk of New Deal public works efforts (at least in terms of cost) were directed at such obvious spurs to growth and productivity as dams, hydroelectric plants, highways, harbors, and other infrastructure projects. But there were also investments (through the WPA and other agencies) in parks, museums, schools, theaters, recreational facilities, and public art—projects that the private sector was unlikely to undertake, whose economic value was not always clear, but that reflected a commitment to building a good society and a healthy community.

Wartime Government and Economic Growth

World War II brought a new urgency to state capitalism. After having survived a decade of excess plant capacity, most capitalists were reluctant to make major investments in new factories, fearing that the need for them would vanish when the war ended and, as many expected, the Depression returned. The New Dealers pressed, therefore, for a massive program of public investment in new plants; as a result of their efforts, the government financed the construction of enormous new industrial facilities, many of which were converted from military to civilian production after 1945 and became essential parts of the postwar industrial boom. Through the RFC and the newly created Defense Plants Corporation, Washington financed over two thousand industrial projects and spent more than $17 billion in the process (substantially more than the private sector invested during the war). By the end of 1945, government-financed plants accounted for 96 percent of all synthetic rubber production, 90 percent of magnesium, 71 percent of aircraft manufacturing, and 58 percent of aluminum. The government had constructed some of the largest and most modern manufacturing facilities in the nation, among them Ford's Willow Run plant near Detroit. State capital was also important in expanding the capacity of the petroleum and chemical industries. With the end of the war, other industrial nations were faced with the task of rebuilding a shattered industrial infrastructure. In the United States, industrialists faced the postwar era with their industrial plant not only intact but greatly augmented by government-financed war plants (Brinkley 1995, pp. 240–45).

In explaining the persistence of the Great Depression, the economic historian Michael Bernstein (1987) and others have argued that the 1929 recession hit the U.S. economy at an unusually vulnerable moment. The traditional engines of economic growth (railroads, construction, and auto-mobiles) had ceased to expand as rapidly as they had in the past; younger in-dustries capable of driving growth in new directions (chemicals, plastics, aviation, petroleum, and others) were not yet strong enough to take up the slack. The wartime public investment in these industries was therefore not just important in meeting contemporary military needs; it was also crucial to positioning the American economy for its dramatic postwar expansion. Without it, the enormous domestic and international demand for industrial products after 1945 would have encountered an economy still several years away from being able to produce them. Postwar economic growth would likely have been slower and less stable.

It would also have been slower and less stable had it not been for the major public spending initiatives of the postwar era: first, the massive gov-ernment military spending on the buildup for the early Cold War and the conflict in Korea; then the Federal Highway Program, the largest public works project in American history, which began in the mid-1950s; and even the space program, which generated large-scale technological benefits for the civilian economy. If the 1950s and 1960s were, as many Americans now re-member them, the golden age of American economic expansion, the reason was not, as many conservatives like to claim, because government stayed out of the way of the private sector. It was in large part precisely the opposite: be-cause government made direct and crucial, if at times inadvertent, contribu-tions to growth.

A Fading Legacy

By almost any measure, then, the federal government's ventures in public in-vestment produced a series of significant policy successes, beginning in the first years of the Republic and reaching their modern peak in the period from the New Deal through the first decades of the Cold War. Those ventures helped open the West to white settlement and economic development (albeit at great cost to the native peoples of the region). They helped create the con-ditions necessary for large-scale industrialization and the formation of na-tional and international markets for industrial goods. They helped end the Great Depression. They helped win the war. They helped create critical pro-ductive resources that made postwar expansion possible in previously un-derdeveloped regions and industries. They contributed to the enriching of public spaces and public life. And yet this substantial social and economic achievement left an insubstantial political legacy (Brinkley 1993). The concept of public investment emerged from the 1940s and 1950s so weak that even liberals failed to advance it with any real vigor or consistency for more than thirty years. Today, advocates of public investment seldom justify their proposals by pointing to previous successes in the United States. They prefer analogies to Germany and Japan (and seldom note that even those nations' economic successes are partly the result of American postwar public investments in Europe and Asia, investments inspired in part by the projects of the New Deal).

Why did the long history of successes in public investment prove so ideologically ephemeral? Part of the answer lies in the way in which the government disposed of its property at the end of the war. Virtually all federally funded plants were leased during the war to private corporations—a substantial proportion of them to such industrial giants as ALCOA, Standard Oil, Ford, General Motors, and Du Pont. The argument over what to do with them once the war was over was resolved quickly, after a special commission on reconversion (chaired by Bernard Baruch and dominated by corporate figures) predictably recommended that the plants be turned over to the private sector. Most were sold to the original lessees (at bargain prices) within a few months of the end of the war. Many liberals were outraged. Some argued that the government should retain ownership and use the plants to pressure private industry to behave responsibly in setting prices and wages. Many more objected to the uncontested ceding of public property to a few large corporations. The experience soured many of them on the possibilities of future public investment; they came to associate large capital projects with public subsidies to monopolies and cartels. It would be better, many liberals came to believe, to use public spending in ways that would redound more directly to the benefit of the consumer.

A second weakness in the legacy was that so much of the nation's public investment, both during and after the war, took the form of military spending. Liberals were quick to see the many ways in which military spending was wasteful and unproductive and how it diverted resources from important civilian purposes. They were less willing to acknowledge that at least some military spending, particularly the large expenditures on research and development, served as an investment in the nation's productive capacities. (The military itself seldom justified its programs on that basis, either; the defense of national security was rationale enough.) A large portion of the nation's public investment was, in short, disguised in ways that left it without any autonomous popular legitimacy.

Another weakness was the failure of the wartime agencies of public investment to legitimize themselves in the popular or political mind. During World War I, the short-lived War Industries Board and its director, Bernard Baruch, were widely lionized for their supposedly herculean achievements. The image of their success inspired progressive hopes for similar economic experiments in peacetime. But the World War II mobilization efforts had no such impact. Throughout the war years, corporate leaders who dominated the agencies succeeded in portraying the production "miracles" of World War II as the achievement of the private sector, which heroically overcame the obstacles that government structures placed in their way. The dismal reputation of the chaotic War Production Board and the even more dismal reputation of its ineffectual chairman, Donald Nelson, obscured the important role that state institutions and state funding had played in ensuring sufficient wartime production.

Reinforcing this growing political bias against public investment was the ideological revulsion with which virtually all Americans, liberals and conservatives alike, responded to the fascist regimes that the United States was fighting during the war. The results of the German and Italian experiments in creating "partnerships" between government and business persuaded many Americans that democratic societies must, as Reinhold Niebuhr once said, "walk warily" before embarking on any comparable statist experiments in the United States—including experiments in public investment (or, as the Germans sometimes called it, "state capitalism"). The ideology of the free market drew heavily from the negative examples of Germany, Italy, Japan, and, later, the Soviet Union and emerged from the war with significant new strength.

But the greatest weakness in the legacy of public investment was a result of the very rationale that liberals used to justify it in the first place. For the great New Deal–World War II expansion of public investment coincided with an important, if only slowly recognized, shift in the way that liberals justified government intervention in the economy and defined the problem that this intervention was designed to solve. For some decades before the New Deal and even during the first years of the Roosevelt administration, those who believed in an active state emphasized problems of production. Free-market capitalism, they claimed, could not be trusted to allocate productive resources wisely or equitably alone. Capitalists, left to their own devices, would form monopolies or cartels or would find other ways to avoid competition. The result would be a system of production that was both inefficient and unjust. One of government's important roles, therefore, should be to compel the private sector to behave in ways that would avoid the problems associated with monopoly.

By the early 1930s, producerist reformers had become even more convinced of the need for government intervention in the private sector. American capitalists, they argued, had responded to the Great Depression by retrenching. They had limited wages and cut production. And they had virtually ceased investing. There was no net private investment in the 1930s; the sum of all new private investment was less than the amount of plant depreciation. Not surprisingly, New Dealers came to believe that it was up to the state to promote policies that would force expansion and growth. There were, of course, many different prescriptions for how government should do that. They ranged from vigorous antitrust efforts to state planning of investment and production to public ownership of the means of production. But however vigorous the debate over the role of the state, the ultimate hope of most of those who engaged in it was to find a way for government to influence the way capitalist institutions behaved and the way the capitalist economy invested. Public investment was, of course, one way for government to achieve that goal. The idea of public investment was strongest, therefore, when it was linked in the 1930s and 1940s to a producer-oriented agenda, when public projects could be seen as a contribution not just to consumption but also to the nation's productive potential.

By the end of World War II, most liberals were coming to embrace a different concept of what the state should do, a concept described (but not wholly created) by Keynesian economic theory. The problems of production now seemed less pressing. The real challenge facing the economy, and hence facing a government committed to assisting the economy, was consumption. The Depression, most New Dealers had come to believe, had resulted from a lack of mass purchasing power. The solution to the Depression was a set of public policies that would increase that purchasing power and hence raise demand. The state should treat its citizens less as producers and more as consumers. Some liberals continued to view capitalist leaders with mistrust and to press for antitrust, regulatory, or planning efforts, but these policies were becoming increasingly secondary to the powerful new belief in using government fiscal policies to stimulate demand and create full employment.

That view of the state was not incompatible with a belief in public investment. Indeed, many liberals argued that the greatest value of public investment was in creating consumer demand—both by creating jobs in the short run and by expanding markets in the long run through regional development. Some Keynesians, among them John Kenneth Galbraith, continued through the 1950s and 1960s to insist that the best use of fiscal policy was to spend public funds on important public projects, that to do so would have the multiple effect of stimulating economic growth, enhancing the nation's productive resources, and improving the quality of public space and public life. But most Keynesians rejected Galbraith's notion and embraced a much more conservative version of the theory—what some scholars have called commercial Keynesianism. Public investment, they argued, worked too slowly to provide a significant economic stimulus in a recession. If increasing consumption was the ultimate goal of public policy, then the most effective way to achieve it was through reducing taxes (the approach that Walter Heller persuaded the Kennedy administration to adopt) or through kinds of public spending that would reach the hands of consumers much more quickly (an idea that helped sustain liberal efforts to enlarge programs of public assistance). Such policies had the additional advantage of seeming much less threatening to the traditional ideology of free enterprise.

Concern about the productive capacities of the American economy did not disappear, but it became so secondary to these newer, consumption-centered concerns that it had increasingly little impact on policy. Production, it seemed, could take care of itself. And for nearly thirty years after World War II, it appeared to do so. At the same time, support for public investment languished—not just among conservatives, who had always scorned it, but also among liberals, who were once its champions. Even the remarkable interstate highway program of the 1950s and 1960s did little to relegitimize the idea of public investment. The Eisenhower administration justified the program in the narrowest possible terms: not as a contribution to the larger health of the economy, but simply as a continuation and expansion of the narrowly defined, widely accepted government responsibility for highways. On the right, public investment continued to attract derision and contempt. On the left, it produced little enthusiasm, as attention turned to other, supposedly more efficient tools for promoting growth.

Renewing Public Investment

Where, then, does the idea of public investment stand today? There is at least one area where it continues to attract enthusiastic support, particularly from the right. Many conservatives (and many liberals as well) are firmly convinced that the government has an important role in ushering in the Information Age—in supporting and expanding the capacities and the accessibility of the Internet and other new technologies. Both the Clinton administration and the House Republican leadership, for example, approve of government support for research and investment in these new technologies, although their models for such support are not always identical.

For conservatives, the promise of the Information Age is not just more growth but less regulation. It is the promise of a new, fluid, individualistic world in which ambitious entrepreneurs can circumvent both public and private bureaucracies, rationalizing their freedom by alluding to the imperatives of a new era. Despite their enthusiasm for government subsidies to new technologies along the way, conservatives envision the information era as a world in which talented individuals are even more independent, even less tethered to the state or the corporation or any other collective entity. For the Clinton administration, meanwhile, commitment to the information superhighway entails encouraging voluntary corporate initiatives and offering modest national incentives for the wiring of public schools. But the Clinton approach lacks any substantial public investment that would spur growth while furthering opportunities and shared purpose.

A genuinely progressive program of public investment will go much further. It will not restrict itself to initiatives designed to free individuals from the restrictions of the social fabric or initiatives that have no significant cost attached to them. It will also look for avenues of investment, both modest and substantial, capable of regenerating communities; expanding opportunities; facilitating more conventional, employment-generating forms of economic growth; and improving the character of public life. Such a program will need to rest on two things: a strategy for making itself politically and economically viable in the new economy, and a vision of its goals fitted to the needs of the contemporary world.

Creating a political strategy for a new program of public investment requires confronting an obstacle that many observers of contemporary politics consider virtually insuperable. One is the fiscal straitjacket that the federal deficit and (more to the point) the preoccupation of both major parties with closing it has created. As long as balancing the budget remains the major goal of public life, it will be difficult for any but the most urgent and the most cagily promoted public projects to win political support or congressional approval. Challenging the largely unquestioned assumption that the deficit is and should be our central public concern is an obvious task awaiting progressives.

One strategy particularly well suited for promoting public investment, less a frontal challenge than a flanking maneuver, is to revive the long-abandoned budgetary distinction between current spending and investment. Separating investment budgets from regular budgets is routine for many state governments and for many national governments outside the United States. The American federal government has itself accepted such a division at various times in its history. But in our recent past, there has been no distinction between current spending and long-term investment either in the budget process or in the larger public discourse surrounding it.

The Clinton administration made an abortive rhetorical effort to revive this distinction with its unsuccessful public investment initiative of 1993. But that hastily drafted and sloppily assembled measure actually did the cause more harm than good by labeling serious and frivolous spending programs alike as investments and thus reinforcing the widespread belief that there is no difference between the two. A real investment budget would have to rest on a rigorous set of standards for distinguishing long-term from short-term projects and for calculating each program's likely contributions to sustained economic growth or other long-term social goals. It would have to rest as well on a systematic effort to educate the public about the difference between spending and investment and about the ways in which investments can in fact benefit rather than burden future generations.

What kinds of programs would produce such benefits? On what should a public investment strategy for today's economy concentrate? To some extent, it should concentrate on the things that such strategies have always concentrated on: significant public projects that benefit large numbers of people and that are unlikely to advance without public support. Such projects would, I believe, fall in two large categories. One would be investments in the physical landscape, and the other, investments in the talent and well-being of our population: on one hand, investments in roads, bridges, dams, airports, and other public facilities that benefit our economy; on the other hand, investments in education, training, and other programs that benefit people. But a truly progressive program of public investment would have a broader vision than infrastructure and education alone.

Galbraith's (1958) critique of the affluent society forty years ago was not based primarily on the cost that public squalor imposed on economic growth. It emphasized even more the cost that it imposed on the character of our society and our ability to survive as a community conscious of our ties and obligations to one another. That critique is no less suitable to today's public world than it was to the world of the 1950s, and it requires a vigorous response.

We expect the public sector to provide us with or support the amenities that our communal life must have in order to exist in the first place: parks, playgrounds, concert halls, libraries, and other public spaces; cultural and artistic life, which are among the most important bonds tying communities together; basic services that enable neighborhoods to remain economically and culturally viable. Such amenities have suffered along with every other area of public life during the fiscal pressures of the last twenty years. Their deterioration not only degrades our life as a society. It also reinforces popular despair about the efficacy of the public sector and poisons progressive hopes in many other areas. Public investment is not simply a vehicle for promoting economic growth, although that should be one of its principal tasks. It is also a vehicle for enhancing our society's shared life and for countering the growing inclination of many Americans (actively encouraged by much of the right) to assume that every citizen is autonomous and can rely on the community for nothing.

The contemporary problems of the American economy—problems that seem increasingly detached from its aggregate performance—reveal some of the costs that the United States has paid by allowing decisions about productive resources and public institutions to move so completely into the private sector. Free-market capitalism does many things very well. But it does not and cannot sustain either a healthy economy or a good society by itself. The private sector is not equipped to maintain and improve the nation's basic infrastructure. It has not been effective in creating a trained and educated workforce. It has not reliably generated the new technologies on which advanced economies depend. And it has not proved capable of sustaining the social and cultural lives of communities without active public-sector engagement. There are, in other words, critical tasks in which the state, in partnership with communities, must play a significant role (as it has in the past), or these tasks will remain undone.

Those who believe in public investment, therefore, face a dual challenge. They must look for ways to convince a skeptical public that government is capable of acting effectively to improve the nation's productive capacities and its social health. But they must also work to redirect progressive thinking away from its almost exclusive preoccupation with consumption. Progressives must articulate a renewed concern with ensuring that America can prosper—both as a producing nation and as a viable community—in a rapidly changing world.

The New Social Inequality and Affirmative Opportunity

William Julius Wilson

A s the turn of the century approaches, the movement for racial equality needs a new political strategy. That strategy must appeal to America's broad multiethnic population, while addressing the many problems that afflict disadvantaged minorities and redressing the legacy of historical racism in America.

The nation seems to have become more divided on issues pertaining to race, especially since the first O. J. Simpson murder trial. And affirmative action programs are under heavy assault. Americans' understanding of the meaning and significance of race has become more confused. Many Americans are puzzled by complex racial changes—not only the growth of socioeconomic inequality among African-Americans, but also the sharp increase in joblessness, concentrated poverty, and welfare receipt among the black poor living in ghettos. Such changes have unfolded in the aftermath of the passage of comprehensive civil rights legislation in the 1960s and the subsequent enactment of affirmative action programs and the antipoverty efforts of the Great Society. By now, some three decades later, not only have many changes transpired for African-Americans and for American race relations. In addition, broad public sympathy for those minority individuals who have suffered the most from racial exclusion has waned.

Indeed, many white Americans have turned against public programs widely perceived as benefiting only racial minorities. Several decades ago, efforts to raise the public's awareness and conscience about the plight of African-Americans helped the enactment of civil rights legislation and affirmative action programs. By the 1980s, however, black leaders' assertions that black progress was a "myth"—rhetoric used to reinforce arguments for stronger race-based programs—ironically played into the hands of conservative critics. Although this strategy may have increased sympathy among some whites for the plight of black Americans, it also created the erroneous impression that federal antidiscrimination efforts had failed. And it overlooked the significance of the complex racial changes that had been unfolding since the mid-1960s. Perhaps most pernicious of all, arguments for more and more race-based programs to help blacks fed growing white concerns, aroused by demagogic messages, that any special efforts by politicians to deal with black needs and complaints were coming at the expense of the white majority.

While these developments happened in politics, Americans confronted jarring new economic conditions. National and international economic transformations have placed new stresses on families and communities—stresses that are hardly confined to blacks. Along with African-Americans, large segments of the white, Latino, and Asian populations are also plagued by growing economic insecurities, family breakups, and community stresses. Such conditions are breeding grounds for racial and ethnic tensions. In this social climate, conservatives have attempted to unite white Americans around anger at the government and racial minorities. Their political message seems plausible to many white taxpayers, who see themselves as being forced to pay for programs that primarily benefit racial minorities.

In this essay I suggest how progressives can redefine the issues so that the concerns of both the larger American population and the racial minority population are simultaneously addressed. Progressives can pursue policies that unite rather than divide racial groups, thus opening the way for the formation of a multiracial progressive coalition in national politics.

The Changing Climate for Race-Based Programs

When affirmative action programs were first discussed in the 1960s, the economy was expanding, and incomes were rising. It was a time of optimism, a time when most Americans believed that their children would have better lives than they had. During such times a generosity of spirit permits consideration of sharing an expanding pie.

In the decades immediately after World War II, all income groups experienced economic advancement, including the poor. A rising tide did indeed lift all boats. In fact, as revealed in figure 1, between 1947 and 1973 the lowest quintile in family income experienced the highest growth in annual income, "which meant that the poor were becoming less poor in both relative and absolute terms" (Bronfenbrenner et al. 1996, p. 14). But this pattern began to change in the early 1970s. Growth slowed, and the distribution of inflation-adjusted income started to become more unequal. Whereas average income gains from 1973 to 1992 continued for the higher quintiles (but at a rate considerably slower than that of the previous two decades), the two lowest quintiles actually experienced annual declines in income during this period. Wage data since 1979, based on percentiles instead of quintiles (see figure 2), show a pattern quite similar to the trends in family income. The wages of those at the top have continued to climb in recent years, while those at the bottom have fallen steadily.

Thus the downward trend in wages during the past two decades has lowered the incomes of the least well-off citizens. This trend has been accompanied by a growing sense among an increasing number of Americans that their long-term economic prospects are bleaker. And they would not be reassured to learn that the United States has had the most rapid growth of wage inequality in the Western world. In the 1950s and 1960s the average earnings of college graduates was only about 20 percent higher than that of high school graduates. By 1979, it had increased to 49 percent, and then it rapidly grew to 83 percent by 1992. "When the American economy rebounded from a recession in the early 1990s, roughly 2 million new jobs were created per year, but a large percentage of these offered wages below $8 an hour (or about $16,000 a year), with few if any health benefits and not much opportunity for advancement" (Bronfenbrenner et al. 1996, p. 117).

In sum, since the late 1970s, real wages (that is, wages adjusted for inflation) have fallen in the United States. Wage disparities between those with college degrees and those without have widened considerably. Working-class Americans feel economically pinched, barely able to maintain current standards of living even on two incomes. Many are insecure about keeping their jobs and fear that they will never be able to afford to send their children to

Figure 1. Family Income in the United States

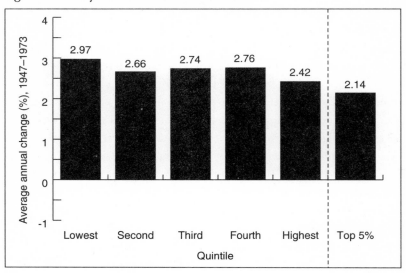

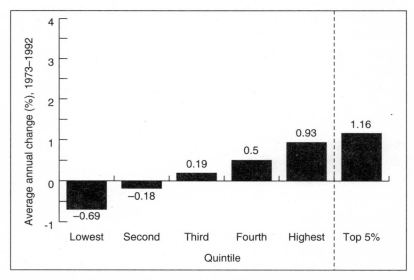

Source: Adapted from Bronfenbrenner et al. (1996). The 1947 figures are from *The Statistical History of the United States, Colonial Times to 1970.* The 1969 and 1992 figures are from the Bureau of the Census, *Income of Families and Persons in the United States, 1990.* Figures are adjusted for inflation based on constant 1992 dollars.

Figure 2. Wage Growth in the United States

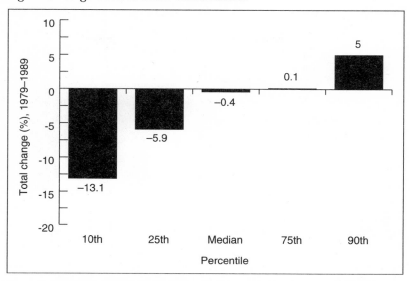

Source: Adapted from Bronfenbrenner et al. (1996). Data reported in the Council of Economic Advisors, *Economic Report of the President, 1995*. Wages are in constant 1982–1984 CPI-U-X1 dollars.

college. Many believe that for all their hard work, their children's lives will be worse than theirs. For example, a 1995 Harris poll, conducted for *Business Week*, revealed that only one-half of all parents expected their children to have a better life than theirs; nearly seven out of ten believed that the American dream has been more difficult to achieve during the past ten years; and three-quarters felt that the dream will be even harder to achieve during the next ten years (cited in Bronfenbrenner et al. 1996).

Unfortunately for those who support race-based programs, this period of economic hard times has not been an ideal climate for a national debate on affirmative action. Despite the recent economic recovery and low rates of unemployment, most families continue to struggle with declining real wages, increasing job displacement, and job insecurity in a highly integrated and highly technological global economy. During periods when people are beset with economic anxiety, they become more receptive to simplistic ideological messages that deflect attention away from the real and complex sources of their problems, and it is vitally important that political leaders channel citizens' frustrations in more positive or constructive directions. For the past few years and especially in 1995, immediately after the congressional elections of 1994, just the opposite frequently occurred. The poisonous racial rhetoric of certain highly visible spokespersons has increased racial tensions and channeled frustrations in ways that severely divide the racial groups. Instead of associating citizens' problems with economic and political changes, these divisive messages have encouraged them to turn on each other—race against race. As I pointed out in a *New York Times* editorial (Wilson 1992), this was a theme repeatedly emphasized by Bill Clinton during his 1992 campaign for the presidency.

Many white Americans have turned against a strategy emphasizing programs that they perceive as benefiting only racial minorities. There has been a growing concern, aroused by demagogic messages, that the politicians' sensitivity to black complaints had come at the expense of the white majority. And undifferentiated black complaints have aggravated the situation because they have reinforced a perception that, whatever our efforts, nothing really works, and a lot of time, energy, and money have been wasted.

The Rising Significance of Class

By the beginning of the 1980s, the accomplishments of the civil rights struggle were clear; among them were the rising numbers of blacks in professional, technical, managerial, and administrative positions. Progress was also evident in the increasing enrollment of blacks in colleges and universities and the growing number of black homeowners. The expansion of participation in these areas was proportionately greater for blacks than for whites because such a tiny percentage of blacks had held property or pursued higher education before this time. As Jennifer Hochschild has pointed out, "One has not really succeeded in America unless one can pass the chance for success on to one's children" (1995, p. 44). Until the 1960s, doing so was quite difficult even for the few members of the old black middle class. Empirical research in the early 1960s provided no evidence that class could rival the powerful effects of race on black occupational and income achievements. In other words, states Hochschild, blacks "experienced a perverse sort of egalitarianism—neither the disadvantages of poverty nor the advantages of wealth made much difference in what they could achieve or pass on to their children. Discrimination swamped everything else" (p. 44).

Research by social scientists, however, reveals that between 1962 and 1973, class began to affect career and generational mobility for blacks as it had regularly done for whites (Wilson 1980; Featherman and Hauser 1978; Hout 1984). In particular, blacks from the most advantaged backgrounds experienced the greatest upward mobility. For the first time in American history, more advantaged blacks could expect their success to persist and cumulate. These trends have continued since 1973 but at a slower rate (Hochschild 1995, p. 44). On the other hand, among the disadvantaged segments of the black population, especially the ghetto poor, many dire problems—joblessness, concentrated poverty, family breakup, and the receipt of welfare—were getting even worse between 1973 and 1980.

The differential rates of progress in the black community have continued through the 1980s and early 1990s. Family incomes among the poorest of the poor reveal the pattern. From 1977 to 1993, the percentage of blacks with incomes below 50 percent of the amount designated as the poverty line, what we call the poorest of the poor, increased from 9 percent of the total black population in 1977 to 17 percent in 1993. In 1977, fewer than one of every three poor blacks fell below one-half of the poverty-line amount, but by 1993 the proportion rose to more than one-half (these figures and those that follow have been adjusted for inflation). In 1993 the average poor black family slipped further below the poverty level than in any year since 1967, when the Census Bureau started collecting such data (U.S. Bureau of the Census, 1994).

From 1975 to 1992, while the average income of the lowest quintile of black families in the United States declined by one-third and that of the second-lowest quintile declined by 13 percent, the average income of the highest quintile of black families climbed by 23 percent and that of the top 5 percent by 35 percent. Although income inequality between whites and blacks is substantial and the financial gap is even greater between the two races when wealth is considered—total financial assets, not just income (Oliver and Shapiro 1995; Wolff 1995)—in 1992 the highest fifth of black families nonetheless secured a record 49 percent of the total income among black families, compared to the 44 percent share of the total income received by the highest fifth of white families, also a record. So while income inequality has widened generally in America since 1975, the divide is even more dramatic among black Americans. If we are to fashion remedies for black poverty, we need to understand the origins and dynamics of inequality in the African-American community. Without disavowing the accomplishments of the civil rights movement, black leaders and policymakers now need to give more attention to remedies that will make a concrete difference in the lives of the poor.

The Achievements and Limits of Affirmative Action

The demands of the civil rights movement reflected a general assumption on the part of black leaders in the 1960s that the government could best protect the rights of individual members of minority groups, not by formally bestowing rewards and punishments based on racial group membership, but by using antidiscrimination legislation to enhance individual freedom. The movement was particularly concerned about access to education, employment, voting, and public accommodations. From the 1950s to 1970, the emphasis was on freedom of choice; the role of the state was to prevent the formal categorization of people on the basis of race. Antibias legislation was designed to eliminate racial discrimination without considering the proportion of minorities in certain positions. The underlying principle was that individual merit should be the sole determining factor in choosing candidates for desired positions. Because civil rights protests against racial discrimination clearly upheld a fundamental American principle, they carried a degree of moral authority that leaders like Martin Luther King, Jr., were able to repeatedly and effectively emphasize.

It would have been ideal if programs based on the principle of freedom of individual opportunity were sufficient to remedy racial inequality in our society. But long periods of racial oppression can result in a system of inequality that lingers even after racial barriers come down. The most disadvantaged minority individuals, crippled by the cumulative effects of both race and class subjugation, disproportionately lack the resources to compete effectively in a free and open market.

Eliminating racial barriers creates the greatest opportunities for the better-trained, most talented, and best-educated members of minority groups because these members possess the resources to compete most effectively. These resources reflect a variety of advantages—family stability, financial means, positive peer groups, good schooling—provided or made possible by their parents (Fishkin 1983).

By the late 1960s, a number of black leaders began to recognize this. In November 1967, Kenneth B. Clark said, "The masses of Negroes are now starkly aware of the fact that recent civil rights victories benefited a very small percentage of middle-class Negroes while [poorer blacks'] predicament remained the same or worsened" (Clark 1967, p. 8). Simply eliminating racial barriers was not going to be enough. As the black economist Vivian Henderson put it, "If all racial prejudice and discrimination and all racism were erased today, all the ills brought by the process of economic class distinction and economic depression of the masses of black people would remain" (Henderson 1975, p. 54).

Accordingly, black leaders and liberal policymakers began to emphasize the need not only to eliminate active discrimination but also to counteract the effects of past racial oppression. Instead of seeking remedies only for individual complaints of discrimination, as specified in Title 7 of the Civil Rights Act of 1964 (which prohibits employers from discriminating against individuals on the grounds of race, color, religion, gender, or national origin), they sought government-mandated affirmative action programs designed to ensure adequate minority representation in employment, education, and public programs.

But if the more advantaged members of minority groups benefit disproportionately from policies that embody the principle of equality of individual opportunity, they also profit disproportionately from affirmative action policies based solely on their racial group membership (Fishkin 1983). Minority individuals from the most advantaged families tend to be disproportionately represented among those of their racial group most qualified for preferred status, such as college admissions, higher-paying jobs, and promotions. Thus policies of affirmative action are much more likely to enhance the socioeconomic positions of the more advantaged minority individuals than the positions of the truly disadvantaged (Loury 1984 and 1995).

To be sure, affirmative action was not intended mainly to benefit the more advantaged minority individuals. As William L. Taylor, the former director of the United States Civil Rights Commission, has stated, "The focus of much of the [affirmative action] effort has been not just on white-collar jobs, but also on law enforcement, construction work, and craft and production in large companies—all areas in which the extension of new opportunities has provided upward mobility for less advantaged minority workers"

(Taylor 1986, p. 1714). As Taylor also notes, studies show that many minority students entering medical schools during the 1970s were from low-income families.

Affirmative action policies, however, did not really open up broad avenues of upward mobility for the masses of disadvantaged blacks. Like other forms of "creaming," they provided opportunities for those individuals from low socioeconomic background with the greatest educational and social resources. A careful analysis of data on income, employment, and educational attainment would probably reveal that only a few individuals who reside in the inner-city ghettos have benefited from affirmative action.

Since the early 1970s urban minorities have been highly vulnerable to structural changes in the economy, such as the shift from goods-producing to service-producing industries, the increasing polarization of the labor market into low-wage and high-wage sectors, the destabilizing innovations in technology, and the relocation of manufacturing industries outside the central city. These shifts have led to sharp increases in joblessness and the related problems of highly concentrated poverty, welfare receipt, and family breakup, despite the passage of antidiscrimination legislation to correct discriminatory patterns through litigation and the creation of affirmative action programs that mandate goals and timetables for the employment of minorities (Wilson 1987, 1995).

On the other hand, affirmative action programs have helped to bring about sharp increases in the number of blacks entering higher education and gaining professional and managerial positions. Moreover, as long as minorities are underrepresented in high-paying, desirable positions in society, affirmative action programs will be needed. Nonetheless, in response to cries from conservatives to abolish affirmative action altogether, some liberals have argued for a shift from affirmative action based on race to one based on economic class or need (Kahlenberg 1995).

The major distinguishing characteristic of affirmative action based on need is the recognition that the problems of the disadvantaged—low income, crime-ridden neighborhoods, broken homes, inadequate housing, poor education, cultural and linguistic differences—are not always clearly related to previous racial discrimination. Children who grow up in homes plagued by these disadvantages are more likely to be denied an equal chance in life because the development of their aspirations and talents is hindered by their environment, regardless of race. Minorities would benefit disproportionately from affirmative opportunity programs designed to address these disadvantages because they suffer disproportionately from the effects of such environments, but the problems of disadvantaged whites would be addressed as well.

An affirmative action based solely on need, however, would result in the systematic exclusion of many middle-income blacks from desirable positions because the standard or conventional measures of performance are not sensitive to the cumulative effects of race. By this I mean having one's life choices limited by race, regardless of class, because of the effects of living in segregated neighborhoods (that is, being exposed to styles of behavior, habits, and the particular skills that emerge from patterns of racial exclusion), because of the quality of de facto segregated schooling, and because of the nurturing by parents whose experiences have also been shaped and limited by race, which ultimately affects the resources they are able to pass on to their children (Heckman 1995).

Thus if we were to rely solely on the standard criteria for college admission, like SAT scores, even many children from black middle-class families would be denied admission in favor of middle-class whites who are not weighed down by the accumulation of disadvantages that stem from racial restrictions and who therefore tend to score higher on these conventional measures. An affirmative action based solely on need or economic class position could create a situation in which African-Americans who are admitted to Harvard represent the bottom half of the socioeconomic continuum in the black community, while those who are in the top half tend to be excluded because they are not eligible for consideration under affirmative action. They would therefore be left to compete with middle- and upper-income whites who are not burdened by the handicaps of race—as their higher scores on the conventional tests reflect.

The extent to which standard aptitude tests like the SAT and tests used for promoting police officers are measuring not privilege but real merit or the real potential to succeed is not readily apparent. Ideally, we should develop flexible criteria of evaluation or performance measures, as opposed to numerical guidelines or quotas, that would not exclude people with background handicaps, including minority racial background, who have as much potential to succeed as those admitted without those handicaps. While some test scores may correlate well with performance, they do not necessarily measure important attributes that also determine performance, such as perseverance, motivation, interpersonal skills, reliability, and leadership qualities. Accordingly, since race is one of the components of being disadvantaged in this society, the ideal affirmative action program would emphasize flexible criteria of evaluation based on both need and race.

The cumulative effects of historical discrimination and racial segregation are reflected in many subtle ways that result in the underrepresentation of blacks in positions of high status and their overrepresentation in positions of low status. Some of these problems can be easily addressed with affirmative action programs that are at least in part based on race; others have to be combated by means of race-neutral strategies. As indicated earlier, less-advantaged blacks are extremely vulnerable to changes in our modern industrial society, and their problems are difficult to solve by means of race-based strategies alone—either those that support equality of individual opportunity, such as the Civil Rights Act of 1964, or those that represent affirmative action. Now more than ever, we need broader solutions than those we have employed in the past.

From Preference to Affirmative Opportunity

Given the current political climate and the new social inequality, any program designed to significantly improve the life chances of disadvantaged minorities, including increased employment opportunities, would have to be broadly applicable. That is, it would have to address the concerns of wide segments of the U.S. population, not just those of minority citizens.

Almost two decades ago, Vivian Henderson argued that "the economic future of blacks in the United States is bound up with that of the rest of the nation. Politics designed in the future to cope with the problems of the poor and victimized will also yield benefits to blacks. In contrast, any efforts to treat blacks separately from the rest of the nation are likely to lead to frustration, heightened racial animosities, and a waste of the country's resources and the precious resources of black people" (Henderson 1975, p. 54).

Henderson's warning seems to be especially appropriate in periods of economic stagnation, when public support for programs targeted to minorities—or associated with real or imagined material sacrifice on the part of whites—tends to wane. The economy was strong when affirmative action programs were introduced during the Johnson administration. When the economy turned down in the 1970s, the public's view of affirmative action increasingly soured.

Furthermore, as Joseph A. Califano, Johnson's staff assistant for domestic affairs, observed in 1988, such programs were generally acceptable to whites "only as a temporary expedient to speed blacks' entry into the social and economic mainstream." But as years passed, many whites "saw continuing such preferences as an unjust insistence by Democrats that they do penance for an era of slavery and discrimination they had nothing to do with." They also associated the decline in public schools not with broader changes in society but with "forced integration" (Califano 1988, p. 29).

The Democrats also came under fire for their support for programs that increasingly were misrepresented as being intended for poor blacks alone. Virtually separate medical and legal systems developed in many cities. Public services became identified mainly with blacks, private services mainly with whites. In an era of ostensible racial justice, many public programs ironically seemed to constitute a new and costlier form of segregation. White taxpayers saw themselves as being forced through taxes to pay for medical and legal services that many of them could not afford to purchase for their own families.

White reaction to race-based problems has several dimensions, however. Over the past fifty years, there has been a steep rise in white support for racial desegregation. For example, although in 1942 only 42 percent of white Americans supported integrated schooling, by 1993 that figure had skyrocketed to 95 percent. Public opinion polls reveal similar patterns of change during the past five decades in white support for integration with regard to public accommodations, mass transportation, and housing (Bobo and Smith 1994).

Nonetheless, the virtual disappearance of Jim Crow attitudes toward racial segregation has not resulted in strong backing for government programs to aggressively combat discrimination, increase further integration, enroll blacks in institutions of higher learning, or enlarge the proportion of blacks in high-level occupations. Indeed, as evidenced in the public opinion polls, whites overwhelmingly object to government assistance targeted to blacks. Whereas eight of every ten African-Americans believe that the government is not spending enough to assist blacks today, only slightly more than one-third of white Americans feel this way. The idea that the federal government "has a special obligation to help improve the living standard of blacks" because they "have been discriminated against so long" was supported by only one in five whites in 1991 and has never exceeded more than one in four since 1975 (Bobo and Kluegel 1994). And the lack of white support for this idea is unrelated to such background factors as age and education level.

Of course, the most widely discussed racial policy issue in recent years has been affirmative action. Despite a slight decrease in opposition to affirmative action programs in education and employment between 1986 and 1990, sentiments against these programs remain strong. In 1990, almost seven in ten white Americans opposed quotas to admit black students in colleges and universities, and more than eight in ten objected to the idea of preferential hiring and promotion of blacks.

Such strong white opposition to quotas and preferential hiring and promotion should not lead us to overlook the fact that there are some affirmative action policies that are supported by wide segments of the white population, regardless of racial attitudes. Recent studies reveal that, while opposing such "preferential" racial policies as college admission quotas or job hiring and promotion strategies designed to achieve equal outcomes, most white Americans approve of such "compensatory" affirmative action policies as race-targeted programs for job training, special education, and recruitment (Bobo and Smith 1994; Bobo and Kluegel 1993; Lipset and Schneider 1978; Kluegel and Smith 1986; Kinder and Sanders 1987). For example, in the 1990 General Social Survey, 68 percent of all whites favored spending more money on schools in black neighborhoods, especially for preschool and early education programs. And 70 percent favored granting special college scholarships to black children who maintain good grades (Bobo and Smith 1994).

Accordingly, programs that enable blacks to take advantage of opportunities, such as race-targeted early education programs and job training, are less likely to be "perceived as challenging the values of individualism and the work ethic." In other words, compensatory or opportunity-enhancing affirmative action programs are supported because they reinforce the belief that the allocation of jobs and economic rewards should be based on individual effort, training, and talent. As sociologists Larry Bobo and James Kluegel (1993) put it: "Opportunity-enhancing programs receive greater support because they are consistent with the norm of helping people help themselves. In addition, opportunity-enhancing programs do not challenge principles of equity. Indeed, requirements that beneficiaries of such programs make the effort to acquire the training and skills needed to improve their economic positions are fully consistent with reward on the basis of individual effort."

Unlike preferential racial policies, opportunity-enhancing programs have popular support and a relatively weak connection to antiblack attitudes (Bobo and Smith 1994). For all these reasons, to make the most effective case for affirmative action programs in a period when such programs are under attack from many quarters, emphasis should be shifted from numerical guidelines to opportunity. The concept that I would use to signal this shift is "affirmative opportunity."* By substituting "opportunity" for "action," the concept "affirmative opportunity" draws the focus away from a guarantee of equality of results, which is how "affirmative action" has come to be understood. It echoes the phrase "equal opportunity," which connotes a principle that most Americans still support, while avoiding connotations now associated (fairly or not) with the idea of affirmative action—connotations like quotas, lowering of standards, and reverse discrimination, which most Americans detest.

However, by retaining the term "affirmative," the concept keeps the connotation that something more than offering formal, legal equality is required to overcome the legacy of slavery and Jim Crow segregation. As a society, we also have the continuing moral obligation to compensate for the enduring burdens—the social and psychological damage—of segregation, discrimination, and bigotry. To practice affirmative opportunity means to renew the nation's commitment to enable all Americans, regardless of income, race, or other attributes, to achieve to the highest level that their abilities will permit. In this sense, the phrase echoes President Johnson's 1965 Howard University commencement speech on human rights, which was uniformly praised by black civil rights leaders.

To repeat, polling data suggest that Americans support the idea of affirmative action programs to enable people to overcome disadvantages that are not of their own making. This should be done, however, by using flexible

---

*My views on affirmative opportunity have greatly benefited from my discussions with Noel Salinger of the Irving B. Harris School of Public Policy at the University of Chicago. Salinger helped me to draft several memoranda on affirmative action for the White House, and my views here were initially developed in those memoranda.

criteria of evaluation, not numerical guidelines or quotas. The obvious rejoinder is that "using flexible criteria" is another way of saying that lower standards will be permitted. On the contrary, using flexible criteria of evaluation will ensure that we are measuring merit or potential to succeed rather than privilege. In other words, we want to use criteria that would not exclude people who have as much potential to succeed as those admitted who have more privileged backgrounds.

The differences in average test scores, touted by some opponents to compensatory social programs and affirmative action, are largely measures of differences in opportunities between the advantaged and the disadvantaged, especially in equal access to high-quality child care and good schooling (Heckman 1995; Neal and Johnson 1995). Flexible criteria accommodate the need to design metrics of ability that predict success and that are not captured by such tests. Indications of these attributes may be obtained from letters of recommendation, past performance, or other measures. Mayor Richard Daley's use of merit promotions in the Chicago Police Department, which are based on such factors as job performance and leadership ability, is an example of how such criteria can be used.

Relying on flexible criteria may be a way of replacing the goals and timetables currently used by government agencies and contractors. Having said that, I should also note that it will be extremely important to calibrate the use of flexible criteria in practice. They must be presented as a way of expanding the pool of qualified applicants by making attributes other than raw test scores count more. Flexible criteria must be applied in thoughtful ways, based on the experience of what works in certain situations and particular institutions. Otherwise, the practice will be infected with arbitrariness, which would quickly undermine public support.

New Social Rights for All Americans
Affirmative opportunity efforts remain vital to a progressive strategy and central to the continuing quest for racial justice in America. But affirmative opportunity programs alone are not enough. They ought to be combined with appropriate race-neutral public policies in order to address economic insecurities that now affect many groups in an era of rising social inequality.

In thinking about social rights today, we must appreciate that the poor and the working classes of all racial groups struggle to make ends meet and that even the middle class has experienced a decline in its living standard. Americans across racial and class boundaries worry about unemployment and job security, declining real wages, escalating medical and housing costs, the availability of affordable child care programs, the sharp decline in the quality of public education, and crime and drug trafficking in their neighborhoods.

Not surprisingly, these concerns are clearly reflected in public opinion surveys. For the last several years, national opinion polls consistently reveal strong public backing for government labor-market strategies, including training efforts, to increase employment opportunities. A 1988 Harris poll indicated that almost three-quarters of its respondents would support a tax increase to pay for child care. A 1989 Harris poll reported that almost nine out of ten Americans would like to see fundamental changes in the health care system of the United States. A September 1993 *New York Times*–CBS poll, on the eve of President Clinton's health care address to the nation, revealed that nearly two-thirds of the nation's citizens would be willing to pay higher taxes "so that all Americans have health insurance that they can't lose no matter what." Finally, recent surveys conducted by the National Opinion Research Center at the University of Chicago reveal that a substantial majority of Americans want to see more money spent on improving the nation's educational system and on halting the rise in crime and drug addiction (General Social Survey 1988–94).

Despite being officially race-neutral, programs created in response to these concerns—programs that increase employment opportunities and job skills training, improve public education, promote better child and health care, and reduce neighborhood crime and drug abuse—would disproportionately benefit the most disadvantaged segments of the population, especially poor minorities. Social programs, too, can further racial justice, provided that they are designed to include the needy as well as the somewhat better off.

A comprehensive race-neutral initiative to address economic and social inequality should be viewed as an extension of—not a replacement for—opportunity-enhancing programs that include race-based criteria to fight social inequality. To repeat, I feel that such programs should employ flexible criteria of evaluation in college admission, hiring, job promotion, and so on, and should be based on a broad definition of disadvantage that incorporates notions of both need and race. Although recent public opinion polls indicate that most Americans would support race-based programs intended to enhance opportunities, mobilizing and sustaining the political support for such programs will be much more difficult if they are not designed to reach broader segments of the American population.

Other programs that can be accurately described as purely race-neutral—national heath care, school reform, and job training based on need—would greatly benefit not only racial minority populations but large segments of the dominant white population as well. National opinion poll results suggest the possibility of a new alignment in support of a comprehensive social rights initiative that would include such programs. If such an alignment is attempted, perhaps it ought to feature a new public rhetoric that would do two things: focus on problems that afflict not only the poor but the working and middle classes as well; and emphasize integrative programs that would promote the social and economic improvement of all groups in society, not just the truly disadvantaged segments of the population.

In the new, highly integrated global economy, an increasing number of Americans across racial, ethnic, and income groups are experiencing declining real incomes, increasing job displacement, and growing economic insecurity. The unprecedented level of inner-city joblessness represents one important aspect of the broader economic dislocations that cut across racial and ethnic groups in the United States (Wilson 1996). Accordingly, where economic and social reforms are concerned, it hardly seems politically wise to focus mainly on the most disadvantaged groups while ignoring other segments of the population that have also been adversely affected by global economic changes.

Unfortunately, just when bold new comprehensive initiatives are urgently needed to address these problems, the U.S. Congress has retreated from using public policy as an instrument with which to fight social inequality. Failure to deal with this growing social inequality, including the rise of joblessness in U.S. inner cities, could seriously worsen the economic lives of urban families and neighborhoods.

Groups ranging from the inner-city poor to the working- and middle-class Americans who are struggling to make ends meet will have to be effectively mobilized in order for the current course taken by policymakers to be changed. Perhaps the best way to accomplish this is through coalition politics that promotes race-neutral efforts—such as jobs creation, further expansion of the earned income tax credit, public school reform, access to excellent child care programs, and universal health insurance. A broad-based political coalition is needed to successfully push such programs through the political process.

Because an effective political coalition in part depends upon how the issues to be addressed are defined, it is imperative for leaders to underscore the need for economic and social reform that benefits all groups, not just America's minority poor. Changes in the global economy are creating growing social inequality and situations which intensify antagonisms between different racial and ethnic groups. Yet groups who often see themselves as antagonists may become allies in a reform coalition to redress common problems—especially problems perceived as caused by forces outside their own control.

In the absence of a broad, effective coalition, disadvantaged groups could find themselves in a very vulnerable political position. According to recent proposals in the House of Representatives, more than two-thirds of proposed spending cuts from the federal budget for the year 2000 would come from programs targeted for low-income citizens, even though these programs represent only one-fifth of the current federal budget. And the situation is even more clear-cut when we consider possibilities for new social programs. Unless progressives can build broad coalitions, it is unlikely that Congress will ever vote to finance the kinds of reforms that are needed to combat the new social inequality. The momentum is away from, not toward, adequate social programs.

Instead of recognizing and dealing with the complex and changing realities that have led to economic distress for so many Americans, policymakers seek to assign blame and associate the economic problems of families and individuals alike with such personal shortcomings as lack of initiative, work ethic, or motivation. Consequently, there is very little support in favor of financing any social programs, even the creation of public service jobs for the limited number of welfare recipients who reach a time limit for the receipt of welfare checks. Considering the deleterious consequences that this shortsighted retreat from public policy will have for so many Americans, it is distressing that progressive groups, far from being energized to reverse the public policy direction in which the country is now moving, at times appear intimidated and paralyzed by today's racially charged political rhetoric.

Comprehensive solutions for the new social inequality stand little chance of being adopted or even seriously considered if no new political coalition begins pressing for economic and social reform. Political leaders concerned about the current shift in public policy will have to develop a unifying rhetoric, a progressive message that both resonates with broad segments of the American population and enables groups to recognize that it is in their interest to join a reform coalition dedicated to moving America forward.

Bridging the Racial Divide

Given America's tense racial situation, especially in urban areas, the formation of a multi-ethnic reform coalition will not be easy. Our nation's response to racial discord in the central city and to the growing racial divide between the city and the suburbs has been disappointing. In discussing these problems we have a tendency to engage in the kind of rhetoric that exacerbates, rather than alleviates, urban and metropolitan racial tensions. Ever since the 1992 Los Angeles riot, the media has focused heavily on the factors that divide rather than unite racial groups. Emphasis on racial division peaked in 1995 following the jury's verdict in the O. J. Simpson murder trail. Before the verdict was announced, opinion polls revealed, whites overwhelmingly thought that Mr. Simpson was guilty, while a substantial majority of blacks felt that he was innocent. The media clips showing public reaction to the verdict dramatized the racial contrasts: blacks appeared elated and jubilant; whites appeared stunned, angry, and somber. America's racial divide, as depicted in the media, seemed wider than ever.

The country's deep racial divisions certainly should not be underestimated, but the unremitting emphasis on these gaps has obscured the fact that African-Americans, whites, and other ethnic groups share many concerns, are beset by many similar problems, and have important values, aspirations, and hopes in common.

For example, if inner-city blacks are experiencing the greatest problems of joblessness, their situation is nevertheless a more extreme form of economic difficulties that have affected many Americans since 1980. Solutions to the broader problems of economic marginality in this country, including those that stem from changes in the global economy, can go a long way toward addressing the problems of inner-city joblessness, especially if the application of resources includes wise targeting of the groups most in need of help (Wilson 1996). Discussions that emphasize common solutions to shared problems promote a sense of unity, regardless of the different degrees of severity in the problems afflicting different groups. Such messages bring races together, not apart, and are especially important during periods of racial tension.

Because the problems of the new social inequality are growing more severe, a vision of interracial unity that acknowledges racially distinct problems but at the same time emphasizes transracial solutions to shared problems is more important than ever. Such a vision should be developed, shared, and promoted by all leaders in this country, but especially by political leaders.

A new democratic vision must reject the commonly held view that race is so divisive that whites, blacks, Latinos, and other ethnic groups cannot work together in a common cause. Those articulating the new vision must realize that if a political message is tailored to a white audience, racial minorities draw back, just as whites draw back when a message is tailored to minority audiences. The challenge is to find issues and programs that concern families of all racial and ethnic groups, so that individuals in these groups can honestly perceive mutual interests and join in a multiracial coalition to move America forward.

Despite legacies of racial domination and obstacles thrown up by recent events, a politics about problems and solutions relevant for people across racial groups is very possible in the United States today. Political leaders— above all popular Democrats—should forcefully articulate such a message and work to fashion the multiracial coalitions that must be at the heart of any progressive new majority in American democracy.

The Case for Social Insurance

Theodore R. Marmor and

Jerry L. Mashaw

Imagine for a moment an America without social insurance—without Social Security, Medicare, unemployment insurance, or any sort of broadly pooled employee health coverage. In this America, middle-aged, middle-income citizens would have to bear the burden of financially supporting their aged parents. They would be at the mercy of corporate downsizings and the vagaries of the business cycle, and they would have to cope entirely on their own with the potentially catastrophic medical costs of their and their parents' illnesses.

Many people would escape most of these calamities, of course, and many more would believe that they could escape them—until the moment disaster struck. Emergency help might be available from private or public charities, but only for people who could prove that they were destitute. Those in dire circumstances but not actually destitute would be a minority, and the majority might believe that these unfortunates were to blame for their fate. The skeptical majority might well give some help, but it would do so grudgingly and in ways that the recipients would likely find humiliating.

An America without social insurance would combine high anxiety about personal security with the self-righteous belief that whatever one has has been individually earned. Splits between haves and have-nots, the lucky and the unlucky, would fester. The nation's politics would likely oscillate between attempts to entrench the status quo by regulation—tariffs, laws about plant closings, job guarantees, employer mandates, and the like—and bitter contests over who among the poor are sufficiently deserving of aid. It is hard to imagine how American workers, without the security of social insurance, could be brought to accept the desirability of an ever-changeable market with flexible and modest legal constraints. The demands of narrow interest groups would proliferate, as those with momentary market advantages sought to lock in a measure of security. In other words, an America without the personal and social protections afforded by social insurance would not be a society that most people would like for their families. Nor would business leaders like the political side effects.

Social insurance programs are, in short, good for American society and good for Information Age capitalism. Democracy works better if citizens participate together in risk-reducing arrangements to which all contribute and of which all can be proud. This is the truth about social insurance. But since the 1970s, the American public has been told a very different story.

Americans have been encouraged to doubt both the financial affordability and the operational manageability of social insurance programs that play such a critical role in holding our economy and society together. Determined to undermine and privatize the nation's publicly managed social insurance systems, antigovernment conservatives have blanketed the media with opinion pieces, whipping up hysteria about entitlements that are supposedly breaking the federal budget while delivering unnecessary benefits to wealthy old people. Following a deliberate, long-term strategy (see Butler and Germanis 1983), the opponents of social insurance have tried to persuade middle-class Americans that Social Security, Medicare, and other universal social insurance programs are problems rather than vital solutions to today's and tomorrow's insecurities.

Against the backdrop of the confusions and misplaced anxiety stoked by the enemies of social insurance, we restate the civic and economic case for America's variant of social insurance. We refute the criticisms that have been leveled against Social Security and Medicare by would-be privatizers, and we show how these valuable pillars of the nation's existing social insurance system can be prudently reformed for the twenty-first century. Now more than ever, the United States needs comprehensive social insurance.

Our nation's universalistic social programs should be adjusted and expanded for the future, not dismantled.

The American Version of Social Insurance

American social insurance rests on the premise that we should protect workers and their families from dramatic losses of economic status and should do so through programmatic interventions that are socially respectable, economically sensible, and politically stable. For virtually all Americans, a socially respectable protection against economic loss means protection that is earned by funding the insurance pool. Whatever the details of particular programs—whether disability insurance, Medicare, unemployment insurance, life insurance, or Social Security pensions—social insurance rejects safety nets made of means-tested welfare programs as stigmatizing and unreliable. The social insurance recipient is neither pauper nor supplicant.

The contributor's Social Security card, not a poverty-level, means-tested safety net, is the central metaphor of social insurance. Rather than symbolically catching those who have fallen through the safety net, the card of social insurance stands for the collective effort to prevent a radical decline in a family's living standards. Modeled after the fringe benefits that economic elites take for granted, American Social Security is meant to protect citizens against the collectively predictable but individually uncertain risks of loss of income in a modern capitalist economy. Social insurance represents an ideal of economic security, one guaranteeing a sense of worthiness and dignity for those working in a cooperative social enterprise.

This social ideal has political consequences. It produces an us/us rather than a we/them political dynamic. The question is not what "we" (the affluent) should do for "them" (the impoverished). Rather, it is how we should manage the risks of economic misfortune that will befall some of us some of the time and threaten all of us over time. This perspective both stabilizes the politics of particular programs and dampens the fires of class conflict that might otherwise destabilize the political order more generally. The second concern—class conflict—was prominent at the beginning of American social insurance in the 1930s. The first concern—the destabilization of longstanding commitments—must occur to anyone who has witnessed the ravaging of antipoverty programs and the corrosive politics surrounding welfare from the mid-1970s to the present.

The economic rationale for universalistic social insurance has several parts. For many American families, low incomes, overoptimism, and a myopic focus on present needs or wants have hampered savings for a secure retirement or for insuring against the loss of income through death or disability. Universalistic insurance also recognizes that people at the start of their working lives have trouble insuring themselves against the possible future loss of earning capacity, for this is when their earnings are relatively low and their family obligations relatively large. Finally, collective insurance against risks also protects the prudent against the "free riding" of the imprudent, who would ultimately claim social support from "pools" (general taxation) to which they had not contributed.

Some financial risks, we should keep in mind, are extremely difficult to insure against through private markets, even if Americans were all responsible, reasonably well-off, and farsighted. The moral hazard inherent in disability insurance, along with the tendency of courts to rewrite contracts, makes market provision for disability risks extremely inefficient for virtually all who really need it. Similarly, rational risk selection by private insurers will exclude from reasonably priced health insurance pools just those persons or families who are most at risk. And no insurance executive worth her stock options would even propose attempting to provide private unemployment insurance. In these situations, not only are broad social insurance programs socially and politically desirable, but they are economically the only game in town.

Worker-Contributors Together

These social, political, and economic advantages notwithstanding, critics loudly complain about the unfairness of America's social insurance arrangements. The character of these complaints reveals the ideological chasm that separates the social insurance vision of economic security from its individualistic, libertarian antagonists.

Talk of fairness is a staple of political conversation, and the debate over Social Security is no exception. Critics of Social Security claim that their real objection to the program is its financial unfairness. Workers who make more and put in more, they say, do not get the same rate of return as the workers who make less and who put in less. This claim of unfairness presumes that if government addresses the economic security of families at all, it should build a system around the idea of the individual "saver-investor." Under such an arrangement, the government would mandate that individuals put aside some percentage of their income for retirement and for insurance against death, disability, and unemployment. Payments made when or if any of these events materialized would reflect the accumulation in each individual's account. Even if such a system were economically feasible—which is true only for retirement pensions—it fundamentally misunderstands the social contract that social insurance entails.

American Social Security pensions treat retired persons as worker-contributors, all of whom have participated in the same insurance pool. Because people do not know in advance who will have high or low earnings over a working life, those paying FICA taxes receive a reasonable base pension in retirement. The aim of Social Security is simple: to guarantee benefits that will provide everyone with an adequate retirement income when combined with some private savings and private pensions. For Social Security to make good on this sensible aim requires some redistribution from people who turn out to earn higher lifetime incomes to those who turn out to earn lower wages.

American workers can rightly expect that the larger their Social Security contribution, the greater their retirement benefits. Larger "contributions" (the conventional euphemism for the taxes that private insurance would call "premiums") mean that higher-wage workers receive larger pensions than do lower-wage workers. But the degree of financial hierarchy in Social Security is reduced by another of its purposes—the commitment to a minimally adequate income for lower-wage workers. The ratio of benefits to former wages is higher for retirees who have earned lower wages during their working lifetimes. In short, America has constructed a worker-contributor, not a saver-investor, version of fairness. The "Every boat on its own bottom" ethos of the market economy is tempered by the "Everybody in the same boat" ethos of social insurance.

To some degree the clash between individualistic and socially shared visions of fairness frames the debate about social insurance in the right terms. We believe that the social, political, and economic arguments for universalistic social insurance are persuasive. And opinion polls show that most Americans agree with us. People have little taste for running the individual risks that privatizers of various stripes believe they should prefer.

Because the critics of Social Security cannot hope to persuade most Americans to become high-wire risk takers, they have switched the line of attack. Opponents claim that America's broad social insurance programs are unaffordable and ungovernable. Without contesting the desirability of social insurance itself, critics want us to believe that socially shared provision for economic security simply cannot be organized successfully. Government cannot be trusted and botches everything it touches, we are told. Outcries about entitlements, big government, and deficit spending are blended in histrionics that capitalize on more generalized anxieties and that bury the truth about social insurance programs.

The attacks of the 1990s are hardly new. Over the past twenty years, we have heard persistent claims of a crisis in American government—with social policy deeply implicated in these troubles. The stagflation of the 1970s provoked distress about the government's capacity to manage its operations, let alone improve social conditions. Some doomsayers argued that shrinking public revenues made it impossible to satisfy the expectations generated by the Great Society programs of the Kennedy-Johnson years. Others claimed that the excessive expenditures from the programs themselves helped to produce the economic difficulty in which we found ourselves. These years of doubt and dismay were followed by the antigovernment politics of the Reagan era. Huge tax cuts created a massive federal budget deficit, and then conservatives pronounced the social programs too expensive to sustain.

We live with the legacy of this rhetoric of failure. Nowhere is this clearer than in the misguided pessimism with which Social Security and Medicare are currently discussed. The task for progressive commentators is not only to attack criticism where unjustified. It is also to recognize that adjusting and improving our social insurance programs is central to sustaining a humane America in the twenty-first century. Unless we renew the inclusive and adaptive dream of Social Security's birth in the 1930s and its continuous adjustments since that time, conservatives will triumph in their decades-long efforts to derail social insurance programs that serve the nation's middle class as well as its poor.

Criticisms of Social Security pensions today are generally presented as a response to "fiscal crisis." But these are merely occasions for replaying in different chords the profound opposition that social insurance has always generated among economic conservatives. The past decade provides ample illustration of this. In the early 1980s, when public officials announced that the Social Security accounts, if unadjusted, would go bankrupt, Americans accepted without commotion the changes made by the 1983 Greenspan Commission. Modestly reducing benefits while modestly increasing social insurance taxes, these changes bolstered rather than revamped Social Security. The public's confidence in Social Security's financial future gradually returned to normal. In opinion polls, popular support for Social Security remained very high—as it still does.

As a result of the early 1980s reforms, surpluses grew in Social Security's accounts. Oddly enough, this too awakened critics. Some fiscal gurus—including Peter Passell, an economics columnist for the *New York Times*—complained that the growing surpluses constituted a "crisis in slow motion." (Collectors of oxymorons take note.) Our point is straightforward: when both deficits and surpluses bring cries of alarm, the evidence points toward ideological opposition.

Today, the rhetoric of imminent disaster has reemerged. It has been primed by the prophets of doom and gloom in the Concord Coalition and reinforced by financial interests eager to gain new business from mandated individual savings accounts for retirement. The case for big changes in America's public retirement arrangements has thus begun to shoulder its way back onto the broader national agenda. Extrapolating short-term trends into the indefinite future, critics once again have portrayed Social Security pensions as "uncertain promises" that are unlikely to be fulfilled unless a strong dose of market medicine is given to put things right. Pointing to the aging of America's population, these critics make the unwarranted extrapolation that Social Security will not be able to pay its bills without draconian tax increases or reductions in retirement benefits.

But this overlooks the complete demographic picture (Leone 1996). Although it is true that there will probably be fewer workers for each retiree in the America of the twenty-first century, there will also be many fewer children for each adult worker. In the near future, working adult Americans may have to take care of parents and grandparents who are living longer, but they will also be raising fewer children. The overall number of Americans dependent on the workforce will stay in the same ballpark over the next four decades—and the proportion of dependents will remain far below what it was in 1960.

A Plan for Sustaining Social Security

A thirteen-member advisory council on Social Security recently issued a report outlining several contrasting views about the future of the Social Security system. One group led by Robert M. Ball, former commissioner of Social Security in both Democratic and Republican administrations, argued that the system can be stabilized through moderate adjustments in pension formulas coupled with a new investment strategy.

As Ball observes, the Social Security system is today accruing substantial surpluses, and total income will exceed outlays until about the year 2020. Thereafter, Social Security reserves must be retired to pay current benefits that exceed the level of current taxes. By 2070—that is, almost three-quarters of a century from now—benefits are projected to exceed taxes by about 5.5 percent of taxable wages. So unless some adjustments are made in benefit levels, taxation levels, or trust fund earnings, Social Security's retirement program may someday be unable to pay all its bills, and some mild trouble could start as early as thirty-five years from now. From this perspective, critics are technically correct when they say that the current system is unsustainable.

But the real issue is whether something like the current system, with slight adjustments, *could* be sustained. On that score, the alarmist claims about Social Security's future are simply nonsense. Even with no changes at all, Social Security is sustainable for a long time. And only prudent adjustments are necessary to keep Social Security fully funded indefinitely. As Robert Ball and his colleagues suggest, by gradually shifting the investment of a portion of Social Security's surplus into equity securities, this projected gap in future funding could be closed, with no tax increases and extremely modest changes in current benefit levels. Under the option proposed by Ball and five other members of the Social Security advisory council, the total seventy-five-year deficit can be eliminated, and then some, by six modest adjustments.

- Extend Social Security coverage to currently excluded state and local employees.
- Increase the length of the computation period for workers' average earnings from thirty-five to thirty-eight years.
- Tax Social Security benefits that exceed already taxed contributions, as with private defined-benefit retirement plans.

- In accordance with a March 1996 proposal by the Bureau of Labor Statistics, correct the current overstatement of the consumer price index, which is used to calculate cost-of-living increases.
- Credit income taxes on Social Security pensions to the pension rather than to the Medicare trust fund.
- Shift approximately 40 percent of the Social Security trust funds, now invested in Treasury securities, into equity securities.

In short, the present system can be sustained and people's retirement benefits maintained with some modest adjustments in the way that Social Security is financed. Proposals for more radical surgery on Social Security—such as the one put forward by a group of privatizers—have aims other than simply "saving" Social Security.

The Attack of the Privatizers

Five members of the thirteen-person advisory council proposed a major overhaul that would break up America's shared Social Security system. Under the scheme of the radical privatizers, every worker would be required to create a personal security account (PSA) funded by diverting part (5 percentage points) of the payroll taxes now collected to finance Social Security pensions. Individual workers could invest the portion in their PSA accounts as they please. Upon retirement, a person would receive the accumulated value in his or her PSA, on top of a small base pension financed through the shared Social Security system. This base pension would be paltry—just $410 per month in today's money, far lower than the poverty threshold.

The PSA proposal would actually require Americans to pay higher taxes while the new scheme was being set up. In order to keep taking care of today's retirees, there would need to be a hike of 1.52 percent in the FICA payroll tax, plus benefit reductions and over $1 trillion of new public borrowing. To make the privatizing proposals work, the retirement age would also need to increase to age sixty-seven by 2011.

According to the Office of the Actuary at the Social Security Administration, each of the alternative proposals for the future of Social Security put forward by subsets of the advisory council successfully meets the federal statutory requirement that the Social Security system (on current projections) be in long-term (seventy-five-year) actuarial balance. But, if that is true, why go beyond the moderate adjustments proposed by the Ball group? Why put Americans through a huge upheaval when a program that has worked well for decades needs only slight adjustments to keep on working? Good question. And answering it requires us to realize that the real debate is between those who think social insurance is worth saving and those who want to reduce government's role in retirement security in favor of Wall Street's.

Shared Investments Versus Individual Accounts

If implemented, both the Ball plan and the PSA privatizing proposal would tie Social Security's fortunes more closely to the performance of private capital markets. (Ball suggests only a study of, not the actual implementation of, Social Security investments in the stock market.) But the Ball plan, if put into force, would manage new investments through a shared fund, whereas the PSA proposal would create individualized accounts. Over the past sixty years (the life of the Social Security pension system), capital markets have outperformed real wage growth by several percentage points. So, in principle, either way of transferring part of our Social Security monies into capital markets might make things better for the future, allowing future retirees to have better pensions at less tax cost to today's and tomorrow's workers.

Nevertheless, there are risks. Tying Social Security retirement pensions to the performance of the capital markets would have looked quite bizarre in 1935, when the Social Security system was launched. Even if we do not experience another Great Depression, the events of October 1987 should remind us that the stock market can make quite precipitous downward "corrections." Although on average, over long periods of time, people tend to do better by investing in the market, some individuals and some cohorts of individuals will do substantially worse.

This concern about smoothing out the vagaries of market returns underscores the first striking difference between the Ball plan and the PSA model. In effect, the Ball approach puts the market risk on the government— that is, on all of us collectively. In sharp and telling contrast, the PSA model puts the risk on individuals. The choice between these proposals is thus similar to the choice between a defined benefit and a defined contribution retirement program. Private savings, whether in IRAs or otherwise, are the equivalent of a defined contribution pension plan: workers save a certain, individually defined amount and end up at retirement with assets equal to the performance of their portfolio. If a person invests wisely and is lucky, great. But if individual investments have not done so well, the person has a poor retirement income.

Social Security, in contrast, has always been similar to a defined benefit scheme. The federal government makes long-term promises to pay certain pension benefits and bears the risks that the performance of the economy will make those promises either harder or easier to fulfill. Historically, many private firms have also provided similar defined benefit retirement plans. But only about 30 percent of Americans now retire with a company pension, and companies are rapidly shifting from defined benefit to defined contribution pension arrangements. This means that Social Security is now the only vehicle available to most Americans in which they, as individuals, do not bear market risks on savings for their basic retirement income. In a world that is becoming riskier in other ways, American working families can still count on promised Social Security pensions to be there.

The Ball plan would keep Social Security secure in this way. The Ball proposal would allow the Social Security system to reap potentially higher returns from financial markets, yet any risks on the downside would be borne by all of us together, not by individuals.

Proponents of the PSA privatizing plan project that on average it might do better in the financial markets than the Ball proposal. But their projections are misleading. A better return for this approach would happen only because it would hike current payroll taxes, not because it would establish individual investment accounts. If we added the same tax hike to the Ball plan, the returns to Social Security would be even greater than the average PSA returns. That is because the Ball plan, as a shared system, would have lower administrative costs; it would not pay billions of dollars in fees to private Wall Street brokers.

The real issue here is not economics but ideology. Most privatizers want to break up Social Security because they do not trust the government, because they believe that the American people do not trust the government, or because they think that Social Security depresses savings rates.

Privatizers argue that Americans who have an individual or personal security account might view their investment as being more secure than a claim on the Social Security system. Privatizers take it for granted that Americans have lost or soon will lose their faith in any system run by the government. Should any such loss of popular faith really happen, though, it would be a triumph of media hype over sober reflection. The Social Security system avoids inflation risks, bankruptcy risks, and market risks. It has been running for sixty years without ever missing a payment.

Social Security continues to have the overwhelming support of the American populace, and Americans say that they are quite willing to pay some additional taxes to ensure the financial soundness of the system into the distant future. Nevertheless, the ongoing drumbeat of privatizers' criticisms of Social Security could make headway, especially with younger workers. Younger Americans may come to prefer risky over nonrisky investments. Nor can we fully discount the Lake Wobegon effect—young workers' overoptimism that they all will have lifetime earnings that are above average.

Some New Democrats want to encourage such youthful overoptimism by instituting a *partially* privatized, two-tier Social Security system, in which a slight increase in today's payroll taxes would be diverted into individual investment accounts proportionately smaller than the accounts envisaged in the full privatizing proposal (see Shapiro 1997). This may sound like a good, Clinton-style, middle-of-the-road proposal. But it really isn't. Partial privatization would probably lead to inexorable pressure for full privatization. And partial privatization would in fact make most Social Security beneficiaries less secure. It would shrink the cushion that the system provides for people with modest earnings and those who become disabled. At the same time, partial privatization could lead more fortunate Americans to believe that they are doing better by virtue of their individual investments.

Here is how that would happen: investment of some Social Security funds in stocks rather than Treasury bonds would likely improve the investment performance of Social Security over the long run. If such new market investments are done collectively, as the Ball group would favor, that will simply strengthen the finances of Social Security as we know it. But if even a small fraction of new market investments were to be structured through mandated "individual" Wall Street accounts, it could appear that any improvement in average retirement returns was coming through the individualization of accounts rather than from the simple shift in investment holdings. Workers—and especially more privileged employees—might press to divert more and more of their Social Security taxes into private accounts. A downward

political cycle would thus be set in motion, leading toward more and more individualization of retirement savings—to the advantage of more privileged
employees. The less stake that American workers believe themselves to have
in the shared provision of retirement benefits through Social Security, the
more likely it is that political support for the system will erode. New
Democrat–style partial privatization, in short, would destabilize rather than
anchor Social Security.

Full and partial privatizers often decry the Ball plan for collectively managed market investment of a portion of the shared Social Security fund, arguing that this plan would amount to government meddling in the capital
markets. But this argument is not compelling. After all, privatizing plans
would themselves use federal regulations to force workers to pay (higher)
taxes to feed mandated individual investment accounts on Wall Street. Privatizing schemes are not "free choice," and they would require a vast government regulatory apparatus, one much more administratively complex than
the system that administers the shared Social Security system. What is more,
the operation of Wall Street itself depends on public regulation. Maintaining
the soundness of and confidence in financial markets by massive governmental "meddling" has been one of the great success stories of American public
policy since the 1930s.

Investing Social Security funds in equity securities would not roil capital markets—as long as investments are limited to broad index funds. As the
Ball plan envisions, such funds would be managed solely in the interest of beneficiaries, with the government as a mere passive shareholder. Such constraints are not difficult to construct, as illustrated by the experience of the
Federal Employees Thrift Plan, the Tennessee Valley Authority, the Federal
Reserve Board's defined benefit retirement programs, and many state retirement funds.

American workers would not, on average, be better off investing pri-
vately for retirement than having those investments made through a common
Social Security index fund. Because private investing directly exposes beneficiaries to temporal fluctuations in the financial markets, privatizing accounts would make many working Americans and their families worse off in
their retirement years. There are obvious profit reasons for private money
managers to want millions of individual accounts to be set up—accounts on
which brokers would collect regular fees. But there is no reason, other than

ideological antipathy to government, for Americans to prefer privatizing schemes to adjustments in Social Security's financial arrangements that retain the system's shared character.

Shifting Fortunes

Critics of Social Security make much of the supposed burden that retirees place on the working young. By now, the image of the affluent old enjoying a secure retirement on the backs of hard-pressed wage earners is an established cliché. But the most recent complete data on the income of the aged (1994) reveal that 56 percent of persons over age sixty-five would be below the poverty line without their Social Security payments. Three-quarters of all recipients have total income, including their Social Security benefits, under $25,000 per year. Fifty percent have income under $15,000 per year. Families with an income of $50,000 or more represent only 9 percent of Social Security beneficiaries. In short, most elderly Americans are not rich.

Reform of Social Security really poses two distributional issues—fairness between generations and fairness between more privileged Americans and less privileged ones within the same age groups. The intergenerational equity issue is mostly a distraction. The first cohorts of Social Security pensioners indeed enjoyed a windfall, getting out much more than they had put in. But that, as they say, is history. Today, both the Ball plan and the privatizing proposals aim to put Social Security pensions into long-term actuarial balance. Given that the burdens on current and future generations under the alternative schemes will be equivalent, the real issue is social-class fairness within generations. Here an ideological chasm separates the Ball plan from the PSA privatizing approach.

The Ball approach maintains the worker-contributor model of equity that currently undergirds Social Security. Distributional fairness in this social insurance model is straightforward but not always well understood. First, workers are insured against a lifetime of relatively low-wage work by a guarantee of a minimally adequate pension in old age. Second, recognizing that a person's level of wages includes some combination of personal circumstance and effort, the size of the pension increases with a worker's level of contribution. But it redistributes by giving lower-wage workers a better "return" on their lifetime earnings. Everyone signs up at the beginning of their working lives for a system that makes two promises: a minimally

adequate retirement income for all workers, and a guarantee of higher returns (in absolute dollar amounts) to those who make higher contributions
over their working lives.

The promises of the system would change fundamentally if privatizing
reforms were implemented. Under the PSA conception, the pensioner is
viewed as an investor. The idea is that higher-wage workers who save more
and workers who make more fortunate investments deserve to have better
financial situations in retirement. The investor notion of fairness seemingly
rewards individual prudence and self-denial—the decision to give up current
consumption as a hedge against an uncertain future. Yet a mandatory requirement to save a fixed percentage of wages rewards neither prudence nor
self-sacrifice. The saver, after all, did not choose to save. And sacrifice in this
scheme is actually inversely related to affluence. Lower-wage workers will do
a lot less well under privatization.

The obvious unfairness of such a change is clear when we look at America's overall retirement system, which is already badly skewed toward helping
the well-to-do. U.S. tax policy offers greater subsidies to the retirement savings of higher earners than lower earners. The home mortgage interest de-
duction, along with tax exemptions for such individual savings vehicles as
IRAs, Keoghs, 401Ks, and defined contribution plans, provide much more assistance for lifetime wealth accumulation to high earners than they do to low
earners. As things are now, the current structure of Social Security pensions
somewhat reduces this imbalance. But a shift to PSAs would eliminate important equalizing features of the overall retirement system, shifting Americans
in general toward more individually variable and socially unequal patterns of
saving for retirement. Proponents celebrate that privatizing schemes would
be sensitive to personal circumstances. But given that the circumstances infl-
uencing lifetime earnings and personal-investment prospects include being
born black or white, male or female, able-bodied or impaired, into a rich family or a poor one, the unfairness of this approach seems manifest.

The imposition of substantial stock market risks on low earners is also
objectionable. The lower one's earnings over a lifetime—the more Social
Security pensions matter to one's bedrock protection against destitution in
old age—the less likely one would be to prefer having that protection subject
to market risks of the sort contemplated by the PSA proposal. After all, if
one's investments went south under the PSA plan, one would be left with a

guaranteed benefit of only $410 per month in 1994 dollars—less than current supplemental security income payments and much less than the poverty threshold.

The PSA scheme also trades a portion of Social Security's protections—survivor benefits—for ownership of the PSA, which passes to one's heirs at death. Security for younger workers and the families of lower-wage workers is again being traded for increased benefits to higher-wage workers, and particularly to the survivors of those who do not outlive the value of their PSAs. This is not a trivial trade. Social Security currently provides life insurance valued at $1.3 trillion, more than all private life insurance policies currently in force in the United States. In short, the PSA proposal piles stock market and other risks on families who are poorly positioned to bear them.

Beneath the surface of the technical debate about Social Security's tax rates, benefit schedules, and long-term financial future, there is a deep ideological divide between defenders and opponents of social insurance. Defenders like us see necessary adjustments as a natural and inevitable evolution of a prized public institution. Opponents see these occasions as opportunities for radical revision. They see this as a moment for convincing Americans, especially the young, that social insurance is an unfair, unsustainable sham. But privatizing Social Security is a contradiction in terms. It would change the dynamics of the program in order to fit the imperatives of private markets. Markets can supply a marvelous array of investment vehicles, but they cannot supply social insurance. The United States has already become more unequal and less economically secure over the past generation, and privatizing Social Security would make it more so.

The Fight over Medicare

Medicare, which was largely ignored in the battle over health care reform in the early 1990s, has returned to the center of American political debate. Given the bipartisan calls for reductions in the nation's budget deficits and longstanding Republican hostility to Medicare as a broad social insurance program, the Republican takeover of Congress in 1994 was almost sure to make Medicare the subject of intense and very public conflict. Moreover, unlike Social Security, Medicare actually is in some fiscal distress. Social Security could proceed as it is for a long time, but projections for Medicare expenditures suggest real worries about unsustainable budget outlays.

Figure 3. Medicare and Private Health Insurance Spending per Enrollee

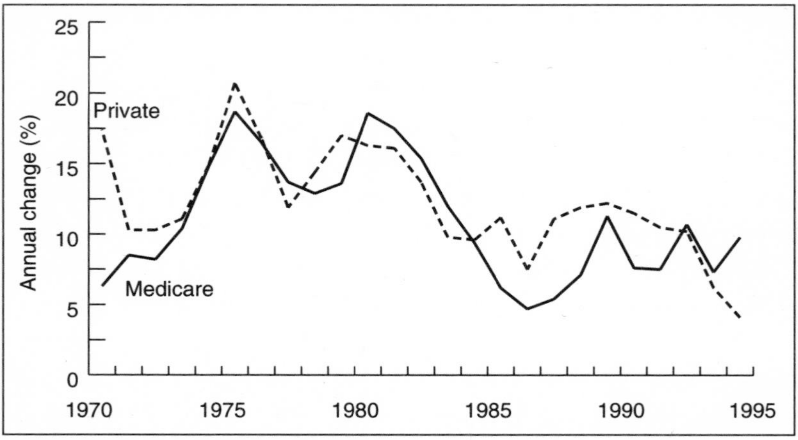

Source: HCFA, Office of the Actuary, 1996. On a per-enrollee basis, private health insurance grew on average 12.2% annually between 1969 and 1994, compared to 10.9% for Medicare.

A somewhat longer view reveals, however, that these projections present a puzzle rather than a crisis. For most of Medicare's history, its expenditures grew at a pace similar to those in the private medical economy. Remarkably, from 1983 to 1993 Medicare outlays grew *less* rapidly than outlays through private health expenditures. Since then, Medicare expenditures have grown a bit more rapidly than expenditures in the private medical economy. This could be seen as atypical against the backdrop of the longer history. But whether atypical or not, critics of the system can now decry its "high costs." Looming shortfalls are projected for the Medicare trust fund, setting the stage for fearful debates about what should be done to "save Medicare."

Privatization is touted by some as the solution to Medicare's problems. In this case, there are two quite different forms of privatization being discussed. One is a broad proposal for Medical Savings Accounts (MSAs). Instead of participating in group insurance at places of employment or paying the health insurance portion of FICA taxes, Americans would be required to contribute (tax free) to MSAs to cover their individual medical needs. Presumably the buildup in these accounts would provide sufficient reserves for medical care, both during years of employment and in old age.

There are major transitional problems with this scheme, but those need not distract us from the main line of argument. For the young, the healthy, and the affluent, the MSA approach is a great deal—particularly if, as is virtually certain, this tax-free saving could be tapped for other purposes once a sufficient cushion was achieved. What happens to the remainder of the population is only slightly less clear, but broadly predictable. With the good risks now not contributing to the insurance pool, the bad risks must be "insured" by general taxation. In short, instead of providing medical care as an aspect of social insurance, the system will move rapidly toward segmentation: private insurance for the relatively well-off; welfare medicine for everyone else.

The alternative privatization approach for Medicare retains social insurance coverage for the elderly, but it attempts to save money by having private managed-care plans compete for Medicare's patients. This alternative poses no direct threat to social insurance. Rather, the worrisome question is whether managed care can simultaneously save money and deliver decent medical care to the elderly or, for that matter, to anyone else. These are crucial questions for the whole of American medicine, not just Medicare. They only distantly connect to the question of whether medical care for the elderly should continue to be provided under American social insurance principles.

Indeed, the current controversies over Medicare's financing divert us from the more fundamental issue of whether the insurance risks of ill health should be dealt with in a universal program or left to a patchwork system of private payment, private insurance, and diverse public programs. While we think of Medicare as the sharing of health risks—which it is—we often forget that Medicare is also an incomplete social insurance program. Historically, Medicare was seen by its progressive supporters as a second-best solution. The campaign for Medicare emerged from the failure of attempts to win universal health insurance for all Americans (Marmor 1973).

The Origins and Character of Medicare

As a program for social security retirees and recipients of disability insurance, Medicare's political origins lie in the United States' rejection of national health insurance. First discussed before World War I, national health insurance fell out of favor in the 1920s. When the Great Depression made economic insecurity a pressing concern, the Social Security blueprint of 1935 enabled both health and disability insurance to be broached as controversial items of social insurance that should be included in a reasonably complete scheme of social protection. From 1936 to the late 1940s, liberals called for incorporating universal health insurance within the emerging social insurance package. But a congressional coalition of conservative southern Democrats and northern Republicans defeated this attempt at expansion of social insurance, despite the great public appeal of full health coverage.

Proponents of an expanded Social Security system reassessed their reform strategy during President Truman's second term of office. By 1952, they had formulated a plan for incremental expansion of government health insurance. The proponents of what ultimately became known as Medicare shifted the category of beneficiaries to elderly retirees while retaining the link to social insurance financing and eligibility. Medicare thus became a proposal for providing retirees with limited hospitalization insurance—a partial plan for the segment of the population whose fears of a financially catastrophic illness were as real as their difficulties in purchasing health insurance at modest cost. With this began the long battle to turn a proposal acceptable to the nation into one that Congress would enact. This reform battle stretched from the formulation of the Medicare tactic in the early 1950s through final legislative success in 1965.

These origins determined the initial design of Medicare and created expectations in the minds of its proponents about how the program should develop over time. The incrementalist strategy assumed that hospitalization coverage was the first step in benefits and that more would follow under the usual pattern of Social Security financing. Supporters thought of Medicare as national health insurance for a population group, universally covering retirees and, later, the disabled. Likewise, proponents presumed that eligibility would be gradually expanded. Eventually, they believed, Medicare would take in most, if not all, of the population, with the first extension perhaps being made to children and pregnant women. The kind of full inclusion envisaged here meant workers and their families, not literally every citizen or person in the land. But there was no mistaking the Medicare strategists' aspiration toward ever broader coverage.

At the time of enactment, all Medicare enthusiasts took for granted that its rhetoric should emphasize the expansion of access, not the regulation and overhaul of American medicine. The clear aim was to reduce the risks of financial disaster for the elderly and their families. And the clear understanding was that Congress would demand a largely hands-off posture toward the doctors and hospitals providing the care that Medicare would finance. Thirty years later, that vision seems odd. It is now taken for granted that how one pays for medical care affects both the care given and the amounts paid. But in the buildup to enactment in 1965, no such presumptions existed.

The incrementalist strategy of the 1950s and early 1960s assumed not only that most of the nation was concerned with the health insurance problems of the aged but also that social insurance programs enjoyed vastly greater public acceptance than did means-tested assistance programs. Social insurance in the United States was acceptable to the extent that it sharply differentiated its programs from the demeaning world of public assistance. "On welfare," in American parlance, was a term denoting failure, and leaders within the Social Security Administration made sure that Medicare fell firmly within the tradition of benefits earned, not given as charity. The aged could be presumed to be both needy and deserving because, through no fault of their own, they had lower earning capacities and higher medical expenses than any other age group. The Medicare proposal avoided a means test by restricting eligibility to persons over age sixty-five (and their spouses) who had contributed to the Social Security system during their working life. The initial plan limited benefits to sixty days of hospital care. Physician services were originally excluded in hopes of softening the medical profession's hostility to the program.

The form adopted for Medicare—Social Security financing and eligibility for hospital care and premiums, plus general revenues for physician expenses—had a political explanation, not a consistent social insurance rationale. The very structure of the benefits, which first provided for acute hospital care (part A of the legislation) and then provided for physician treatment as an afterthought (part B), was not primarily linked to the special circumstances of the elderly. Left out were provisions that addressed the problems of the chronically sick elderly—those whose medical conditions would not dramatically improve and whose needs related to maintaining independent functioning rather than recovering from discrete illnesses or injuries.

Viewed as a first step, of course, the Medicare strategy made sense. But after thirty years, with essentially no serious restructuring of the benefits, Medicare deserves a sober review, though certainly not a panicky retreat.

From the standpoint of universalism, Medicare is only partially success-ful. It separates retired workers from those still on the job, thus breaching one version of social solidarity. (The response, of course, is that all of us hope to become retired, so that part-A Medicare taxes on workers are just down pay-ments on our own hospital insurance as retirees.) Perhaps more worrisome is that because Medicare covers only some parts of the population (the elderly and the disabled), disputes over it can take on the coloration of interest-group politics (though not the us-versus-them vitriolics of welfare policy). In short, while critical to the well-being of the aged, Medicare cries out for expansion to make good on the social, political, and economic promise of universal pro-vision. For now, however, we will concentrate on the debate over Medicare's finances.

How to Reform Medicare

Coping sensibly with Medicare's problems requires, for a start, putting to rest two misleading claims in the recent debate. One is the mistaken view that because Medicare faces financial strain, the program requires immediate and dramatic transformation. The experience of the 1980s demonstrates that Medicare administrators, when given appropriate tools and political support, can limit the pace of increase in the program's costs. Cost escalation is not a necessary feature of the Medicare program. It is an artifact of particular tech-niques of monitoring and reimbursement.

The second misleading notion has to do with the very language used to define the financial problems that Medicare undoubtedly faces. Critics (and some defenders) continue to use the alarmist language of insolvency to de-scribe Medicare's future, projecting a dreadful scenario in which the pro-gram's trust fund will literally run out of money. This language represents the triumph of metaphor over thought. Government, unlike a private household, adjusts its patterns of spending and fund-raising by democratic decisions. The "trust fund" is an accounting term of art, one applied in this case to Medicare. The term reflects the convention we have developed for describ-ing earmarked revenues for spending both now and in the future. But we should always keep in mind that Congress can change the taxes that finance Medicare, if it has the will. It can likewise change the benefits and reim-bursement provisions of the program. Or it can do some of both. Channeling the fiscal consequences through something called a "trust fund" changes nothing in the real political economy. Fretting constantly about the trust fund is the cause of much muddle, unwarranted fearfulness, and misdirected energy.

To view the debate about Medicare's crisis-ridden finances as misleading is not to suggest that the program is free of problems. Far from it. But it is important to understand that Medicare can be adjusted in ways that fully preserve the national commitment to health insurance for America's elderly and disabled.

What should be done? One place to start is to reduce the growing gap between the benefits that Medicare offers and the obvious needs of its beneficiaries. What Medicare pays for should be widened to include the burdens of chronic illness; that means incorporating prescription drugs and long-term care into the program, which is precisely what the Clinton administration had hoped to do in its ill-fated health insurance overhaul.

Widening the benefits package does not mean, contrary to what many claim, that total expenditures must rise proportionately. Expenditures represent the volume of services times their prices. Many other nations have not only universal coverage and wider benefits than Medicare, but they spend less per capita than we do for their elderly. Canada, for example, is able to do this because they pay their medical providers less, spend less on administration, and use expensive technology less often.

There is no reason that Medicare's outlays need rise at twice the rate of general inflation (or more). To achieve lower rates of increase in Medicare's expenditures does not require changing the program's status as a promise to elderly Americans and their loved ones. What does have to be changed is the amount of income that medical providers of all sorts receive from the Medicare program. The restraint of costs necessarily means reductions in payments to those in the medical industry. The real question is whether the reduction comes from fewer needed services, fewer unneeded services, or lower payments for services, needed or not.

Medicare's financing also could use some overhauling. Raising taxes will have to be part of the answer. For some this is simply ruled out of current discussion, a good example of fearfulness defeating evidence. The breadth of public support for Medicare suggests that it is possible to mobilize popular opinion in favor of tax increases when the problem is clearly defined and the justification convincingly offered.

We need debate over how Medicare should be improved. What we do not need is debate that scares the country about its future by disseminating false claims about Medicare's unaffordability. It would indeed be a crisis if the legitimate health care costs of our aged and disabled were unaffordable. And it is true that a pattern of health care expenditures increasing at twice the rate of national income growth is unsustainable over the long run. But there is no reason to believe we must tolerate this future.

The politics of budget deficits, not Medicare's aims or operations, is what has brought the program to renewed prominence on the nation's agenda. In the process, another highly misleading claim about reforming Medicare's "premiums" has arisen, one with profound implications for American social insurance. It is the view that Medicare's financial troubles require means-testing the program in the form of income-related premiums for part-B physician insurance coverage. Indeed, one constituency in the Washington political community regards such a policy change as simply common sense. Defying hundreds of years of common usage, these actors have developed a new jargon, one where means-testing does not mean what ordinary language suggests. Tests of means are normally understood as a way of settling issues of eligibility—who is in and who is out of some program. Such tests suggest the distinction between us (the generous) and them (the needy); means-testing conveys exactly the connotation that generations of Americans have associated with being "on welfare."

The world of public finance provides a quite different vocabulary, one largely free of such associations. Using the language of public finance, one refers to progressive, proportional, or regressive ways of paying for government programs. Or one discusses the redistributive effects of either the financing or the benefits of a program.

Not so with the 1997 Congress, where Republican leaders suggest means-testing Medicare in the sense of having premium levels rise with the income of retired beneficiaries. This appeal to "soak the rich" populism is dangerous. It threatens social insurance principles and constitutes another technique for unraveling the broad political support that social insurance programs have by virtue of their eligibility and financing. Here is why. The purpose of insurance is to spread the costs of a risk, not to concentrate those costs. Spreading costs over a lifetime of work is precisely what the current financing of Medicare's part-A hospitalization coverage does. Imagine now subjecting upper-income retirees to a premium for their medical insurance set at, to use the current idea, 50 percent of the average Medicare expenses for physician and related coverage (part B). The medical expenses of the elderly, as with any group, are wildly uneven. The top 10 percent of users have expenditures more then twenty times those of the cheapest 90 percent. Any benefits manager of a moderately sized corporation with relatively healthy retirees will be able to provide them with policies that will compete with a means-tested Medicare part-B program financed by income-related premiums. This is an obvious road to undermining the broader risk pool upon which Medicare, as social insurance, depends. If better-off Americans pull out, the system cannot survive.

The appeal to means-testing Medicare is but one of the misconceived approaches to dealing with the financial pressures on the program. If there were wide support for financing Medicare more progressively, it would be worth reconfiguring the sources of payment for Medicare's bills. One obvious possibility would be to increase the use of general revenues, including general income taxes that both the elderly and the nonelderly pay, or to express the part-B premium as a small proportion of one's Social Security pension. But there is very little to be said for adjusting premiums, as the means-testing enthusiasts suggest. First of all, it is dangerous as a matter of social solidarity. Moreover, such changes not only fail to raise significant funds but are also administratively cumbersome and costly. Only in the world of the blinkered technocrat—without attention to linguistic sensitivities or implementation barriers—would such an idea appear appealing.

Medicare's early implementation stressed accommodation to the medical world of the 1960s. Its objective was to keep the economic burden of illness from overwhelming the aged or their children. It was assumed then that incorporating the elderly into the wonders of American medicine was the welcome task at hand. Thirty years later, the setting is radically different. The difficulties of Medicare are those of American medicine. We pay too much for some procedures, and we do too many things that either do little good in relation to their costs or even do some harm. In the world of American private health insurance, cost control has now arrived with a vengeance. Medicare is unsettled and is likely to remain so in the context of budget deficit politics unless we accept that limiting what we spend on Medicare need not mean eviscerating or even radically transforming the program. The price of cost control will undeniably have to be borne, but that burden should be borne, as social insurance would prescribe, proportionately.

Defending and Expanding American Social Insurance

Between exaggerated fears of unmanageable budget deficits and mindless incantations about the unsustainability of "big government programs," sensible discussion regarding the American public household has been largely paralyzed. Presidents announce the end of big government. Fiscal elites wring their hands about the affordability of public budgets. Conservatives in both political parties embrace risky privatizing schemes. A kind of collective amnesia blots out the reasons that the nation embarked on social insurance programs in the first place and keeps us from thinking realistically about where gaps remain that only social insurance can fill efficiently, equitably, and affordably.

The most prominent gap remains in medical care. Undertaking enormous risks, some 40 million Americans and rising went without health insurance for all or part of 1996—mostly adults and children in working families. The situation seems intolerable now, but it is likely to become worse. When the uninsured become acutely ill, they may receive emergency treatment. But this does not remove the constant insecurity that people feel or make it easier for uninsured families to get the steady, good, preventive health care that all adults and youngsters need. In the past, moreover, hospitals and doctors may have been able to shift the cost of treating the uninsured onto patients covered through Medicare, Medicaid, or employer-provided health plans. But now such room for maneuvering is disappearing. In the brave new world of managed health care and draconian public and private budget cutting, doctors and hospitals have shrinking fiscal room to be charitable. Universal health coverage becomes more, not less, essential.

The case for widening coverage and expanding America's shared pools for financing health care is familiar and powerful. Most Americans are healthy most of the time, so in any given year most health outlays go to help the sickest 10 percent of the population. In the absence of vigorous new legislative steps, however, the impact of competitive pricing and budget cuts in health care will be that the sick pay more or get much less. A race to the bottom in health care will proceed relentlessly unless the principle of widely and fairly sharing the costs of illness is once again brought into prominence.

The real crisis of American social insurance is thus not what the conservatives claim. The real crisis is not in Social Security or even in Medicare, because both of these shared and popular programs can be adjusted for the future. But meanwhile a much worse doomsday scenario looms: working people and their families, contending with ever more intense demands at work and at home, suffer a steadily deteriorating access to decent health care. In this scenario, which is already unfolding apace, 1 million more working parents and their children lose health insurance each year. And ordinary working families get less adequate and more bureaucratic forms of care, as employers, governments, and health care providers all enforce budget stringency in the health care system.

These worsening problems are why America's broadly shared social insurance should be not only defended but extended. As we have argued, the case for protecting Social Security and Medicare against those who falsely claim that they are unaffordable and unmanageable is compelling. Supporters of social insurance can and must counter those in either party who, for reasons of ideology or profit, aim to turn social protection over to the harsh mercies of the market. But the present challenges to the ideals and practices of American social insurance require more than a defense and suggestions about adjustment. They call for the creation of the political space for achieving extensions of social insurance so that all Americans can be cushioned against the predictable risks of postindustrial capitalism and the costs of modern medicine.

The future of American social insurance is politically uncertain. Fears about the future are stoked by those who hope to profit from privatized schemes of one sort or another. To counter these economic and ideological interests will require the mobilization of ordinary Americans—something that can happen only if people rediscover why arguments for social insurance made sense in the first place. Rediscovering this for ourselves, we can appreciate how grotesquely opponents of social insurance have miscast the challenge that we as Americans now face. That challenge is twofold. We must preserve and adjust America's inherited systems of social protection and at the same time fight for better protection in the future.

A Partnership with American Families

Theda Skocpol

Americans barely arrived home from the polls in November 1996 before pundits and politicos grabbed the airways to declare that the voters did not mean what they had just said about sustaining social supports for families.

The popular message was clear. Because most voters wanted to preserve domestic programs from conservative "revolutionaries," Bill Clinton became the first Democrat since Franklin Roosevelt to win a second presidential term, and Republicans very nearly lost control of the House of Representatives. Female voters were especially concerned that Medicare, Medicaid, and federal education supports be protected. So were working people of modest means, many of whom had stayed home in 1994 yet returned to the voting booths to boost the Democrats in 1996 (Teixeira 1996). Opinion polls during the last election cycle revealed that Americans still strongly support Social Security as they know it. And despite memories of the health reform debacle of 1994, most still want health coverage for all working parents and children. An immediate post-election survey reaffirmed this longstanding popular priority (Greenberg 1996d), while also noting that the American public "is focused on protecting Medicare from cuts, not on entitlement reform."

But people and pundits are not on the same wavelength. Post-election editorials declared that Americans want "centrist" government to "rise above partisanship" and undertake far-reaching "entitlement reforms" (for examples of such claims, see Meyerson 1997). Editorialists called for expert-led commissions to restructure Social Security and Medicare into partially individualized, market-driven programs—cutting retirement benefits promised to the middle class in the process.

Naturally, Republicans and Wall Streeters are delighted to have public opinion interpreted in this way. What is more, they do not have to push too openly for big cuts and fundamental restructuring of federal social programs, because a goodly number of Democrats are leading the charge. Senator Bob Kerrey champions the cause. And so does the dominant official in the second Clinton White House, Treasury Secretary Robert Rubin, whose "priorities are ones moderate Republicans could embrace." "Balancing the budget has taken on an importance that goes beyond the economic benefits of getting the deficit to zero as opposed to just getting close," Rubin explained to *Wall Street Journal* reporter David Wessel (1997, p. A18), who observed that Rubin "is pressing the president to join with Republicans to tackle 'at least one' of the big benefit programs for the elderly."

Secretary Rubin inclines toward market-oriented reforms advocated by leading "new Democrats" (see Marshall 1997). Right after the 1996 election, Al From of the Democratic Leadership Council declared that the voters had "issued a deliberate call for a new centrist politics," which would inevitably include a "fundamental restructuring" of "our biggest systems for delivering public benefits—Medicare, Social Security, and public education, for openers," in order "to meet the challenge of the Information Age." It was fortunate that the Democrats had failed to retake Congress, said From (1996), because this creates a "rare window of opportunity" for "centrist politics" to address the "challenges of the 21st century."

You Are on Your Own

Working Americans are not imagining things when they say that the system is not supporting them or listening to their concerns (Greenberg 1996b). People of modest means who work for a living have every right to feel abandoned on questions of social support—not just by retrenchment-minded businesses and antigovernment conservatives, but by leading new Democrats as well. Despite important differences between right-wing Republicans and new Democrats, there are some uncanny similarities in the way that Newt Gingrich and Al From envision restructured social programs for the Information Age. Both Newt and Al imagine a new-millennium scenario that goes something like this:

> Ben Jones, a single, thirty-something middle manager with bright career prospects, is sitting in front of his home computer at ten o'clock at night. After a challenging day at work, Ben stopped off at his health club, ate a sensible light supper at a trendy restaurant, and now has his feet up while he manages his life. After doing a little banking and booking his own airline tickets for a weekend getaway to the Caribbean, Ben is ready to make choices about health care and retirement security. He orders his broker to redirect some of the dollars mandated for his personal security account (the privatized portion of Social Security). Then Ben costs out the possibility of switching from his employer's health plan into a tax-advantaged medical savings account that would let him purchase back-up coverage for a medical catastrophe while pocketing an extra few thousand dollars for personal expenditures every year for as long as he expects to remain healthy. It looks like a good deal to Ben, so he sends a message to register the change. Delighted with the new control over his own life that America's Information Age government allows, Ben turns off his computer and hits the sack.

What is missing from this picture? Most working families, obviously. Lurking in the shadows of this snazzy picture are people like eighty-five-year-old Edith Ames, who, after a lifetime of work and child-rearing, cannot get a place in a decent nursing home and cannot survive at home on her shrinking Social Security benefit, and a retired salesman like Barney Palaccio, who ends up with a lousy pension for himself and his wife because his investment choices were unwise or unlucky. Also missing are Jeff and Roseanne Cunningham, young working parents who have just learned that the HMO health plan that they "chose" with their fixed voucher does not offer the specialized medical treatments that their five-year-old daughter unexpectedly turns out to need. And we must not overlook Cheryl Smith. Should the marketizing reforms imagined by Newt and Al actually come to pass, we can expect Cheryl's story to happen much more often than Ben's happy fable.

It is eleven o'clock at night, and Cheryl, a forty-year-old working wife and mother, is sitting at her kitchen table poring over some brochures while talking with her distraught seventy-five-year-old mother on the telephone. This is the end of a long day for Cheryl. She got home at 6:00 P.M. after commuting from her job as a data-entry clerk for an insurance company. She prepared dinner for her husband, Bob, and their two children, ten-year-old John and four-teen-year-old Sally. Afterward, Cheryl and Bob washed the dishes while they talked about how to handle a call from Sally's teacher, who reported that Sally's grades are falling and she is hanging out with some rough older boys. (Bob and Cheryl worry about Sally's future as well as her present, because they know that Sally has to do well enough in high school to earn some sort of college scholar-ship.) After this discussion, Bob paid a few bills and went upstairs to watch TV, while Cheryl helped John with his math problems. Now the youngsters have gone to bed, and Cheryl is talking with her mother about how to use her Medicare voucher to buy an affordable health plan for next year. The voucher seems less adequate than last year, and Cheryl's mom is very worried that she won't be able to keep her doctors or get regular visits and medicine for her chronic heart and arthritis problems. Cheryl's mom begs for answers. But the brochures are very confusing, with a lot of fine print, and it is hard to know what the best choice might be. Cheryl gives up for the night. She is exhausted, and she has to get up at 6:00 A.M. and start all over again.

Will Democrats Stand with the People?

The Cheryl Smiths of America mostly voted for Democrats in the last elec-tion, and so did the Ediths, Barneys, and Jeffs and Roseannes. But these vot-ers and millions of others like them can hardly be sure where the Democratic Party is headed on questions of social support for families of modest means and prospects. If the Democratic Leadership Council achieves the bipartisan deals that it wants, the Ben Joneses of Information Age America may do just fine. But what will happen to Cheryl, her mother, and the other working Americans that we glimpsed?

Progressive Democrats have an opportunity to take up the cause of strong social supports for American families; the virtual betrayal of popular concerns by antigovernment Republicans and leading new Democrats leaves this way wide open. But progressives must first decide where supports for families fit in their own political project.

Progressives, like other Democrats, feel burned by social policy disputes. In the aftermath of the health security debacle of the early Clinton years, Democrats are understandably wary. Launching a grand health reform plan that apparently bridged popular and business concerns led to disaster rather than renewal for Democrats in 1994 (Skocpol 1996a). Given Congress's and the president's declared commitment to quick federal budget balancing, there seems little possibility for using social spending to deal with popular concerns. Meanwhile, Democrats are coping with the 1996 legislation to "end welfare as we know it." This travail goes on and exacerbates divisions between urban and suburban Democrats.

Social policy has been subtly marginalized in recent discussions among progressives. Labor-oriented populists (Campaign for America's Future 1996; Faux 1996; Sweeney 1996) call for Democrats to respond to macroeconomic trends hurting working families through regulation of international trade and measures to tame corporations and strengthen labor unions. Labor populists want to build a class-based politics around the quest for higher wages and enhanced workplace protections. To be sure, they also voice support for Social Security and Medicare; but this is just one on a list of priorities, and not at the top.

Along with other liberals, some progressive Democrats think of Social Security and Medicare as programs for the elderly—ever so subtly buying into the conservative presumption that "entitlements" for retirees hurt the young and undermine investments in the future. But to peg Social Security and Medicare in this way fails to recognize how vital they are for working-age families. From the point of view of working parents—men and women trying to hold down unglamorous jobs while caring for aging parents and growing children—many things that look from Washington, D.C., like discrete programs are actually part of a system of support, however incomplete. Families are on tight budgets of money and time. Working-age adults—especially working mothers—benefit if grandmother and grandfather can count on Social Security and Medicare without a lot of bureaucratic hassles. Some 70 percent of adult American women are in touch with their mothers at least weekly (Lawton, Silverstein, and Bengston 1994, pp. 26–27), so they are the first to hear if grandparents are having problems. At the same time, working parents must worry about health care coverage for themselves and their children and provide their offspring with decent schools and safe neighborhoods, community and after-school activities, and affordable access to college. The entire set of caring concerns, focused on older and younger family members alike, come together for working-age adults. Liberals occasionally deride "family issues" as mere cultural diversions from more fundamental economic and workplace concerns. But family supports have both a normative and a very material dimension, and they are very much at the center of concern for most voters.

Championing a full range of social supports for families should also be at the center of Democratic Party politics—certainly if Democrats want to build a strong new majority. But if popularly oriented progressives are to push our party in this direction—if we are to become effective champions of public social provision for the twenty-first century—we first need to reappropriate the past. We need to understand that broad social supports for families are not only momentarily popular; they are central to the best and most longstanding traditions of American democratic government.

The Formula for Success

A historical perspective on U.S. social policymaking reveals no more of a split among economic, moral, and family considerations than we would hear in kitchen-table conversations today. Again and again—and starting long before Franklin Roosevelt's New Deal—successful social policies have furthered economic security and opportunity for many American families while simultaneously expressing and reinforcing mainstream moral values about family integrity, individual responsibility, and the mutual obligations of individuals and the national community. Popular progressive Democrats who decide to champion family security do not need to imitate foreign models or take unprecedented leaps into an unhinged future. Popular progressives today do not even have to cling to the New Deal as their sole precedent. They can discover fresh ways to renew and extend longstanding traditions of American social provision.

While some might quibble here or there, most would agree that America's finest social policy achievements have included the following milestones. Whether a single program or a set of related measures, each milestone has offered security and opportunity to millions of individuals, families, and communities, inspiring broad and enduring political support in the process. The milestones of American social provision span most of the nation's history.

In *public education,* the United States led the world in creating widely accessible systems of public schools (Heidenheimer 1981). During the nineteenth century, primary schools and then secondary schools were founded throughout most localities and states.

Civil War benefits provided disability and old-age pensions, job opportunities, and social services to millions of Union veterans and survivors. By 1910, more than a quarter of all American elderly men and more than a third of northern men over age sixty-two were receiving regular payments from the federal government on terms that were extraordinarily generous by the international standards of that era. Many family members and survivors were generously aided as well (Skocpol 1992, pp. 129–35).

Programs to help mothers and children proliferated during the 1910s and early 1920s. Forty-four states passed laws to protect women workers and also "mothers' pensions" to enable poor widows to care for their children at home (Leff 1973). Congress established the Children's Bureau in 1912 and in 1921 passed the Sheppard-Towner Act to fund health education programs open to all American mothers and babies (Ladd-Taylor 1986).

The *Social Security Act,* which was passed in 1935, included unemployment insurance and public assistance to the poor along with Old Age Insurance (OAI), which subsequently became its most popular part. OAI eventually took the name Social Security and expanded to cover virtually all retired employees, while providing survivors' and disability protections as well (Derthick 1979). Most employees and their dependents were included in Social Security by the 1960s. Modeled in part on retirement insurance, Medicare was added to the system in 1965 (Marmor 1973).

The *GI Bill of 1944* offered a comprehensive set of disability services, employment benefits, educational loans, family allowances, and subsidized loans for homes, businesses, and farms to 16 million veterans returning from World War II (Mosch 1975; Olson 1974).

Although these giant systems of social support developed in different periods of American history and varied in many ways, they have important features in common. The shared characteristics are worth describing, because they add up to a recurrent formula for successful social support in U.S. democracy. Again and again, Americans have asked their government to further opportunity and security for millions of families. Here are the features that have made such efforts successful:

- American social policy milestones and the movements supporting them have aimed to give social benefits to large categories of citizens in return for either past or future service to the community.

The most enduring and popularly accepted social benefits in the United States have never been understood either as poor relief or as mere individual entitlements. From public schools to Social Security, they have been morally justified as recognitions of or as prospective supports for individual service to the community. The rationale of social support in return for service has been a characteristic way for Americans to combine deep respect for individual freedom and initiative with support for families and due regard for the obligations that all members of the national community owe to one another.

A clear-cut rationale of return for service was invoked to justify the veterans' benefits expanded in the wake of the Civil War and World War II (Skocpol 1992, pp. 148–51; Ross 1969). Less well understood, though, is the use of civic arguments by the educational reformers and local community activists who originally established America's public schools. They argued for common schools not primarily as a means of furthering economic efficiency or individual mobility but as a way of preparing all children for democratic citizenship (Emirbayer 1992; Tyack and Hansot 1982, part 1). Similarly, early

1900s programs for mothers were justified as supports for the services of women who risked life to bear children and devoted themselves to raising good citizens for the future (Skocpol 1992, part 3).

Today's Social Security and Medicare systems likewise have a profound moral underpinning in the eyes of most Americans (Kingson, Hirshorn, and Cornman 1986; Greenberg 1996b). Retirees and people anticipating retirement believe they have earned benefits by virtue of having made a lifetime of payroll contributions. But contrary to what pundits and economists often assert, the exchange is not understood as narrowly instrumental or individualistic. Most Americans see Social Security and Medicare as a social contract enforced by and for contributors to the national community. The benefits are experienced as just rewards for lifetimes of work on the job and at home, not simply as returns-with-interest on personal savings accounts.

- Successful U.S. social policies have built bridges between more privileged and less privileged Americans and across lines of race and region, bringing people together as worthy beneficiaries and as contributing citizens.

Even if policy milestones started out small compared to what they eventually became, the key fact has been the structure of contributions and benefits. Because successful social policies have built bridges linking more and less privileged Americans, they have not been considered or labeled as welfare programs.

Public schools, for example, were founded for most children, not just the offspring of privileged families, as was originally the case with schools in other nations (Katznelson and Weir 1985, chap. 2). Civil War benefits and the GI Bill were available to all eligible veterans. Although mothers' pensions eventually deteriorated into what we now call welfare, they were not originally so stigmatized (Skocpol 1992, chap. 8). During the early 1900s, most American mothers who lost a breadwinner-husband suddenly found themselves in dire economic need. What is more, early federal programs for mothers and children were universal. The Children's Bureau was explicitly charged with serving all American children (Skocpol 1992, chap. 9); its first chief, Julia Lathrop, reasoned that if "the services of the [Sheppard-Towner] bill were not open to all, the services would degenerate into poor relief" (from a letter quoted in Covotsos 1976, p. 123).

Social Security and Medicare are today's best examples of inclusive social programs with huge cross-class constituencies. Although Social Security is the most effective antipoverty undertaking ever run through government in the United States, its saving grace over the past several decades—during an era of tight federal budgets and fierce political attacks on social provision—has been its broad constituency of present and future beneficiaries, none of whom understand it as welfare (Heclo 1986). As Theodore Marmor and Jerry Mashaw explain elsewhere in this volume, were Social Security and Medicare to be divided into residual social safety nets via individualistic private market accounts, they would soon be on the road to moral, political, and fiscal demise. America would not just be making a technical or budgetary adjustment. Especially in the case of Social Security, even partial privatization would undercut a successful solidaristic program that, with minimal bureaucratic hassle, enhances dignified security for millions of working families.

- Broad U.S. social policies have been nurtured by partnerships between government and voluntary associations. There has been no zero-sum relationship between state and society, no trade-off between government and individuals, and no simple opposition between national and community efforts.

The policy milestones that I have identified were developed (if not always originated) through cooperation between government agencies and elected politicians on one hand and voluntary associations on the other hand. I am not referring merely to nonprofit, professionally run social service agencies. I mean voluntary citizens' groups. The associations that have nurtured major U.S. social programs have usually linked national and state offices with participatory groups in local communities.

Public schools were founded and sustained by traveling reformers, often members of regional or national associations, who linked up with leading local citizens, churches, and voluntary groups (Tyack and Hansot 1982, part 1). In the early 1900s, the movers and shakers behind state and national legislation for mothers and children were the Women's Christian Temperance Union, the General Federation of Women's Clubs, and the National Congress of Mothers, which later became the PTA (Skocpol 1992, part 3). Civil War benefits ended up both reinforcing and being nurtured by the Grand Army of the Republic (Skocpol 1992, chap. 2). Open to veterans of all economic, ethnic, and racial backgrounds, the Grand Army was a classic three-tiered voluntary civic association, with tens of thousands of local posts, whose members met regularly, plus state and national affiliates that held big annual conventions (McConnell 1992).

Social Security has had a complex relationship to voluntary associations. During the Great Depression, a militant social movement and voluntary federation of older Americans, the Townsend Movement, pressed Congress to enact universal benefits for elders (Holtzman 1963). But Social Security definitely did not embody specific Townsend preferences, and the movement itself withered away during the 1940s (Amenta, Carruthers, and Zylan 1992). Today over 35 million Americans ages fifty and older are enrolled in the American Association of Retired Persons (AARP), whose newsletters and magazines alert older voters to maneuvers in Washington, D.C., that affect Social Security and Medicare (Morris 1996). The AARP does not have very many local membership clubs (though it is currently working to establish more of them). Still, many elderly Americans participate in locally rooted seniors' groups, including the union-related National Council of Senior Citizens, which has played a key role in advocating for Medicare. Along with unions and religious congregations, moreover, federal, state, and local governments have done a lot over the past thirty years to create services and community centers for elderly citizens. An important side effect has been to foster considerable social communication, civic voluntarism, and political engagement among older Americans.

The final example of government-association partnership in the expansion of inclusive U.S. social provision is perhaps the most telling. A nationwide veterans' federation, the American Legion, was critical in the enactment of the inclusive and generous GI Bill of 1944 (Ross 1969; Skocpol 1997c). New Democrats today often praise the GI Bill for giving benefits in return for service and in ways that maximized the choices of individual veterans, who could enroll in any training program, college, or university. All very true, and worthy of emulation (Skocpol 1996b). But what new Democrats need to notice is that the GI Bill took this shape only because the American Legion pressured both conservatives in Congress and the somewhat elitist planners of the wartime Roosevelt administration (Skocpol 1997c). The legion was a locally rooted, cross-class, and nationwide voluntary association that developed in close symbiosis with two very strong federal bureaucracies—the U.S.

military and the Veterans Administration (Pencak 1989). In this story, there are no oppositions of state versus civil society or of government versus individual autonomy and community engagement. The post–World War II American Legion—along with half of the nation's young workers and families—was enormously helped by an active federal government and by very generous public spending.

The Missing Middle

Having surveyed American social politics across 150 years, we can now take a closer look at the recent events so critical for Democrats. From the New Deal to the present, the Democratic Party has been at the vortex of developments—and crucial nondevelopments—in American social policymaking.

During the Depression and World War II, many Western nations launched comprehensive systems to guarantee citizens full employment and social security. In the United States, too, New Deal reformers battled for broad protections for all citizens or wage earners. But by the 1950s, the United States was left with only one relatively universal permanent program—Social Security's contributory disability and retirement insurance. Other attempts to institutionalize broad social programs were defeated, and America was set on the road to a "missing middle" in social provision—the relative absence of protections for working-age adults and their children that pertains today.

True, gaps in social protection were temporarily filled for many younger American families by the GI Bill of 1944 and subsequent veterans' legislation. Generous social investments in many young men and their families, along with hearty postwar economic expansion, ensured opportunity and security for millions of child-rearing families. Especially well-served were those working and middle-class whites who entered the labor force, married, and raised children from the late 1940s into the 1960s. But after that, the impact of the GI Bill faded, just as the American economy was about to take a turn for the worse for young workers and families (Danziger and Gottschalk 1995; Blank 1997).

Taken together, the War on Poverty, the Great Society, and many of the social policy initiatives sponsored by moderate Republican president Richard M. Nixon aimed to help poor children and working-age adults, especially African-Americans, who had not been fully incorporated into the economic growth or social insurance protections of the postwar era. But when the dust settled, the broadest and costliest achievements focused on the elderly. The most important federal innovations were Medicare, enacted in 1965, and the indexing of Social Security pensions to inflation, which occurred in 1972. During the Reagan era of the 1980s, moreover, cutbacks occurred primarily in welfare programs for the poor and not in the popular social insurance programs, which covered the middle-class elderly along with working and poor retirees.

Today, American social provision is very generationally skewed, and grand schemes for reconstructing social policies are fought out in generational terms. The Concord Coalition asserts that too much is being done for the elderly (Peterson 1993), while the Children's Defense Fund (1994) insists that more must be done to uplift poor children. With only these alternatives, it is a no-brainer what progressive Democrats must do: oppose those wanting privatization for Social Security and Medicare, and at the same time try to do more for poor children. But this approach risks overlooking millions of midlife adults and their children, often in working families of modest means. Of course, most working-age parents, especially wives and mothers, feel a strong stake in Social Security and Medicare. But young men in particular may see themselves primarily as taxpayers within late twentieth-century America's uneven system of social provision.

Popular progressives need to change the terms of the policy debate. Rather than accepting zero-sum generational conflicts—allowing conservatives to pit poor children against the elderly, while ignoring the needs of many working families—progressives should pursue options that unite rather than divide generational and class groups. We must advocate social support for *all* working families, fighting for revisions of the nation's system of social provision to allow better support for employed as well as retired people.

Of course, I am not the first person to imagine a more seamless and complete system of social insurance and family supports. This was the dream of many Progressives and New Dealers, not to mention the hope of farsighted black and white leaders during the 1960s. But regional and racial divides dashed hopes for completing a comprehensive American welfare state at the end of World War II. And since the 1960s, possibilities to achieve more complete social supports for all American families have been undercut, again and again, by bitterly racialized disputes over welfare.

Divisive Battles over Welfare

A new era of progressive cross-racial politics might have blossomed after African-Americans finally achieved civil rights. Briefly in the mid-1960s, liberal Democrats gained executive power and majorities in Congress, and some dreamed of completing the social and economic reforms left over from the unfinished agendas of the 1930s and 1940s. New full-employment programs might have jointly benefited the black poor along with white and black unionized workers, offering help to all citizens willing to serve the nation through work. Progressives in the 1960s might also have fashioned such new security programs as universal health coverage (and it would have been easier to do it then, before the runaway inflation in health costs in the 1970s).

But alas for progressives during the 1960s, it was hard to unite unions and civil rights activists, despite the best efforts of leaders like Walter Reuther, Bayard Rustin, and Martin Luther King, Jr. Institutional and policy legacies encouraged policymakers to model Medicare on Social Security (Marmor 1973), while relying on Keynesian tax cuts for businesses to stimulate the national economy (Weir 1992). Tiny training programs and targeted welfare efforts were what remained to help the very poor. Between the mid-1960s and mid-1970s, millions of needy single-parent families were added to the welfare rolls, becoming eligible as well for Medicaid and other means-tested assistance as well (Patterson 1981, chaps. 10–11).

A fierce conservative backlash soon gathered force (Edsall and Edsall 1991). As many Americans faced declining economic prospects from the early 1970s, as African-Americans poured into the cities and found too few stable jobs, and as more and more women entered the wage-labor force by choice or necessity, welfare programs targeted for some very poor mothers could easily be portrayed as unfair. Conservatives used this tactic for all it was worth—and many ordinary Americans responded, especially white southerners and northern Catholics. True, most welfare mothers have had to work part-time off the books just to survive. But this hardly mattered, because the point is more cultural and political than narrowly economic. Benefits from Aid to Families with Dependent Children (AFDC), originally conceived as mothers' pensions, lost their legitimacy in an era of racial conflict, declining wages, and widespread female entry into the wage-labor market.

For more than a generation, welfare has served as a spectacularly successful political battering ram against liberals. President Nixon expanded welfare benefits (as well as affirmative action), then turned around and attacked them to encourage conflicts among Democrats. Ronald Reagan featured antiwelfare appeals as part of his winning campaign for the presidency in 1980. Intellectual and political attacks on welfare subsequently deepened and spread to Democrats, culminating in the bipartisan congressional majorities that voted to "end welfare as we know it" in August 1996. In U.S. politics it has always been difficult to justify social benefits for the poor alone, and never more so than in the recent era.

After the New Deal, in short, liberal Democrats missed opportunities and worked themselves into political impasse. After the GI Bill, the long-standing formula for successful American social provision—giving support to people who are seen as contributors to the community, regardless of their social class—was *not* extended into broad new social supports for working-age families. Welfare programs proliferated instead, but they soon became racially controversial and culturally delegitimated in an era of changing roles for women. After the 1960s, nobody in the Democratic base was happy. Welfare efforts failed to reverse economic and family trends that were simultaneously generating more poor families (Blank 1997), while millions of Americans working for modest wages were left without forms of assistance (Medicaid, for example) offered to the very poor. Here was simply an untenable situation for Democrats. They came to be seen as champions of paltry and ineffective "poverty programs" rather than as advocates of opportunity and security for all working families.

Toward a Partnership with Working Families

What should Democrats do to escape the political impasse of the past generation? Although Democrats must defend Social Security and Medicare and adjust these programs in socially shared ways, the time has come to look beyond rear-guard actions toward a vision of social supports for all American families coping with our era's unsettling economic and social changes.

Popularly oriented progressives can and should lead the way in defining a family-oriented vision for the nation—along with a practical political strategy for Democrats. All kinds of families at various stages of life must be part of our family-oriented politics, of course. Yet there are strong social, economic, and political reasons why popular progressives should put *working parents* at the center of the new family politics.

As we have seen in earlier essays in this book, since the 1970s most working families have become increasingly hard-pressed in an unforgiving economy. Except for elites, regular wage increases are few and far between, and ordinary employees cannot be certain of health coverage and other employer-provided benefits that are vital for them and their families. Yet the problems that today's families face are more than economic. Working parents in particular face a double squeeze—not only a squeeze of economic resources but also a squeeze on the time and energy needed to raise children and engage in activities in churches, schools, neighborhoods, and civic life.

With both men and women juggling jobs and family duties at the same time, stable marriages are often difficult to form or sustain, and home and community life may suffer. Even among families that do hold together, at the very time when most working people are grappling with unnerving changes in the economy, domestic demands are greater and certainly more pressing. Grandparents live longer, and while they often help to succor their children and grandchildren, the elders themselves need caring attention from their adult children. But at the same time, children require plentiful reserves of parental guidance and a very long-term commitment of family resources if they are to flourish and prepare to succeed in tomorrow's demanding world. Working fathers and most especially working mothers find themselves under extraordinary pressures today.

Stronger, more coherent support for America's families is not just a matter of giving benefits to individuals. Equally at stake are social honor and our sense of mutual obligation between the community and the individuals who serve it—just as such matters have always been at stake in each era of American social policymaking. The future of the nation as a whole depends vitally on the work that families do—and especially on the efforts of parents during the years when they are both wage-earners and caregivers. The future growth of the economy, the vibrancy of our civic life and culture, and the well-being of the retirees of tomorrow—all depend on how well families can manage to do both economically and culturally as they raise the children who will become the citizens and workers of tomorrow.

Of course, child-rearing families have always been important, so in a sense the current situation is nothing new. But in other ways, the challenges families must meet are greater than ever. In a high-tech, fast-changing economy, the rearing of children and young people into productive workers and participating community members demands much greater reserves of parental and institutional support than ever before. But marriages are fragile, and men and women alike face intense demands on the job. In short, if ever there was an era when American working families *need* strong social support, this is it. And the people who most require—and deserve—extra support are working parents. They are the ones at the vortex of today's economic and family pressures. Working parents deserve honor and support from the nation as a whole, because, under increasingly difficult conditions, they are doing vital service on which all of us depend, today and tomorrow.

Ironically, a progressive vision of family support is "conservative" in the best sense of the word. Whatever proponents of unfettered markets and unbridled individualism may claim, Americans throughout our national history have flourished with the aid of shared social supports, not in their absence. Those who want to dismantle existing family supports, such as Medicare and Social Security, and those who struggle to preclude new supports for working parents, such as "health care that is always there"—they are the true wild-eyed radicals of our time. In contrast, popular progressives who champion an inclusive vision of social supports for families are the ones remaining in touch with—and striving to revitalize—the best traditions of American democracy.

A Family Message for Popular Progressives

If a family-oriented politics focusing especially on working parents is the right strategy for popular progressive Democrats, then our message to our fellow Americans should contain the following points.

Now more than ever, it is time for America to honor and reward the vital contributions of parents—and of all others across our land, from grandparents and aunts and uncles to neighbors, religious congregations, and employers—who take substantial steps in making the good work of parents possible. Families need a sense of security, working adults should have opportunities to get ahead, and mothers and fathers must be able to afford to spend time at home and in their communities. Children need safe and excellent schools and supportive activities. Parents are the ones who must take the lead, working with teachers and neighbors to ensure good schools and engaging activities.

Right now, America is treating parental work as a kind of private luxury. Higher incomes and glamorous freedoms go to individuals who take off on their own or shirk their responsibilities. Workplaces and the economic rules of the game make life hard for family men and women. Parents end up making disproportionate sacrifices to do the work of raising the children on which we all depend. We Americans have to change this, by fashioning a more family-friendly economy and society. We must arrange our public social supports and our employment system to honor and facilitate the work of parents. Parental service to the community and nation is vital, and we must reward and honor that contribution.

To support parents, while promoting security and opportunity for all American families, Democrats propose to pursue the following goals. We know that it will be difficult to legislate all the changes we need in the current fiscal and political climate. But here are the steps that we want to take whenever we can:

Make the economy family-friendly. Parents will make their way for themselves and their children through work, so adults must be able to find jobs and take advantage of opportunities for education or training. All jobs must have decent wages and health and pension benefits, which make family life viable. There must be rights to family leave on terms that make it truly available to all employees. And because parents need time as well as money, we as a nation should work toward the norm of a thirty-five-hour workweek (with pay remaining at least at the level it was before the reduction in hours).

Ensure that every child has sustained contributions from both parents. We progressives want public policies—taxes, benefits, and marriage rules—that encourage married parenthood. At the same time, we recognize that there are many divorced and single parents doing the best they can. If marriages fail, we want rules to help children and the parent who takes responsibility for them, including automatic systems of child support that allow a custodial parent to work less than full time and still provide for children.

Make communities and institutions safe and supportive for families with children. We progressives support tough crime laws and active measures to make neighborhoods safe, clean, and orderly. We want schools that are held to high standards, are able to afford small classes, and whose administrators and teachers are free to innovate. Governments at all levels must have the wherewithal and inspiration to encourage private-sector and voluntary activities to nurture and supervise children—and to honor and support mothers and fathers.

Why Family Populism Is Smart Politics

At a juncture when Democrats need to build a new electoral majority and when grand battles over public budgets and the very shape of public institutions loom ahead, progressives must connect with popular concerns and moral energy. A family-oriented populism focused especially on working parents can revitalize the tradition of successful social policymaking in American democracy, generating political dividends for progressive Democrats in the process. Americans believe in linking national supports to important individual contributions to community well-being. Mobilizing government to work with nongovernmental institutions to better support parents is an endeavor very much within this vital tradition.

Pursuit of supports for working families can strengthen Americans' sense of community—not just in particular localities, but also across lines of class and race. As William Julius Wilson argues eloquently in this book, progressives must combine continuing efforts to carve out new opportunities for African-Americans with pursuit of social programs relevant to Americans of all ethnic and racial groups. A family-oriented strategy does both of these things. Supports for working families are especially vital for African-Americans, who often find themselves in a tighter economic and family squeeze than other Americans. Yet Americans of all ethnic and racial groups also need economic redress and social support. Shared programs will do the most for the severely disadvantaged while significantly helping everyone.

A family-oriented politics does not depend on everyone being a parent or part of the same kind of family. The issue is not sheer numbers of potential voters counted up as isolated individuals. Not every American adult is a parent (in fact, there are more U.S. adults living alone and proportionately fewer families with children than ever before). But simple demography has never been destiny for social policy in the United States. Perceived contributions to the community matter more, as do possibilities for cross-class ties. Issues of parental responsibility and social support for parents can become a sympathetic focus for almost all Americans.

Consider retirees, for example. They may not be active parents right now, but most are grandparents who care about their children and grandchildren. Elders also understand the nation's and their own stake in productive workers (Adams and Dominick 1995). It is an odd feature of U.S. politics today that so many pundits are declaring "generational warfare" just as the country faces the prospect of more elders but fewer dependent children per adult worker (Leone 1997). If work and family can be made to mesh more smoothly—helping adults to become optimally productive even as they are engaged and effective parents—then retirees, working-age adults, and children will all do well together. An aging society is not at all a zero-sum game.

Some may feel that it is best to avoid talking about families, lest we exacerbate racially charged divisions between dual- and single-parent families. But I disagree. Family-friendly conditions are vital for both sets of families. And progressives need not adopt a morally relativist stance. We can champion moral understandings and practical measures that acknowledge the complexities that all Americans live with on a daily basis. Most people accept that two married parents are best for children, even though each of us is personally acquainted with mothers or fathers who have to soldier on outside this ideal situation. As policies are formulated, progressives can acknowledge the tension between ideals and second-best necessities.

For example, tax and social benefits can be designed to support and marginally favor married parents, and divorce laws can be designed to protect children. At the same time, there can be automatic wage withholding and refundable tax credits designed to deliver at least minimal child support to all noncustodial parents. Such arrangements can clearly proclaim that America will not let deadbeat parents shirk all responsibility and that the nation will make sure that lone custodial parents get some help without having to go on welfare. But the nation need not offer help that fully substitutes for a married partner. We can aid children and single parents while still expressing a concrete and normative preference for married parenthood.

Support for families and working parents holds out the prospect of broad electoral appeals and alliance building. Women voters currently favor Democrats by a large margin, and a parent-centered strategy can help to cement the party's relevance for middle-class as well as less privileged women. Yet this strategy should not alienate most men, because it calls for improving wage and benefit conditions vital to husbands and fathers. A vision built

around the well-being of families is also likely to prove very appealing to Hispanic voters, who (as Paul Starr points out) represent a vital new voting bloc
for Democrats. And it should help to mobilize cross-racial support in the
South as well (thus contributing to "reversing southern republicanism," as
Ira Katznelson advocates).

Family Populism or an Appeal to Class?

A morally grounded appeal to shared concerns will always do better in American politics than any explicit call for class-based mobilization. The needs of
less privileged Americans must be at the center of progressive politics, but I
doubt that Democrats should adopt an overtly working class–oriented populism. It is not just that there are too few unionized employees in late
twentieth-century America. There certainly *are* too few—and unions need to
be supported and strengthened by everyone who professes concern for a vital
civil society. But even if unions were to regain the leverage that they enjoyed
during the 1950s, explicitly class-oriented politics cannot suffice for a popular Democratic revival. A popular politics featuring a vision of solidarity and
security for all families can resonate with a revitalized labor movement and at
the same time facilitate broader electoral coalitions and ties between middle-
class and downscale Americans. This kind of progressive strategy may also
be the best way for populists to incorporate valid themes espoused by new
Democrats while remaining true to the needs and aspirations of working
Americans (see Skocpol 1997b on the need to synthesize populist and new-
Democrat concerns).

Unions, churches, responsible businesspeople, parent-teacher associations, and all kinds of community groups can find common ground in a parent-friendly politics. This matters, because popular-progressive Democrats
need to activate ongoing social and institutional linkages that go beyond the
unionized workforce while not being at odds with the unions. As concrete
victories are achieved, parent-friendly policies can generate new resources
and social connections in local communities, at workplaces, and across the
nation. People can be reconnected to civic life and meaningful politics, as
Margaret Weir and Marshall Ganz advocate elsewhere in this volume. New
resources for parents and new connections involving them will not usually
happen in overtly partisan forms. But in real life such new resources and connections may nevertheless help family-friendly Democrats run for and win

public office. Equally pertinent, movements of parents and families can help Democrats to accomplish worthwhile things once they get into office. More civic infrastructure centered on parents will surely be good for popular progressive politics.

Pitfalls to Avoid

Obviously, a family-oriented politics can be pursued in various ways. I have stressed overarching goals here, without going into a lot of policy details. Democrats never seem to lack policy proposals. At a moment's notice, they can draw up lists of ten big ideas or three modest alternatives or twenty-five teensy-weensy possibilities. Whatever, as Bob Dole would say.

But Democrats may not think hard enough about how to coordinate policy choices with an overall political strategy that must play out over time. Right-wingers in America have been very good at this sort of dynamic strategizing (for examples, see Butler and Germanis 1983 and Gingrich 1984). Progressives have not been anywhere near as skillful at coordinating a medium-term strategy with tactical choices that can move us closer to where we want to go politically. Instead, the Democratic Party is surrounded by policy wonks who spend a lot of time thinking up ideal plans and paying little attention to the political context within which the plans would have be enacted and implemented. (The consequences of such policy planning are often unfortunate, but the wonks rarely take any responsibility for the outcomes, attributing the spoiled plans to mere "politics.")

Not everything with a "family" label is automatically worthwhile. Popularly oriented progressives should be wary, I think, of forever fiddling with welfare reform or trying to help children apart from their parents. Perhaps most of all, progressives should worry about empty family symbolism— promising help through oversold regulations that in fact do next to nothing for working people of modest means. Each is a family tactic favored by some Democrats right now. Let me conclude by explaining why each of these tactics can be problematic and suggesting how progressives can do better.

Redo Welfare Reform? Some Democrats—liberals and new Democrats alike—are still thinking of family issues primarily in terms of welfare reform. Some argue that party leaders should strive to make welfare reform work by subsidizing businesses and local governments that hire people leaving the rolls. Others want all-out efforts to fix the Republican-sponsored Personal Responsibility Act, which President Clinton signed in August 1996, largely by restoring funds or attempting to loosen time limits.

Of course, Democrats presently in Congress should do what they can to help the desperately poor. But the last thing that progressive Democrats should *feature* in national politics are modifications of pitifully inadequate assistance programs restricted to a fraction of the very poor. As state and local governments implement welfare changes, progressives should look for ways to integrate former welfare clients into the same programs that address the needs of all low-income workers and families (along the lines suggested by Riemer 1996). In national-level politics, progressives should take the opportunity that the demise of AFDC now thrusts upon us—by stressing new ways to help all hard-pressed working families.

Strides toward "making work pay" for all low-wage workers have been made through recent increases in the earned income tax credit and the minimum wage. Now progressives need to press for jobs, educational and training opportunities, and family supports for all Americans who need them—regardless of whether people have previously cycled through the welfare system. Whatever is immediately feasible on the legislative front, Americans should understand that making wage-work universally available on family-friendly terms is the progressive goal. That is the only way to get beyond endless wheel-spinning over welfare toward something better for working Americans.

Focus on Kids Alone? Despairing of tight budgetary constraints, some progressives are placing top priority on legislating inexpensive new social benefits targeted solely at children. Helping children is a worthy goal, and Democrats should not vote against measures that expand resources for this purpose. Practically speaking, goals like "health care for kids" may be the only way to achieve partially offsetting social spending during a period of Republican congressional dominance and draconian cutbacks in existing federal social programs. But, looking to the future, popular progressives should avoid an overall political strategy and message focused on children rather than working parents *and* their children.

Americans may hear mixed or misleading messages when politicians talk about helping children. Some suspect that children's programs are merely new or expanded welfare programs in disguise (Taylor 1991; Heclo forth-coming). But the issue is deeper than that. Children are obviously tied to par-ents and families, and voters want to know what is going on with the adults. Are they responsible parents? Are they working and adequately caring for their children? Benefits or services administered by social service profes-sionals are not seen as an acceptable substitute for parental care. Above all, Americans want parents to do their job. Consequently, most voters may be-come receptive to a politics about responsible parenthood *and* new social supports for working parents, especially if actual parents are included as citizen-partners in this politics.

How wise is it for progressives to concentrate on expanding health cov-erage just for kids, at a time when more and more working parents are losing employer-provided health coverage or paying more for fewer benefits? Opin-ion polls consistently show continuing majority support for the ideal of basic health coverage for everyone—and adults, after all, are the ones who vote. Adults are also the ones who must care for children. All of us who fly in air-planes are accustomed to the standard safety message about the oxygen masks: "If the masks drop down and you are traveling with a child, put your own mask on first and then help the child." This makes good sense, we real-ize, because children need their parents to be in good shape, fully functional. The same holds true for access to health care. It may be a good thing to as-sure that all children can go to the doctor regularly. But it surely would be better—and more understandable to average voters—to make sure the parents are covered, too. Children need healthy parents who can earn a living and care for them, just as much as they need visits to the doctor.

Even if universal health care is not immediately attainable, progressive Democrats should search for a series of expanding incremental ways to en-sure that all families with one or more working adults have basic coverage. Supporting expanded coverage for kids may be reasonable right now, but our larger goal should be to require prorated contributions to family-sized health care for all full- and part-time workers. This remains a simple, understand-able ideal that, over time, is sure to attract more and more popular support.

Let Them Eat Symbolism? One more dead end for progressives is the easy path toward symbolic pro-family regulations that help only the econom-ically privileged. Unfortunately, many Democrats are already speeding into this byway—again, because it seems the easy way to go in an era of tight federal budgets and intense business lobbying.

Some sorts of symbolic regulatory steps may be acceptable. The V-chip is a good example. Very few Americans are likely to be fooled into thinking that this will automatically do the work of parents. People understand that the V-chip is an expression of the community's desire for parents to supervise children's television watching. At the same time, the V-chip constitutes a warning shot across the bow of the television industry, pressuring it to cut back on the screening of sex and violence. Nobody expects wonders from this legislation. If not much happens, or if unintended bad consequences emerge, then Hollywood and the networks will be blamed, not the Democratic Party.

But other symbolic regulatory measures are not so harmless. Consider the 1993 Family and Medical Leave Act (FMLA), which was celebrated in so many Democratic television ads during the 1996 campaign. The ads made wonderful election-year theater against the hapless Bob Dole, who insisted on portraying himself as the enemy of a man who needed to stay home with his dying daughter (Republicans in the future will not be so stupid). Democratic-sponsored ads for the FMLA created the impression that American workers now have the possibility of staying at home with sick children or relatives. But that is absolutely not true; many low-wage employees are not covered, and most of those who have the right to take leave cannot afford to forego their usual wages (Shellenbarger 1996; Commission on Family and Medical Leave 1996). For Democrats to make exaggerated claims about a primarily symbolic regulatory measure risks making the party look fraudulent among working people of modest economic means—in short, among exactly the people that the party is supposed to represent.

Popularly oriented progressives need to get smart about incrementalism. We need to scrutinize proposed symbolic or regulatory measures with care, championing only those that really express shared goals without dividing downscale from upscale Americans. There are contrasting kinds of incrementalism. Some initially limited measures are progressive entering wedges. A prime example from the past is old age insurance in the Social Security Act of 1935, which built bridges across classes and planted seeds of expansion to include groups that were initially left out. A present-day instance is the Clinton administration's proposal for refundable tax credits for the first two years of college. This holds the promise of delivering real benefits to less privileged Americans, while at the same time building a political alliance across socioeconomic strata—and bolstering social groups and educational institutions that tend to help Democrats.

But other supposedly preliminary measures—particularly regulations that help privileged employees while leaving everyone else out in the cold—are really foreclosing incrementalisms likely to politically isolate downscale Americans. Progressives should do what they can to head off regulatory family measures that truly foreclose future steps. If such measures are enacted anyway, we should try to transform them into platforms from which to demand further change in an inclusive direction. No matter how nice today's television ads about partial measures may seem, the Democratic Party cannot build a new majority on false promises. More distrust of government and cynicism about politics will be the only result of overselling measures that make little practical difference in the daily lives of ordinary American families.

The Way Forward

Like conservative Republicans after 1964, popular progressive Democrats must devise a realigning strategy primarily aimed beyond the beltway—a strategy that looks further ahead than the usual Washington, D.C., time horizon of the day after tomorrow. With public intellectuals self-consciously taking bolder stands than most elected politicians can be expected to embrace at any given moment, progressive Democrats must outline a new moral vision. The new vision must be embodied in specific proposals that can bring Democrats together and appeal to other Americans at the same time.

The pursuit of social supports for America's families, with a special emphasis on moral and material sustenance for working parents, is surely a promising way to tackle these tasks. Debates about this vision can be healthy for America, even if a lot of legislation cannot be moved in Congress tomorrow. At the same time, espousing family populism can help progressive Democrats to make headway within—and on behalf of—their own party. Security and opportunity for all families, honor and support for all parents—these are goals that can help Democrats to build a new majority. These goals can unite millions of Americans in support of public undertakings to address the real challenges of our time.

part two

Reclaiming Democratic Politics

The Political Economy of Citizenship

Michael J. Sandel

I n order to succeed, a progressive political movement needs to revise the terms of American political debate.* This requires more than a political strategy. It requires a new public philosophy, one that draws on stronger notions of citizenship and civic virtue than those informing our present politics. In recent years, cultural conservatives have invoked the language of virtue, while liberals, for the most part, have resisted it. But this is a mistake. The tradition of civic virtue contains important resources for contending with our political condition, and liberals should not ignore them. Central among these is an emphasis on the civic consequences of economic arrangements, what I shall call the political economy of citizenship.

Jeffersonian Political Economy

Consider the way that we think and argue about economics today, in contrast with the way that Americans debated economic policy through much of our history. These days, most of our economic arguments revolve around two

*This essay is adapted from Michael J. Sandel, *Democracy's Discontent: America in Search of a Public Philosophy,* Cambridge: Belknap Press of Harvard University Press, copyright 1996 by Michael J. Sandel. Reprinted by permission of the publisher.

considerations: prosperity and fairness. Whatever tax policies or budget proposals or regulatory schemes people may favor, they usually defend them on the grounds that their policy will increase the size of the economic pie or distribute the pieces of the pie more fairly or both.

So familiar are these ways of justifying economic policy that they might seem to exhaust the possibilities. But our debates about economic policy have not always focused solely on the size and distribution of the national product. Throughout much of American history they have also addressed a different question, namely, What economic arrangements are most hospitable to self-government? Along with prosperity and fairness, the civic consequences of economic policy have often loomed large in American political discourse.

Thomas Jefferson gave classic expression to the civic strand of economic argument. In his *Notes on the State of Virginia,* Jefferson (1787) argued against developing large-scale domestic manufactures on the grounds that the agrarian way of life makes for virtuous citizens well suited to self-government. "Those who labour in the earth are the chosen people of God," the embodiments of "genuine virtue." The political economists of Europe claimed that every nation should manufacture for itself, but Jefferson worried that large-scale manufacturing would undermine the independence that republican citizenship requires. "Dependence begets subservience and venality, suffocates the germ of virtue, and prepares fit tools for the designs of ambition." Jefferson thought it better to "let our work-shops remain in Europe" and avoid the moral corruption that they bring, better to import manufactured goods than the manners and habits that attend their production. "The mobs of great cities add just so much to the support of pure government, as sores do to the strength of the human body. It is the manners and spirit of a people which preserve a republic in vigour. A degeneracy in these is a canker which soon eats to the heart of its laws and constitution."

Whether to encourage domestic manufacturing or to retain the nation's agrarian character was the subject of intense debate in the early decades of the republic. In the end, Jefferson's agrarian vision did not prevail. But the republican assumption underlying his economics—that public policy should cultivate the qualities of character that self-government requires—found broader support and a longer career. From the Revolution to the Civil War, the political economy of citizenship played a prominent role in American national debate. In fact, the civic strand of economic argument extended even into the twentieth century, when Progressives grappled with big business and its consequences for self-government.

The Curse of Bigness

The political predicament of the Progressive era bears a striking similarity to our own. Then as now, Americans sensed the unraveling of community and feared for the prospect of self-government. Then as now, there was a gap or lack of fit between the scale of economic life and the terms in which people conceived their identities—a gap that many experienced as disorienting and disempowering.

The threat to self-government at the turn of the century took two forms. One was the concentration of power amassed by giant corporations; the other was the erosion of traditional forms of authority and community that had governed the lives of most Americans through the first century of the republic. A national economy dominated by vast corporations diminished the autonomy of local communities, traditionally the site of self-government. Meanwhile, the growth of large, impersonal cities, teeming with immigrants, poverty, and disorder, led many to fear that Americans lacked sufficient moral and civic cohesiveness to govern according to a shared conception of the good life.

Despite the dislocations they wrought, the new forms of industry, transportation, and communication seemed to offer a new, broader basis for political community. In many ways, Americans of the early twentieth century were more closely connected than ever before. Railroads spanned the continent. The telephone, telegraph, and daily newspaper brought people into contact with events in distant places. And a complex industrial system connected people in a vast scheme of interdependence that coordinated their labors. Some saw in the new industrial and technological interdependence a more expansive form of community. "Steam has given us electricity and has made the nation a neighborhood," wrote William Allen White (1910, pp. 250, 252–53). "The electric wire, the iron pipe, the street railroad, the daily newspaper, the telephone, the lines of transcontinental traffic by rail and water . . . have made us all of one body—socially, industrially, politically. . . . It is possible for all men to understand one another."

More sober observers were not so sure. That Americans found themselves implicated in a complex scheme of interdependence did not guarantee that they would identify with that scheme or come to share a common life with the unknown others who were similarly implicated. As the social reformer Jane Addams (1907, pp. 212–11) observed, "Theoretically, 'the division of labor' makes men more interdependent and human by drawing them together into a unity of purpose." But whether this unity of purpose is achieved depends on whether the participants take pride in their common project and regard it as their own; "the mere mechanical fact of interdependence amounts to nothing."

Political debate in the Progressive era focused on two different responses to the power of big business. Some sought to preserve self-government by decentralizing economic power and rendering it amenable to democratic control. Others considered economic concentration irreversible and sought to control it by enlarging the capacity of national democratic institutions. The decentralizing strand of Progressivism found its ablest advocate in Louis D. Brandeis, who before his appointment to the Supreme Court was an activist attorney and outspoken critic of industrial concentration. Brandeis's primary concern was with the civic consequences of economic arrangements. He opposed monopolies and trusts, not because their market power led to higher consumer prices but because their political power undermined democratic government.

In Brandeis's view, big business threatened self-government in two ways—directly, by overwhelming democratic institutions and defying their control, and indirectly, by eroding the moral and civic capacities that equip workers to think and act as citizens. Both in his fear of concentrated power and in his concern for the formative consequences of industrial capitalism, Brandeis brought long-standing republican themes into twentieth-century debate. Like Jefferson and Jackson, he viewed concentrated power, whether economic or political, as inimical to liberty. The solution was not to confront big business with big government—that would only compound "the curse of bigness"—but to break up the trusts and restore competition. Only in this way would it be possible to sustain genuine competition and preserve a decentralized economy of locally based enterprises amenable to democratic control.

Beyond the direct dangers to democracy of concentrated power, Brandeis worried about the adverse effects of industrial capitalism on the moral and civic character of workers. He favored industrial democracy, not for the sake of improving workers' incomes, desirable though that was, but for the sake of improving their civic capacities. For Brandeis (1915, pp. 73, 81), the formation of citizens capable of self-government was an end even higher than distributive justice. "We Americans are committed not only to social justice in the sense of avoiding . . . [an] unjust distribution of wealth; but we are committed primarily to democracy." The "striving for democracy" was inseparable from a "striving for the development of men. It is absolutely essential in order that men may develop that they be properly fed and properly housed, and that they have proper opportunities of education and recreation. We cannot reach our goal without those things. But we may have all those things and have a nation of slaves."

The New Nationalism

The other branch of the Progressive movement offered a different response to the threat posed by corporate power. Rather than advocating a decentralized economy amenable to democratic control by local political units, Theodore Roosevelt proposed a "New Nationalism" to regulate big business by increasing the capacity of the national government. "Big business has become nationalized," Roosevelt declared in 1910, "and the only effective way of controlling and directing it and preventing the abuses in connection with it is by having the people nationalize the governmental control in order to meet the nationalization of the big business itself" (reprinted in Leuchtenburg 1961, p. 53).

Like Brandeis, Roosevelt feared the political consequences of concentrated economic power. Big business corrupted government for the sake of profit and threatened to overwhelm democratic institutions. "The supreme political task of our day," Roosevelt proclaimed, "is to drive the special interests out of our public life" (in Leuchtenburg 1961, p. 85). Where Roosevelt disagreed with the decentralizers was over how to restore democratic control. He considered big business an inevitable product of industrial development and saw little point in trying to recover the decentralized political economy of the nineteenth century. Since most big corporations operated in interstate or foreign commerce, beyond the reach of individual states, only the federal government was suited to the task of controlling them. The power of the national government had to grow to match the scale of corporate power.

Like republicans since the day of Jefferson, Roosevelt worried about the civic consequences of economic arrangements and sought to cultivate in citizens the qualities of character essential to self-government. Roosevelt's aim was not only to reduce the domination of government by big business but also to enlarge the self-understandings of American citizens, to instill what he called a "genuine and permanent moral awakening," a "spirit of broad and far-reaching nationalism" (in Leuchtenburg 1961, pp. 38, 36). More than a program of institutional reform, the New Nationalism was a formative project that sought to cultivate a new sense of national citizenship.

If Roosevelt was the leading spokesman for the New Nationalism, Herbert Croly was its leading philosopher. In *The Promise of American Life,* published in 1909, Croly laid out the political theory underlying the nationalist strand of Progressivism. Unlike Brandeis and the decentralizers, Croly argued for accepting the scale of modern industrial organization and for enlarging the capacity of national democratic institutions to control it. The Jeffersonian tradition of dispersed power was now a hindrance, not a help, to democratic politics. Given "the increasing concentration of American industrial, political, and social life," American government "demands more rather than less centralization" (Croly 1965 [1909], pp. 272–75). But according to Croly, the success of democracy required more than the centralization of government; it also required the nationalization of politics. The primary form of political community had to be recast on a national scale. This was the way to ease the gap, so acutely felt in the Progressive era, between the scale of American life and the terms of American identity. Given the national scale of the modern economy, democracy required "an increasing nationalization of the American people in ideas, in institutions, and in spirit."

Although Croly renounced Jefferson's notion that democracy depends on dispersed power, he shared Jefferson's conviction that economic and political arrangements should be judged by the qualities of character they promote. Croly wrote of the "formative purpose" of democratic life. For him, the project of nationalizing the American character was "an essentially formative and enlightening political transformation." American democracy could advance only as the nation became more of a nation, which required in turn a civic education that inspired in Americans a deeper sense of national identity.

The decentralizing and the nationalizing versions of progressive reform found memorable expression in the 1912 contest between Woodrow Wilson and Theodore Roosevelt. In retrospect, however, the greater significance of the 1912 campaign lay in the assumptions that the protagonists shared. Wilson and Brandeis on one side and Croly and Roosevelt on the other agreed, despite their differences, that economic and political institutions should be assessed for their tendency to promote or erode the moral qualities that self-government requires. Like Jefferson before them, they worried about the sort of citizens that the economic arrangements of their day were likely to produce. They argued, in different ways, for a political economy of citizenship.

The economic arguments of our day bear little resemblance to the issues that divided Roosevelt and Wilson, Croly and Brandeis. They were concerned with the structure of the economy and debated how to preserve democratic government in the face of concentrated economic power. We are concerned with the overall level of economic output and debate how to promote economic growth while assuring broad access to the fruits of prosperity. In retrospect, it is possible to identify the moment when our economic questions displaced theirs. In the late 1930s, the terms of economic debate began to shift from considerations of self-government to considerations of consumer welfare. Beginning in the late New Deal and culminating in the early 1960s, the political economy of growth and distributive justice displaced the political economy of citizenship.

The New Deal and the Keynesian Revolution

As the New Deal began, political debate continued to reflect the alternatives defined in the Progressive era. When Franklin Roosevelt took office in the midst of the Depression, two traditions of reform offered competing approaches to economic recovery. One group of reformers, heirs to the New Freedom and the philosophy of Brandeis, sought to decentralize the economy through antitrust and other measures aimed at restoring competition. Another group, indebted to the New Nationalism, sought to rationalize the economy through national economic planning. They argued that concentrated power was an inevitable feature of a modern economy; what was needed was systematic planning and rational control of the industrial system.

Despite their differences, both the planners and the antitrusters assumed that overcoming the Depression required a change in the structure of industrial capitalism. They also agreed that the concentration of power in the economy, left to its own devices, posed a threat to democratic government. Like Croly and Brandeis before them, they differed on how best to preserve democracy in the face of economic power—whether to form a rival concentration of power in the national government or to decentralize economic power in hopes of making it accountable to local political units.

These competing approaches persisted, unresolved, through much of the New Deal. In different policies and different moods, Roosevelt experimented with both, never fully embracing or rejecting either. In the end, however, neither the planners nor the antitrusters prevailed (Brinkley 1995). Recovery, when it came, was due not to structural reform but to massive government spending. World War II supplied the occasion for the spending, Keynesian economics the rationale. But Keynesian fiscal policy had a political appeal that appeared even before the war demonstrated its economic success. For unlike the various proposals for structural reform, Keynesian economics offered a way for government to control the economy without having to choose among controversial conceptions of the good society. Where earlier reformers had sought economic arrangements that would cultivate citizens of a certain kind, Keynesians undertook no formative mission; they proposed simply to accept existing consumer preferences and to regulate the economy by manipulating aggregate demand.

By the end of World War II, the central issues of economic policy had little to do with the debates that had preoccupied Americans from the Progressive era to the New Deal. The old debates about how to reform industrial capitalism faded from the scene, and the macroeconomic issues familiar in our day came to the fore. By 1960 most economists and policymakers agreed that "the chief economic problem of the country was to achieve and maintain high and rapidly rising total output" (Stein 1969, pp. 381–82). Steps to make the distribution of income more equal were also deemed desirable, but secondary to the aim of full employment and economic growth.

Debate would continue, of course, about the relative claims of economic growth and distributive justice, about trade-offs between inflation and unemployment, about tax policies and spending priorities. But these debates reflected the assumption that economic policy is concerned above all with the size and distribution of national wealth. The old questions about what economic arrangements are hospitable to self-government ceased to be the subject of national debate. With the triumph of fiscal policy, the political economy of citizenship gave way to the political economy of growth and distributive justice.

Keynesianism and Liberalism

The advent of the new political economy marked a decisive moment in the demise of the republican strand of American politics and the rise of contemporary liberalism. According to this liberalism, government should be neutral about conceptions of the good life in order to respect persons as free and independent selves, capable of choosing their ends for themselves. As Keynesian fiscal policy emerged from the late 1930s to the early 1960s, it both reflected this liberalism and deepened its hold on American public life. Although those who practiced Keynesian economics did not defend it in precisely these terms, the new political economy displayed two features of the liberalism that defines the procedural republic. First, it offered policymakers and elected officials a way to bracket, or set aside, controversial conceptions of the good life and so promised a consensus that programs for structural reform could not offer. Second, by abandoning the formative project, it denied government a stake in the moral character of its citizens and affirmed the notion of persons as free and independent selves capable of choice.

The clearest expression of faith in the new economics as a neutral instrument of national governance was offered by President John F. Kennedy. In a commencement address at Yale University in 1962, he argued that modern economic problems could best be resolved if people set aside their ideological convictions. "The central domestic issues of our time," he observed (Kennedy 1962, pp. 470–71, 473), "are more subtle and less simple" than the large moral and political issues that commanded the nation's attention in earlier days. "They relate not to basic clashes of philosophy or ideology but to ways and means of reaching common goals. . . . What is at stake in our economic decisions today is not some grand warfare of rival ideologies which will sweep the country with passion but the practical management of a modern economy." Kennedy urged the country "to face technical problems without ideological preconceptions," to focus on "the sophisticated and technical issues involved in keeping a great economic machinery moving ahead."

As Keynesian fiscal policy took hold in the 1950s and 1960s, the civic strand of economic argument faded from American political discourse. Economic policy attended more to the size and distribution of the national product and less to the conditions of self-government. Americans increasingly viewed economic arrangements as instruments of consumption, not as schools for citizenship. The formative ambition gave way to the more mundane hope of increasing and dispersing the fruits of prosperity. Rather than cultivate virtuous citizens, government would take people's wants and desires as givens and would pursue policies aimed at satisfying them as fully and fairly as possible.

At the time, Americans did not grasp the import of this change. Animated by the civic conception of freedom, Americans from Jefferson and Lincoln to Brandeis and Croly and Theodore Roosevelt had struggled to assert democratic mastery over economic power and to cultivate in citizens the virtues that would suit them to self-government. Now Americans seemed ready to give up the struggle or, more precisely, to give up the conception of freedom that made the struggle necessary. Confronted with an economy too vast to admit republican hopes of mastery and tempted by the prospect of prosperity, Americans of the postwar decades found their way to a new understanding of freedom. According to this conception, our liberty depends not on our capacity as citizens to shape the forces that govern our collective destiny but rather on our capacity as persons to choose our values and ends for ourselves.

From the standpoint of republican political theory, this shift represents a fateful concession; to abandon the formative ambition is to abandon the project of liberty as the republican tradition conceives it. But Americans did not experience the new public philosophy as disempowering, at least not at first. To the contrary, in the day of its arrival, the procedural republic appeared to be a triumph of mastery and self-command. This was due partly to the historical moment and partly to the promise of the liberal conception of freedom.

The Moment of Mastery

The procedural republic was born at a rare moment of American mastery. At the end of World War II, the United States stood astride the world, an unrivaled global power. This power, combined with the buoyant economy of the postwar decades, accustomed a generation of Americans to seeing themselves as masters of their circumstance. John Kennedy's (1961) inaugural address gave stirring expression to a generation's conviction that it possessed powers of Promethean proportions. "The world is very different now," he proclaimed. "For man holds in his mortal hands the power to abolish all forms of human poverty and all forms of human life." We would "pay any price, bear any burden," to assure the success of liberty.

Beyond the bounty of American power, the promise of mastery in the postwar decades had another source in the public philosophy of contemporary liberalism itself. The image of persons as free and independent selves, unbound by moral or communal ties they have not chosen, is a liberating, even exhilarating ideal. Freed from the dictates of custom or tradition, the liberal self is installed as sovereign, cast as the author of the only obligations that constrain.

This image of freedom found expression across the political spectrum. Lyndon Johnson rested the case for the welfare state not on strong notions of communal obligation but instead on the idea of enabling people to choose their ends for themselves: "For more than 30 years, from social security to the war on poverty, we have diligently worked to enlarge the freedom of man. And as a result, Americans tonight are freer to live as they want to live, to pursue their ambitions, to meet their desires, . . . than at any time in all of our glorious history" (1964, pp. 1012–13). Welfare rights advocates opposed work requirements, mandatory job training, and family planning programs for welfare recipients on the grounds that all persons, including the poor, "should have the freedom to choose how to express the meaning of their lives" (U.S. Senate 1967). For their part, conservative critics of Johnson's Great Society also made their arguments in the name of the liberal conception of freedom. The only legitimate functions of government, Barry Goldwater (1990 [1960], pp. 52–53) insisted, were those that made it "possible for men to follow their chosen pursuits with maximum freedom." The libertarian economist Milton Friedman (1962, p. 200) opposed Social Security and other mandatory government programs on the grounds that they violated people's rights "to live their lives by their own values."

And so, for a time, the special circumstances of American life obscured the passing of the civic conception of freedom. But when the moment of mastery expired—when 1968 brought the shattering of faith in Vietnam, riots in the ghettos, campus unrest, and the assassinations of Martin Luther King, Jr., and Robert Kennedy—Americans were left ill equipped to contend with the dislocation that swirled about them. The liberating promise of the freely choosing self could not compensate for the loss of self-government more broadly conceived. At home and abroad, events spun out of control, and government seemed helpless to respond.

Reagan's Civic Conservatism

There followed a season of protest that is with us still. As disillusion with government grew, politicians groped to articulate the frustrations that the reigning political agenda did not capture. The most successful, at least in electoral terms, was Ronald Reagan. Although he ultimately failed to allay the discontent he tapped, it is instructive nonetheless to consider the source of his appeal and how it departed from the reigning terms of political discourse.

Reagan drew, in different moods and moments, on both the libertarian and the civic strands of American conservatism. The most resonant part of his political appeal derived from the second of these strands, from his skillful evocation of communal values such as family and neighborhood, religion and patriotism. What set Reagan apart from laissez-faire conservatives also set him apart from the public philosophy of his day. This was his ability to identify with Americans' yearnings for a common life of larger meanings on a smaller, less impersonal scale than the procedural republic provides.

Reagan blamed big government for disempowering citizens and proposed a "New Federalism" that would shift power to states and localities, recalling the long-standing republican worry about concentrated power. But Reagan revived this tradition with a difference. Previous advocates of republican political economy had worried about big government and big business alike. For Reagan, by contrast, the curse of bigness attached to government alone. Even as he evoked the ideal of community, he had little to say about the corrosive effects of capital flight or the disempowering consequences of economic power organized on a vast scale.

For their part, Reagan-era Democrats did not challenge Reagan on this score, nor did they otherwise join the debate about community and self-government. Tied to the terms of rights-oriented liberalism, they missed the mood of discontent. The anxieties of the age concerned the erosion of those communities intermediate between the individual and the nation, such as families and neighborhoods, cities and towns, schools and congregations. But the public philosophy of Reagan-era Democrats lacked the civic resources to respond. Democrats, once the party of dispersed power, had learned in recent decades to view intermediate communities with suspicion. Too often such communities had been pockets of prejudice, outposts of intolerance, places where the tyranny of the majority held sway. And so, from the New Deal to the civil rights movement to the Great Society, the liberal project was to use federal power to vindicate individual rights that local communities failed to protect. This unease with the middle terms of civic life, however honorably acquired, left Democrats ill equipped for attending to the erosion of self-government.

The civic and communal strand of Reagan's rhetoric enabled him to succeed, where Democrats failed, in tapping the mood of discontent. In the end, however, Reagan's presidency did little to alter the conditions underlying the discontent. He governed more as a market conservative than as a civic conservative. The unfettered capitalism that he favored did nothing to repair the moral fabric of families, neighborhoods, or communities.

The Return of Civic Virtue

It remains to be asked how a renewed attention to republican themes might better equip us to contend with our condition. How would a political agenda informed by the civic strand of freedom differ from the one that now prevails? Is self-government in the republican sense even possible under modern conditions, and if so, what qualities of character would be necessary to sustain it?

A partial, inchoate answer can be glimpsed in the shifting terms of political argument. Some conservatives and recently some liberals have gestured toward a revival of civic virtue, character formation, and moral judgment as considerations in public policy and political discourse. From the 1930s to the 1980s, conservatives criticized the welfare state on libertarian grounds. However desirable old-age pensions or school lunches or aid to the poor might be, argued conservatives like Milton Friedman and Barry Goldwater, it was a violation of liberty to use state power to coerce taxpayers to support these causes against their will. Since the mid-1980s, however, the conservative argument has begun to change. Increasingly, conservatives focus their criticism on the moral and civic consequences of federal social policy. Welfare is at odds with freedom, many conservatives now argue, not because it coerces taxpayers but because it breeds dependence and irresponsibility among recipients and so deprives them of the independence that full citizenship requires.

Conservatives were not the first to worry about the damaging effects of welfare on moral and civic character. The first major political figure to criticize welfare from the standpoint of the civic conception of freedom was not Ronald Reagan or Newt Gingrich but Robert F. Kennedy. Shortly before his assassination in 1968, Kennedy stated that welfare was perhaps "our greatest domestic failure," because it rendered "millions of our people slaves to dependency and poverty, waiting on the favor of their fellow citizens to write them checks. Fellowship, community, shared patriotism—these essential values of our civilization do not come from just buying and consuming goods together. They come from a shared sense of individual independence and personal effort." The solution to poverty, Kennedy argued (reprinted in Guthman and Allen 1993, pp. 208–9), was not a guaranteed income paid by the government but "dignified employment at decent pay, the kind of employment that lets a man say to his community, to his family, to his country, and most important, to himself, 'I helped to build this country. I am a participant in its great public ventures.'"

Had Democrats taken up the moral and civic concerns for which Kennedy spoke, they would have been less vulnerable to the politics of virtue advanced by social and cultural conservatives of the 1980s. But liberals came belatedly to the revolt against the procedural republic. Not until the 1990s did they too began to articulate civic themes. In November 1993, speaking in the Memphis church where Martin Luther King, Jr., preached before his assassination, Bill Clinton (1993) ventured onto moral and spiritual terrain that liberals of recent times had sought to avoid. Restoring work to the life of the inner city was essential, he explained, not only for the income it brings but also for its character-forming effects, for the discipline, structure, and pride that work confers on family life. In his 1994 State of the Union address, he continued to trespass on value-laden territory once occupied by conservatives and the religious right. Our problems "are rooted in the loss of values, in the disappearance of work, and the breakdown of our families and communities," Clinton (1994) declared. Among the sources of family breakdown was the soaring number of children born outside marriage. Clinton allowed that former vice president Dan Quayle had been right when he maintained that having children out of wedlock was wrong and that government should act to discourage it.

Other Democrats of the 1990s have also joined the call to restore moral and religious discourse to public life and to repair the character-forming agencies of civil society. The political agenda of recent decades, mainly concerned with adjudicating the roles of market and government, did not address the loss of community and the erosion of civic life. In an address to the National Press Club, Senator Bill Bradley (1995) called for a politics that focused more on the institutions of civil society. Neither the market nor government is "equipped to solve America's central problems, which are the deterioration of our civil society and the need to revitalize our democratic process." Politics should be concerned, he urged, with restoring "churches, schools, fraternities, community centers, labor unions, synagogues, sports leagues, PTAS, libraries, and barber shops" as "civic spaces," sites of deliberation about the common good. The "distinctive moral language of civil society"—the language of community, family, citizenship, and mutual obligation—should play a more prominent role in our "public conversation."

By the 1996 election, the themes of family, community, and civil society had become a pervasive but largely hortatory feature of American political discourse. Any serious effort to shore up value-laden communities must face up to the forces that have undermined them. It is here that a progressive political movement inspired by ideals of citizenship and civic virtue should join the debate with conservatives who speak of virtue. Conservatives like William Bennett (1995) locate the threat to virtue-sustaining institutions in two sources: popular culture and big government. Rap music and vulgar movies corrupt the youth, they argue, while big government and the welfare state sap individual initiative, enervate the impulse for local self-help, and preempt the role of mediating institutions. Prune the shade tree of big government, they insist, and families, neighborhoods, and church-based charities will flourish in the sun and space now crowded out by the overgrown tree.

The cultural conservatives are right to worry about the coarsening effects of popular entertainment, which, taken together with the advertising that drives it, induces a passion for consumption and a passivity toward politics that are at odds with civic virtue. But they are wrong to ignore the most potent force of all—the corrosive power of an unfettered market economy. When corporations use their power to extract tax reductions, zoning changes, and environmental concessions from cities and states desperate for jobs, they disempower communities more profoundly than any federal mandate ever did. When the growing gap between rich and poor leads the affluent to flee public schools, public parks, and public transportation for privileged enclaves, civic virtue becomes difficult to sustain, and the common good fades from view (Reich 1991).

The purpose that should animate a new progressive politics is the project of reconstructing the infrastructure of civic life—not just for the sake of better public services but primarily for the sake of creating public spaces that draw people out of their identity as consumers and cultivate their identity as citizens. This project depends in turn on recalling a tradition of political argument, running from Jefferson to Brandeis to Robert Kennedy, that in recent decades has been eclipsed. Central to that tradition is the question of what economic arrangements are hospitable to self-government and the civic virtues that sustain it. Liberals and progressives should join the debate with conservatives about character, community, and virtue. We need to reconstitute the political economy of citizenship and translate it into terms relevant to our time.

Reconnecting People and Politics

Margaret Weir and Marshall Ganz

> One may think of political associations as great free schools to which all citizens come to be taught the general theory of association.
>
> —Alexis de Tocqueville

Amid the media exposés about money in the 1996 campaign were several less prominent stories about the frustrations of ordinary people who tried to participate in the elections but couldn't find a way in. A Connecticut woman sent a check to the Democratic Party, attaching a note asking how she could volunteer. Although the party sent her many more fund-raising solicitations, no one ever contacted her with information about how to get involved, and she never found any local campaign organization on her own. A woman in New York actually put together a volunteer organization for a local candidate, but the party showed no interest in her efforts (Weine 1996, p. C1).

The difficulty that ordinary people have in participating in political campaigns highlights a central challenge to progressives: How do we get people back into politics? For most people, as political parties have ceased to be mass-based political organizations—becoming instead national (and international) fund-raising organizations—politics has become simply another form of advertising, and a particularly noxious one at that. Interest groups flourish, but they too have lost much of their popular base, focusing instead on Washington-based, staff-led activities. Politics and policymaking have become unanchored, susceptible to pressures from more mobilized minorities on the right or foundering in search of some acceptable "center." But in a largely demobilized political context, the center has little organizational reality and, as a consequence, little dependable political force. Over the past four years, the so-called center has lurched toward the antigovernment right for lack of any meaningful grounding in the everyday experiences of most Americans, much less any strong counterpressure from progressive forces.

As ever fewer people are drawn into organized political endeavors, American democracy suffers from declining voter participation, distrust of government, and a widespread cynicism about politics, especially among the young. This disengagement has policy consequences as well. Increasingly, the assumptions that determine the menu of policy options considered in Washington and many state capitols reflect the narrow interests of elites whose primary concern is to shield themselves from the social and economic costs of growing income inequalities and social dislocations. Tapping into broad-based disillusionment with government, those who dominate today's public discussions offer well-off Americans a range of private and individualized solutions to pressing issues of economic security and well-being: medical savings accounts, privatized Social Security with individual investment accounts, and moves to ever more distant suburbs in search of physical security and decent schools for their children. In this version of the future, not only are the middle class and the poor left to the discipline of the market, but the search for common interests is abandoned. And the scope of what is public shrinks.

The challenge for progressives is to renew the connection between people and politics. There are two critical elements of such a new politics. The first is to redefine the organizational role of state and local parties in ways that make them genuine vehicles for participation, deliberation, and accountability. In particular, progressives should explore new opportunities afforded by recent court rulings that free state party organizations from regulation by state legislatures and permit them to establish their own rules, including those governing the nomination of candidates. The second is to redefine the political role of progressive constituency organizations, including unions, churches, and civic associations, in order to restore them to a central place in shaping participation and the search for common purposes in American public life.

To succeed, a new progressive politics must be grounded in an organized citizenry rooted in specific communities and at the same time linked together in larger networks with the capacity to deliberate about, develop, and carry out local, state, and national strategies. This requires the development of a critical intermediate level of leadership able to link local leaders with their regional and national counterparts. Only through mobilization across localities and levels of government will citizens begin to develop broader understandings of common interests as well as the capacity for coordinated political action on behalf of those interests. This approach calls for a clear break with the pattern of narrow interest representation that has predominated among Democratic Party constituencies since the 1970s.

Finally, if a renewed popular progressive politics is to shape public opinion rather than simply taking it as a given, it must grow out of certain moral sources that have long been part of the American civic tradition and that have so often provided the underpinning for progressive politics in the past. These moral commitments, however, must be translated into a proactive public policy agenda, an agenda that can inspire the support needed to make it achievable at local, state, and national levels. People will continue to withdraw from politics unless they believe that by taking an active part they can achieve something of real moral consequence to their everyday lives.

Not Invited to the Party

Why have Americans become so disengaged from politics? Prominent explanations point to the roles of television, the suburbanization of the population, and the general distrust that Americans have toward government (Putnam 1996). Undoubtedly there is something to each of these points, but explanations that look only at individuals do not see the transformations in the world of parties and groups that shape American politics. Instead of asking why so many people are pulling back from politics, we should wonder why they are offered so few opportunities for effective participation. What levers can citizens use to influence politicians and government? What incentives do political leaders have to respond to their fellow citizens and invite their involvement? The most fateful developments in politics over the past thirty years have been the decay in institutions that gave people the opportunity to make a difference in politics and the simultaneous waning of incentives for leaders to mobilize people into politics.

To appreciate these changes, contrast the way that politics worked right after the New Deal. For most of American history, national political parties were federations of locally rooted county and state electoral organizations, which were responsible for nominating candidates, deploying resources needed to elect them, and distributing the fruits of office. The Democratic Party was made up of these state and local party organizations (Mayhew 1986). In many major cities, patronage-based political machines—and in a few places, reform political movements—brought people into politics. Labor unions, which organized 35 percent of the labor force at their zenith, had a strong mass base and organizational presence. Significantly, unions took an active role in politics that went beyond simply representing the narrow interests of their members. In cities across the nation, labor brought new groups into the Democratic coalition (Greenstone 1969). Because these party activities built bridges between different local groups, they reduced the role of narrow interests at the national level. This style of party organization also gave politics something of a bottom-up flavor, connecting state and local organizations to national politics.

Another feature of political organization at this time were large, widespread, but locally rooted civic organizations through which networks of local, state, and national leaders could connect with ordinary people to consider politics and public policy issues (Skocpol 1997a). While not specifically partisan, many of these organizations interacted with partisan electoral politics in ways that enhanced the connection of ordinary people to politics—often in support of a Democratic agenda.

Although local party, union, and civic organizations provided Democrats with the means for connecting people with their political leaders, this form of popular mobilization should not be romanticized in retrospect. Local party organizations and unions were both regionally concentrated in the Northeast and Midwest. In contrast, there was little popular involvement in the weak parties of the West or in the racially exclusive and elite-dominated political organizations of the South. And even in the North, mobilization was often selective. Political machines often ignored voters—especially minorities—whom they viewed as dangerous to their political objectives. Nor were machines necessarily friendly to outsiders, as the story of Abner Mikva's efforts to volunteer for the Chicago machine attested. When it became clear to ward leaders that this would-be volunteer and future judge was politically unconnected, they sent him away, declaring, "We don't want nobody nobody sent" (Rakove 1979).

The transformation of political parties from the bottom-up organizations that mobilized voters yesterday into the top-down organizations that raise money today is key to understanding how people became disengaged from politics. In the 1970s and 1980s, the parties were transformed into today's national "service" firms with state "branches," through which they allocate resources—including the party label—to candidates able to win primaries with their own campaign organizations (Reichley 1992; Aldrich 1995). Where resources once flowed from the bottom up, they now flow from the top down. In the states, the political center of gravity shifted from state or local party organizations—which barely exist on their own today in many places—to state legislative caucuses able to raise large sums of money from interest groups and allocate it to favored candidates. State legislative leaders thus gained the power to turn "spigots" of support for individual candidates on and off regardless of the interests of voters in a particular district. Although mayors and city councils remain tied to networks of local voters or political clubs in some cities, they came to play a far less significant role in state and national politics than they once did—even as their own campaigns have come to resemble those of candidates for state and national office.

Driving this transformation were changes in presidential nominating procedures, campaign finance reform, the eclipse of patronage employment, and new electoral technologies. Ironically, the changes that Democrats initiated in presidential nominating procedures in order to widen participation ended up weakening the connection between people and politics (Polsby 1983). The older system in which party leaders selected delegates to national nominating conventions kept new groups out of the process. The reforms created a system in which campaign organizations of individual presidential candidates competed directly to elect slates of delegates already committed to them, thus transforming the nomination of presidential candidates from a deliberative process among state and local party leaders into plebiscites of individual voters. In fact, the proportion of the Democratic electorate participating in the delegate selection process increased only modestly after the reforms (Advisory Commission 1986). At the same time, state and local party leaders who linked networks of individual voters to larger partisan structures were replaced by consultants commanding new "voter contact" technologies and those able to raise the money to fuel their campaigns. Although national nominating conventions became far more inclusive of blacks, women, and young people, they also became far more elite affairs (Advisory Commission 1986).

Campaign finance reforms enabled national parties to find a new role in the direct-mail solicitation of small contributions that could be funneled into presidential, congressional, and legislative campaigns. State parties also became important vehicles through which contributors could channel soft money to support coordinated campaigns and party-building work that benefited federal candidates whose individual campaigns could not receive the funds directly.

The emergence of new electoral technologies made it possible for consultants to contact voters directly through mail, telephone, and television. As the cost of this technology rose, it became more cost effective to concentrate on persuading voters already likely to vote, but uncertain for whom, and to avoid investing in mobilizing citizens unlikely to vote, even if they were supporters (Ganz 1994). Politicians thus found it no longer necessary to depend on what they came to view as unreliable battalions of party workers, local community leaders, and volunteers to contact, persuade, and turn out voters.

These changes in the organization of politics affected the strategies of interest groups as well, pointing them away from local organizing and toward Washington. As a consequence, much of the energy unleashed by the new social movements of the 1960s did not leave behind organizational structures designed to regularly engage a grassroots constituency. The civil rights movement and the environmental movement, for example, lost much of their organized base during the 1970s, evolving into Washington-based lobbies, where the staff called the shots, or into groups of local activists who shunned electoral politics altogether. Cultivating ties with Democratic members of Congress and pursuing legal and regulatory strategies achieved the policy results that these groups sought; they had little incentive to organize a grassroots base. These groups boasted large memberships because of their direct-mail operations, but such membership was largely meaningless in terms of activated support. And although some local chapters of organizations like the NAACP and the Sierra Club did have real vitality, national staffers gave them no real role in mobilizing support for a public policy agenda.

This system of Washington-based interest representation encouraged groups to become even more narrow in their approaches to politics. Instead of pursuing political alliances that would help build common interests and resources, each major interest group forged its own particular national strategy. Not entirely without reason did critics tag the Democratic Party as the party of special interests.

The transformation of national parties from bottom-up deliberative organizations into top-down campaign organizations has enormous implications for politics and policymaking. By linking distinct networks of interest groups, local political organizations, and national politicians, parties helped to stabilize electoral coalitions and create a measure of continuity between the resources needed to get elected and those needed to govern. They also provided a critical intermediate level of leadership that could link local and national networks. In the past two decades this force for coherence in politics and policymaking has been replaced by a more complex configuration that makes the task of governing much more difficult.

The Sway of Advertising Politics

Three distinct types of linkages now organize politics: a "detached middle" in the electorate, consisting of individuals only loosely connected to politics through the advertising efforts of parties and interest groups; a politics of highly organized Washington-based interest groups often with very weak constituent ties; and pockets of grassroots political organization. Each type of politics pushes policy in a different direction, confronting politicians and policymakers with conflicting pressures and distinctive obstacles.

Designed to appeal to a detached middle that no longer has any stable connections to politics, the advertising strategy dominates presidential, congressional, and increasing numbers of state and local elections. This strategy is also important in policymaking and governing: presidents make extensive use of public-opinion soundings as they develop their policy agendas and as they seek to win support for their policies. The strategy of "going public"—

attempting to build public support in order to increase pressure on Congress—reflects the declining ability of presidents to rely on party loyalty to pass their programs in Congress. This advertising strategy is especially associated with the president but is increasingly practiced by interest groups and state and local politicians as well (Kernell 1986). It is a top-down approach to politics in which the grass roots is part of an overall public affairs strategy executed by inside-the-beltway firms that specialize in grassroots database management.

The second type of politics is that of Washington-based interest groups. In the past twenty years, the number of these interest groups has soared, but most of them approach policy from a narrow perspective and have only tenuous grassroots ties. On the Democratic side, as new groups clamored for entry, the decline of organized labor and local party organizations broke the links that had once existed. In the 1970s, labor grew increasingly defensive and inward looking, beginning to function more as a narrow interest group for its embattled members than as an aggregating force for the Democratic Party. In contrast, new groups associated with the Democratic Party adopted a very different organizational strategy than the one labor had once followed. Rather than grounding their strength in a local base associated with the party, these new organizations were Washington-based staff operations from the start. Their grassroots links were often limited to mail-in memberships. These groups sought to influence policy through their ties with Democratic congressional members and the courts. The growing decentralization of Congress facilitated this strategy by making it easier for lobbyists with little grassroots support to gain a hearing from sympathetic subcommittee and committee staffers. It was not just on the liberal side that interest groups grew. One of the most significant developments of the early 1970s was the mobilization of business organizations opposed to growing federal safety, consumer, and environmental regulation. Likewise, organizations associated with particular policies—such as advocacy groups for the aged—grew dramatically in the 1970s, but the impetus for such groups often came from within the government and remained based in Washington (Walker 1991).

The third type of politics consists of organizations with genuine grassroots organization and mobilization capabilities. Remnants of party organizations in some cities and counties continue to have such capabilities, mainly where they retain a role in nominating candidates for state or local office. But the energy in this form of organization in recent years has been on the right, particularly among groups associated with the Christian Right (Balz and Brownstein 1996). Although these groups constitute a distinct minority in the electorate, their political significance is magnified by the breakdown of established party ties and the atrophy of other organizations with the capacity to mobilize voters at the grass roots. In the relatively demobilized political world that constitutes American electoral politics today, such strongly organized groups can have a disproportionately important impact (Green 1995).

Because each of these three types of politics pulls in a different direction, reconciling them poses difficult strategic choices for politicians and complicates the task of policymaking. The advertising model suggests that finding the average voter and gearing political appeals and policy toward the center is the optimal strategy. Yet, as President Bill Clinton has repeatedly discovered, majorities discerned through public-opinion polling are difficult to activate and unreliable as a political resource. Washington-based interest-group politics is characterized by a narrow, self-interested perspective in which there is little incentive for subordinating narrow priorities to larger goals. The proliferation of such specialized groups and their skill in blocking aspects of policy that they oppose raise a formidable barrier to enacting major policy changes. Yet, on occasion, these groups do build coalitions among themselves, and when they do, they can be a powerful political force. Finally, the ability to mobilize at the grass roots is a prized political resource in this relatively demobilized electoral world, but because it is animated by volunteers whose zeal for a particular issue drives them into politics, grassroots movement-oriented politics tends toward single-minded or extreme views (Mansbridge 1986). This may pose costs in broader political support that offset the benefits of support from grassroots organizations.

Organizationally, this politics is far more top down than the political system that emerged after the 1930s. It is fueled by money, not by people. The connections between leaders and their fellow citizens are looser; indeed, state and national politics may have little organized local activity. Because national and even state politicians now have more incentive to raise money and support from the interests controlling financial resources than they do to mobilize voters in their own districts, when organized mass politics does appear, it does so independently of most established political leaders. Politicians focus their efforts on winning over narrow slivers of swing voters already most likely to vote, deploying the tools of the new advertising politics: computer-targeted direct mail, polling, and television.

Grassroots Politics, Right and Left

Despite these changes in the organization of politics, activists on the right and the left continued to organize. Both encountered significant obstacles, but the right has been more successful in connecting its local efforts to state and national politics. Although some of this success can be explained by the greater challenge that progressives face in uniting a far more diverse set of people with far fewer financial resources, there are also important differences in how conservatives and progressives have gone about connecting people to politics.

Although the national electoral debut of the modern conservative movement, the 1964 Goldwater campaign, resulted in a major defeat, its organizers used it to create a grassroots foundation on which they continued to build. When the conservative movement eventually regrouped, a number of the national right-wing organizations that emerged—such as the Moral Majority and the National Conservative Political Action Committee—operated through direct mail. But others did not. The 7-million-member National Right to Life Committee, the 3-million-member National Rifle Association, and the 2-million-member Christian Coalition developed ongoing organizations capable of intervening in politics from the grass roots up. These organizations have an advantage that labor unions in their heyday possessed: they tap into preexisting religious, recreational, and social networks that have real and continuing significance in their members' lives.

In addition to groups motivated primarily by social issues, federations of business organizations are also based on local chambers of commerce and other small business associations. These groups are organized on at least three levels—local, state, and national. They are based in membership groups, and at each level, members participate in programs, join in deliberation, and select leadership. Leaders of these groups thus have the opportunity to come together, deliberate about their purposes, develop leadership skills, and support one another in a variety of ways. And although funds are often available from state or national organizations for the development of particular initiatives, their local organizations rely on a local dues structure.

These organizations of the right have become increasingly partisan, generally in reaction to federal policies or laws that they oppose, such as *Roe v. Wade*, the tax status of Christian schools, and gun control legislation. The Christian Coalition has from its inception been involved in electoral politics, having formed from the organizational base created by Pat Robertson's 1988 run for the presidency. Furthermore, by making use of surviving precinct, county, and state partisan structures, the Christian Coalition has consciously sought to replicate the kind of organizations that once made the unions such an important presence in national policies. Organized through church networks, the Christian Coalition recruits and supports candidates for school boards, city councils, county commissions, and legislative races, creating new depth in the ranks of conservative Republican officeholders. Given the current weakness of much local political organization, the Christian Coalition was able to colonize the state and local Republican Party apparatus so effectively that by 1994 it was the dominant influence in a majority of Republican state parties.

Conservatives have also built strong leadership networks to connect with grassroots activity. As the engine behind the insurgent congressional conservatives, Newt Gingrich built a candidate recruitment machine that developed a strong farm team of Republican candidates. Most significantly, however, in the 104th Congress Gingrich melded this network of politicians with the popular base of the National Rifle Association and the Christian Coalition. Such cooperation allowed the Republicans to come very close to commanding the kind of power that they needed to oversee major transformations in the social role of the federal government.

The problem for the Republicans was that this interlocking network was still a decided minority, with ideas significantly to the right of the detached center. Republican efforts to reframe the issues for advertising politics—their claims to be saving Medicare, for example—were not sufficient for them to win the advertising game, especially with a Democratic president who was a master at that political genre.

Impressive as they are, the durability of these connections between politicians and voters on the right should not be taken for granted. Much has been made of the fact that the Christian right now controls a considerable portion of the Republican Party state apparatus. Yet the 1996 election revealed that the ties between state parties and the national party are actually contingent. In the past, when parties were more bottom-up affairs, local organizations were the building blocks of national parties. Today they are more like parallel organizations with many overlapping interests, but given the different natures of their tasks—national parties for fund-raising and electing a national candidate, local organizations for attracting and mobilizing supporters—their fundamental interests also conflict. These organizational characteristics suggest that the ties between mass and elite politics on the right may be inherently unstable and difficult to sustain over the long run.

Although the unsuccessful 1964 Goldwater campaign laid a foundation for subsequent grassroots organization on the right, the equally unsuccessful 1972 McGovern campaign seemed to have just the opposite effect on the left. Indeed, one of the most striking features of the political upheavals of the 1960s is their paltry legacy of grassroots political organization. Activists formed many new groups—especially in the areas of civil rights, environmentalism, and women's rights—but while some abandoned grassroots organizing as they came to focus on specific policy objectives, others, who remained committed to grassroots organizing, abandoned electoral politics. To be sure, the movements of the 1960s created grassroots groups committed to local organizing, but most of it was nonpartisan, focused on limited policy goals, and fragmented along lines often dictated by funding sources (Paget 1990).

As a consequence, politics on the left had only weak ties linking national, state, and local politics, creating a political configuration of headless bodies and bodiless heads. In addition, groups organized around different goals—such as cities or the environment—found little need to consider what interests they had in common. These divisions fostered an advocacy system that promoted distinctive national strategies for each set of interests and spurred the formation of thousands of local groups that largely abandoned efforts to influence national public policy directly. This is one reason that progressive politics seems to be far less than the sum of its parts.

From the 1970s on, advocacy organizations run by professional staff members at the state and national levels found that they could operate most effectively if they focused on single issues that could be addressed with specific insider strategies based on lobbying, litigation, and fund-raising. This was true even for coalitions, which focused on one issue at a time to maximize their effectiveness. The direct-mail, telemarketing, and canvassing fund-raising (largely directed at upscale contributors) that these groups came to rely on could all be done more effectively when focused on a single issue. In addition, the funding for many of these groups came from foundations whose tax exemptions permitted issue advocacy but not partisan politics, encouraging a single-issue, nonpartisan focus disconnected from an active grassroots base. Even major national membership organizations that grew during this period—such as the American Association of Retired Persons (AARP), with some 35 million members—are essentially benefit associations with a mailing-list membership.

A second major legacy of the 1960s was the revival of local organizing activities. Some of these groups, supported by small grants from liberal foundations, served as incubators for the emergence of various forms of identity politics, often thriving on their distinctiveness from other similar groups. An organizational culture suspicious of authority, leadership, and orderly democratic process also made collaboration across groups and levels of governance and coordination very difficult.

Community development corporations (CDCs) and local social service providers were a specific legacy of the War on Poverty, which was targeted primarily on low-income communities of color. Most community development activities, which are widespread in many urban neighborhoods, also draw on foundation support and are explicitly nonpolitical. Many of these groups have become so heavily focused on development they do not engage in organizing. Others must avoid controversy because they depend on local politicians for funding. Led by their full-time staff, most CDCs try to make the most of the meager resources available to them, rather than join in a broad political assault on the inequalities responsible for their difficulties in the first place (Weir 1997).

Another current of local organizing was initiated by networks of organizers in the Alinsky tradition—the Industrial Areas Foundation (IAF), the Pacific Institute for Community Organizing, the Gamiliel Foundation, and others. These organizations, rooted primarily in local churches and neighborhoods within low-income communities of color, focus on intensive leadership development, training in civic deliberation, and mobilization on local issues. They are not strictly local, however, because their activities are often supported by national organizing networks that develop organizing models, disseminate information, pass on experience, train organizers, and provide ongoing guidance to organizing efforts. Supported by churches and foundations, these networks have made organizing a more stable profession than ever before, one with higher salaries and pensions and other benefits. For the most part, however, they have not been able to connect local organizing activities to broader political or policy goals. The IAF, for example, with a staff of about 120 professional organizers and fifty-five local organizations around the country, has imaginatively leveraged its influence with public institutions and politicians to achieve concrete community improvements, such as Project Quest in San Antonio and the Nehemiah Homes in New York. Unlike groups on the right, however, they refrain from partisan electoral involvement, especially as tax-exempt funding is usually involved. Until recently they also avoided entering into broader coalitions or becoming involved in proactive advocacy of public policy. While this "outsider" strategy may have made sense in Alinsky's day, when claims could be made on a strong liberal establishment, it makes little sense today, when that establishment has long since passed into history. Further, when most decisions that affect the fortunes of local communities are made at regional, national, or international levels, the network's failure to create bodies of elected leadership capable of deliberating over and implementing strategies beyond the local level is a serious limitation.

Exceptions to this local apolitical stance of community organizing groups do exist. For example, in the late 1970s the National People's Alliance, a coalition of neighborhood organizations, was instrumental in passing the federal Home Mortgage Disclosure Act and the Community Reinvestment Act, which have been critical tools for local nonprofit housing organizations all over the country. These laws' requirements that banks invest in communities in which they do business have provided a lever for broad local campaigns to promote new investment in poor neighborhoods. They have been particularly important in providing poor neighborhoods with access to resources when public funds fell substantially in the 1980s. Significant as this legislative achievement and the organizing that it facilitated were, they did not provide hooks for broadening the focus beyond poor neighborhoods and beyond the functional area of community development.

Despite the transformation of the party in the 1970s and 1980s, not all groups on the left abandoned attempts at electoral politics. In California, the Campaign for Economic Democracy (CED), which grew out of Tom Hayden's unsuccessful 1976 campaign for the U.S. Senate, attempted to create an ongoing electoral organization. The porous organization of the California Democratic Party made it a good target for the CED but also made it a prize hardly worth winning. The CED elected delegates to the Democratic State Central Committee, but the central committee could not nominate candidates, determine policy goals, or control money; nor could it get anyone elected (since 1989, the party has been permitted to make preprimary endorsements). Although the CED tried to build local chapters, they took root only in countercultural communities like Santa Monica and Santa Cruz. And once its first leaders won state or local public office, they took little interest in the further development of the organization. Unlike many groups on the left, the CED did not have a money problem because it was endowed with profits from Jane Fonda's workout book. The fact that it could not survive points to a deeper difficulty in maintaining ongoing electoral organization when political parties are so weak. When they cannot link up to ongoing partisan institutions, grassroots campaign organizations disintegrate because successful candidates have little reason to maintain them. In fact, most candidates prefer forms of "instant organization," such as paid canvassing, bounty registration, and bounty absentee-ballot programs, which conveniently disappear when the election is over.

A more sustained effort to engage in electoral politics was undertaken by Citizen Action, an electoral coalition created by a network of organizers trying to build a progressive political base within working and middle-class communities in the late 1970s. Citizen Action has taken shape as a federation of some thirty-two state coalitions, such as the Massachusetts Commonwealth Coalition, Connecticut LEAP, Ohio Public Interest Campaign, and Illinois Public Action Council. A number of the state groupings that founded Citizen Action, such as Massachusetts Fair Share, initially set out to become local chapter–based organizations. But they soon found themselves financially constrained by the difficulty of creating self-sustaining local chapters, the volatility of public financial support, the limited reliability of funding by supportive unions, the electoral limitations tied to tax-exempt foundation grants, and the attractiveness of canvassing and telemarketing fund-raising technologies.

Because they were fundamentally motivated by a commitment to progressive policy goals, Citizen Action organizers responded to these challenges by shifting their focus from local grassroots organization to mobilization around specific issues, candidates, and campaigns. The state coalitions that emerged encompassed progressive organizations (unions, senior groups, pro-choice groups, and so on) called upon to mobilize for specific campaigns at specific times and places. In often unfriendly political settings, Citizen Action has built a 2-million-person contributor base that is more populist than that of most issue organizations, and it has won notable electoral and policy victories. But its reach has remained limited because it has a limited local base. Citizen Action has created little deliberative capacity beyond the board meetings of representatives of their affiliated organizations, while executive leadership remains in the hands of the professional organizing staff. Its members have no real access to local organizations through which they could participate. And even when it has elected candidates to state legislative office, it has few resources of its own to use in challenging the powerful leadership of more conservative legislative caucus organizations.

The most important organizational exceptions to this pattern are public sector unions such as the 1-million-member American Federation of State, County, and Municipal Employees (AFSCME) and the 2-million-member National Education Association. Particularly at the level of state and local politics, these organizations play an increasingly important role in electoral politics and policymaking. These statewide groups are rooted in local organizations that generate both financial and human resources. They act through local, state, and national elected deliberative bodies, command their own resources, and are capable of coordinating state and national campaigns. Indeed, the virulence with which the right has targeted them is itself the best evidence of their significance. Teachers are now routinely replacing lawyers as an important source of candidates for state legislative offices and constitute the largest blocks of delegates at state and national Democratic conventions. Yet because these unions are weakly connected to any broader political movement, their defense of the public sector can appear increasingly self-serving and unconcerned with the public good. Alone, these unions are more likely to take narrow approaches to public problems, and alone, they cannot articulate a convincing rationale for a strong public sector, particularly when faced with counterarguments that define the public good as less government.

Organizationally, then, the politics of the left that emerged after the 1960s was ill equipped to support broad coalitions. Above all, it was ill suited to support a new version of the bottom-up coalition that had been the keystone of Democratic political strength during the New Deal era.

Building Civic Engagement

Bringing people back in to politics is more than a "nice thing to do," and it requires more than a gesture in the direction of grass roots. The real problem is that ordinary people—their ideas, time, energy, commitment—have come to count for very little in determining who is nominated for public office, who is elected, and what they do when they are elected. Unless ordinary people resume a role in the processes of nomination, election, and policy development, we cannot hope to build a genuinely progressive politics. Because control of the new electoral technology that dominates politics today rests squarely in the hands of those with the most money to buy it, it is urgent to find ways to create new, powerful, democratic alternatives. Getting money out of politics is important, but getting people back in is more important.

Getting people back into politics requires a dual effort. On one hand, powerful membership organizations have to be rebuilt—organizations that are locally widespread, nationally coordinated, and oriented to the accomplishment of public purpose. On the other hand, partisan mechanisms also have to be rebuilt in order to restore links between fractured elements of a progressive coalition and to reconnect citizens and their leaders in pursuit of their common interests.

Local organization that links networks of individuals to broader political structures is crucial to rebuilding a progressive infrastructure. Through local organization, new people are recruited, new networks form, deliberative engagement occurs, genuine commitment emerges, new leadership develops, and real mobilization takes place. Local organization cannot be sustained, however, unless it is rooted in activities of importance in people's everyday lives and unless it can generate the revenue needed to support itself. To be effective, local groups must be connected to broader networks that can operate in state and national centers of economic and political power. Such coordination cannot be limited to a few professionals but should include deliberative bodies at state and national levels so that elected local leaders can take part in state and national decision making. In this way they can bring a local perspective to national decisions and gain a national perspective on local decisions. Local leaders can also earn the right to occupy state and national office.

If popular progressives are to move beyond mere public opinion, organizing must tap into those sources of moral energy that inspire people to make the commitments, take the risks, and endure the sacrifices required to do new things. It is the combination of interest and moral purpose that can draw us into deliberative engagement with others through which we begin to discover new common interests even while constructing the capacity to act on them. This sense of public purpose drove the labor movement, the civil rights movement, and other movements of democratic renewal in the past—and continues to animate the environmental movement, the women's movement, and the commitment of so many young people to public service. The challenge will be translating this sense of purpose not only into proposals for policy but also into campaigns capable of mobilizing enough public support to enact such policies.

Three kinds of organizations provide the building blocks for this kind of political engagement: unions, churches, and civic organizations. Union leaders have a crucial role to play in rebuilding a progressive infrastructure—not only because of their constituency or the work that their members do (increasingly, human service work in the public sector) but because of the unique organizational capacity that they possess. Unions are locally based, capable of coordinated strategies, and beginning to rediscover their sense of moral purpose. Their funding base is tied to organization building—the more members, the more dues—and is relatively unrestricted by nonpartisan requirements. Through local labor councils and state federations, unions have organizational mechanisms for mobilizing coalitions of other groups. The major challenge facing union leaders is to accept their responsibility for leadership of a coalition that can grow only if they are committed to nurturing it rather than dominating it. Labor leadership must also come to understand its interests far more broadly than it often has in the recent past. Fortunately, precisely this kind of move may offer unions the best hope for broadening their support among unorganized workers, the public, and the committed leadership they must attract to their ranks. If it chooses to do so, labor *can* go beyond the politics of "message manipulation" and undertake the serious work of reconstructing a constituency for progressive politics in America.

Urban churches and some national denominations have been active supporters of community organizing around the country, but with a few exceptions, these have been nonpartisan efforts limited to the inner city. Perhaps it is time for mainstream suburban congregations—many of which played major roles in the civil rights and antiwar movements—to return to the fray. After many difficult years focused within, struggling with vexing but important issues involving gender and governance, religious leaders may be able to renew their focus on questions of justice in the community as a whole. In particular, polarization around the abortion issue has seriously dampened the political significance of a generally progressive Roman Catholic position on economic and social issues. And women's religious organizations remain among the most dynamic multitiered voluntary associations in America. Although middle-class churches are solicited to support inner-city efforts, they could play a far stronger role as collaborators in a common effort to address *shared* community, regional, and national concerns—something that is being attempted by the IAF's metropolitan-wide Greater Boston Interfaith Organization.

Civic associations have always played a crucial role in progressive politics in America, a role that they must recapture if the progressive enterprise is to succeed. Locally based organizations that are already part of wider networks, like those affiliated with the IAF, must develop structures that permit them to address the real problems that their members face. They also need to reach out to other partners, as has already occurred in the association of BUILD with AFSCME in their campaign to establish a living wage for employees of city contractors in Baltimore.

Issue advocacy organizations, on the other hand, must confront the fact that their opposition will always have the upper hand in a politics organized around money and technology. Some organizations, such as the Sierra Club, are based on local chapters but have had difficulty mobilizing them to take effective political action. Indeed, because so many young people are attracted to it, the environmental movement as a whole is an important and growing source of progressive energy. Other organizations, such as the AARP, are trying to bring viable state and local organizations into being and may be encouraged to do so as part of a broad strategy of rebuilding democratic infrastructure. Still others, such as Working America, are trying to address the needs of newly mobile professional workers. The redefining of gender roles at work and at home has generated a raft of new challenges for both men and women, but it has also released enormous energy for addressing these challenges, especially among women. Indeed, one of the most positively regarded accomplishments of the Clinton administration was the Family and Medical Leave Act of 1994. Perhaps there is an opportunity for something new, a variation on something old: the mutual benefit association, focused not only on retirement but on the wide range of family security concerns that face most working families—child care, medical care, educational needs, and so on. This could take the form of, say, the League of American Families, an alliance composed of local groups, coordinated at state and national levels, and tied to a moral purpose central to the lives of most Americans.

Revitalizing the Democratic Party

But what of the second part of the puzzle? Revitalization of constituency organizations alone is not enough to relink people to politics. Direct participation in electoral campaigns is one tried-and-true way of generating new volunteers. In the 1996 elections, organized labor's efforts to reengage politically were particularly notable. Although much of their highly publicized budget of $35 million was spent on advertising, unions also sought to energize more local political activity. Because the Democratic Party's coordinated campaign was primarily a vehicle for moving money around and because little effective party infrastructure existed on which to build, labor jerryrigged its own field operation. The aim was to mobilize labor activists for door-to-door campaigning, and the AFL-CIO claims to have recruited twenty thousand of them. In addition to labor's operation, selected candidates, foremost among them Minnesota senator Paul Wellstone, consciously built field organizations to supplement other campaign activities.

Campaign field organizations can provide short-term forums for building connections across different constituency groups, thus helping to generate a broader progressive perspective, but they provide no enduring organizational structure between elections. As a result, organizers have to recreate the activity anew for each race, and politicians, once in office, are unaccountable to a grassroots base. Individual groups attempting to build participatory structures designed to operate between elections face considerable obstacles.

Organizations whose main focus is not electoral soon move to other priorities. These electoral step-children are extensions of the parent organization,
offering limited leadership roles for those from other groups. One possibility,
which organized labor is now considering, is to engage more fully in state and
local elections, including elections for school boards, much as the Christian
Right does.

An effective progressive politics must go further and systematically link
ongoing grassroots activism with party—a route pursued by the Christian
Coalition and its allied groups with considerable success. Although the party
reforms of the 1970s eventually established a fairly uniform presidential
nominating process, as we have seen, nominating procedures for candidates
for state and local offices—the vast majority of the more than 490,000 elec-
tive offices in the United States—remained under the control of state legislatures. As a result, wide variation exists in the regulations governing 50 state,
3,600 county, and more than 150,000 precinct-level party organizations:
these range from such "party-friendly" states as Colorado, Connecticut, New
York, Minnesota, and Pennsylvania to such "party-unfriendly" states as
Alaska, Hawaii, Louisiana, Montana, and Vermont. A variety of measures
affect the strength of state and local party organization, including closed primaries, "sore loser" laws, and straight party ballots. Most significant, however, are nominating conventions and preprimary endorsements—ways in
which party organization can affect the selection of the party's candidates.
Conventions provide opportunities for potential candidates and party leaders to negotiate differences and offer an avenue of participation and influence
for party activists and local party organizations (Advisory Commission
1986). Preprimary endorsements by state and local party organizations or
control over ballot positioning gives local leaders an opportunity to influence
the electoral process based not on how much money they can raise but on
how good a job they can do in turning out their supporters. In New Jersey,
for example, county committees remain active year-round largely due to their
ongoing role in nominating candidates for the local freeholder races held
every off year. It is also no coincidence that the site of the effective Wellstone
field organization was Minnesota, a state in which caucuses continue to have
an active part in nominating Democratic candidates. Not surprisingly, in
states where local party organization continues to play a role in the nomination procedure, local organization tends to remain strong. And where party

organization remains strong, party-affiliated candidates have a better chance of being elected (Bibby 1994).

Progressives should take advantage of recent court rulings (*Tashjian v. Connecticut* [109 SC 1013 1989]) that free state parties from legislative regulation and permit them to establish their own governance procedures. These changes provide an opportunity to put people back into the electoral process by strengthening the role of caucuses and conventions in preprimary endorsements. In the 1960s and 1970s, progressives sought ways around state and local party organizations because they were often controlled by the Democratic old guard. Rather than challenge entrenched party leadership for control of the organizations responsible for deliberating about candidates, policy, and accountability, progressives supported the very measures, such as direct primaries, that now make politics the advertising game that they ultimately cannot win. A concerted effort to nominate progressive candidates for public office through caucuses and conventions could help shift the electoral battle to an area where organizing has a chance to compete with fund-raising. Winning nomination by a caucus or state convention requires organizing people, turning them out, and getting them elected. If progressives cannot out-organize their opposition, they have little claim to being advocates of a popular politics that supports the interests of ordinary Americans.

People with doubts about this approach are haunted by the specter of the 1972 McGovern campaign; they warn of a nominating procedure likely to produce candidates who are too "extreme" to get elected. By privileging the mobilizing capacity of groups able to draw on high levels of commitment from their supporters, they fear, caucuses and conventions will become meetings of zealots in which the most righteous, not the most electable, will be nominated. There is undoubtedly some truth to this. But the current system, which privileges the capacity to mobilize money, not people, and which sustains an electoral process almost devoid of real debate, is certainly not one that we should prefer. Nor should we prefer a politics only of the immediately possible, which is characterized by the familiar culture of world-weary cynicism, over a politics of engagement, which holds out the prospect of genuine change. Indeed, although the zealous religious right has from time to time nominated unelectable candidates, by taking control of the Republican nominating machinery they not only gained a major influence over Congress but also shifted sharply to the right the political debate within the country as a whole. Those who wish to restore a progressive sense of moral purpose to public life must risk outcomes in which dedication to moral purpose really matters.

Other skeptics argue that trying to take control of the state and local Democratic nominating mechanism is a waste of time. But we disagree. Although state and local party organizations may have little widespread presence and few resources of their own with which to elect candidates, they do control the party's name. Despite extraordinary levels of alienation and disaffection, millions of ordinary Americans continue to think of themselves as Democrats. This is no trifling matter. People do not think of themselves as members of the New Party or Citizen Action or as participants in a progressive electoral coalition. As long as America retains its "first by the post" elections and single-member representative districts, it is much more meaningful to contend for influence over Democratic Party nominations and candidates than it is to contest elections through alternative groups with much less popular meaning.

Bringing People Back

We have argued that progressive Democrats need to place a priority on bringing people back into politics. This is not to suggest that the moral commitments and policy choices required to renew the American social contract matter less than the way politics is practiced. Vision, program, and practice must be transformed together. Nor are we opposed to legal reforms designed to reduce the role of big money in politics. Still, popularly oriented progressives need to be very clear about what really ails the system today. Campaigns, advocacy, and elections have lost their moorings. We cannot rest content with getting big money out of politics; we must find new and better ways to bring people back in.

The revitalization of American democracy cannot come from politicians always searching for some chimerical and receding center. Nor can it come from national issue advocacy or local organizing alone. Renewal depends on making new linkages, on promoting groups and networks that pull people in, tie them together, and enable two-way conversations between leaders and their fellow citizens. The reconnection of people and politics has to be made, day to day, in how we actually *do* politics, not only in how we talk about it.

The Battle for the States

Karen M. Paget

W hat I can do between now and Easter is break up the Washington logjam, shift power back to the fifty states, break up all the liberal national organizations—and make them scramble to the state capitals in Texas, Georgia, and in Missouri." Having just taken over as new majority leader in the 104th Congress in early 1995, Newt Gingrich of Georgia was exuberantly regaling journalist Elizabeth Drew with his game plan for the conservative Republican revolution. Gingrich's friend and former House colleague, Vin Weber, interpreted and expanded on the Speaker's remarks. "He wants to change the political dynamic that was put in motion at the time of the New Deal. He believes that to triumph politically you have to smash 'tax-and-spend liberalism,' which has dominated our domestic politics for sixty years" (Drew 1996, p. 26).

Several years later, the scramble to the states is well under way. The waning of Gingrich's personal popularity should not obscure Republican successes in the last Congress. Conservative columnist George S. Will (1996) calculated a success rate of 65 percent for the seventy-four items included in the Republican Contract with America. The leading achievement, of course, was "welfare reform," which ended a sixty-year-old guarantee of federal support for poor women and children and gave the states authority to set the scope of their own safety nets. "More conservative than even the aspirations of the Reagan administration," is how Will described Republican achievements, lauding the big cuts that had been made in discretionary federal spending for the first time since 1969.

The conservative crusade to shrink the federal government and dismantle New Deal–style programs remains vigorous, seconded by those, including many Democrats, who simply want to "devolve responsibility" to the state or local level. A primary weapon in the movement's arsenal is a Balanced Budget Amendment (BBA) to the U.S. Constitution, which would prohibit deficit spending. In 1995 and again in early 1997, this amendment fell barely short in Congress. For the 105th Congress, Speaker Gingrich and Senate Majority Leader Trent Lott have pledged to keep trying to assemble the two-thirds congressional majorities necessary to launch this amendment into the state-level ratification process. The BBA remains a very high priority for today's Republican Party.

Repeated votes on the BBA will happen and continue to be close. Stopping the effort in this Congress should be considered a temporary reprieve, not a permanent victory. What is more, the very possibility of a ratification battle in the states should spur us to look closely at how well prepared progressives are, not only for a BBA ratification struggle but more generally for the state-level tax and budget fights that promise to recur for years to come.

The challenges for progressives are considerable. As Speaker Gingrich told Drew, forcing Democrats to fight on multiple state fronts plays to Republican strengths and may greatly exacerbate Democratic weaknesses. State legislatures, whether nominally Republican or Democratic, tend to be conservative on matters of fiscal policy. Most legislatures have been the target of vigorous antitax movements. In addition, in many states, the best mobilized constituencies are antigovernment groups that tend to support Republicans.

The problem for progressives is even deeper. Fights in the states tend to lay bare progressive incapacities to wage battles requiring an *overall* understanding of tax and budget issues. Advocates of particular programs can be quite knowledgeable and effective. But struggles over taxes and budget cuts expose and frequently exacerbate powerful tensions among constituencies labeled moderate, liberal, or progressive.

In order to construct a durable center-left electoral majority, progressives must do more than deliver votes for a presidential candidate once every four years. Progressives must build a strong base at the state level, not only among voters but also among legislators and governors. A firm base among state legislators, always important, is nowadays absolutely vital, as new budgetary and policy challenges are passed downward by conservatives or by bipartisan Congressional coalitions of devolutionists. And in order to compensate for atrophied party institutions, progressives must knit together state and regional organizations that perform some traditional party functions—such as mobilizing and educating people about the new budgetary realities and pulling disparate groups together to counter overarching threats in a way that avoids zero-sum tactics.

In this essay I consider what is at stake in the ongoing struggle against the Balanced Budget Amendment, asking what may happen if progressives lose the congressional battle and have to fall back into defensive warfare in dozens of states. Because the Congress is committed to balancing the federal budget by 2002, with or without the BBA, I also investigate the capacity of progressives to deal with the fiscal challenges that they must address even in the absence of a ratification fight. Having observed and interviewed activists in the states, I probe analytical resources and consider tensions and resource deficits in order to learn how progressives can do better as they undertake to wage battle on fifty state fronts.

Throughout, I keep the focus on tax and budget issues. Unglamorous as these issues may seem, they are central to the development of any center-left project. If our local, state, and national governments cannot raise and deploy resources, how can we hope to further the security of ordinary families or use government to address the problems of our society? As determined conservatives well realize, governments that cannot tax and spend are easy targets for public frustration and anger. A first set of cuts or fiscal shackles can soon lead to additional cuts or shackles, as people decide that government does not work. This process feeds on itself, unless and until progressives find ways to turn the spiral around.

A Decisive Fight About the Balanced Budget Amendment
The Balanced Budget Amendment is a measure whose ratification would fundamentally change the rules of the game for both the federal government and the states. Of all the measures associated with the "new federalism" or the "devolution revolution," the BBA poses the most danger—to Democrats,

to progressives, and, most important, to the nation's economy. If ratified, the BBA would virtually end the federal government's capacity to counter economic recessions. It would mean leaving state legislatures on their own and facing a trade-off between two bad options—raising taxes or cutting spending—each of which could worsen a recession.

The purpose of the BBA is *not* to achieve fiscal discipline. The intent and driving force behind this amendment is to shrink government expenditures, to reduce safety-net programs and weaken constituencies that support them, to inhibit federal tax increases by requiring a majority of all elected members (not just those present) to vote, and to induce the need for continuous spending cuts. If these assertions seem to border on hyperbole, consider how the amendment was characterized by William Kristol, a Republican strategist and the editor of the *Weekly Standard*. Kristol (1996) calls the BBA "a dagger aimed at the heart of the Democrats."

The amendment would affect most constituencies that compose the Democratic base. Its effects would include spending cuts that would fall heavily on the states and, in turn, on local governments, especially inner cities. Other sure effects would be a hobbling of the federal government in mitigating recessions, especially because the rigid new limits on federal spending for social programs (such as food stamps or unemployment benefits) would prevent automatic expansion in response to numbers of clients in need. Finally, the BBA would also create massive indirect pressure to either cap spending on expensive entitlement programs such as Medicaid or transform them into fixed and dwindling grants to the states in order to limit federal obligations.

The prospect of a constitutional BBA is particularly painful because none of the arguments in favor hold up (and the same can be said for arguments in favor of draconian federal budget balancing by the year 2002, even if it is done simply by congressional legislation). "States and families have to balance their budgets, so why not the federal government?" proponents often ask rhetorically. But though popular and apparently commonsensical, such analogies are patently false. States have capital budgets; householders incur plenty of long-term debt in the form of mortgages and loans to cover their children's educations. Further, America's economic experience since World War II does not substantiate folksy conservative fables about economic growth and deficit spending. The United States has grown, in significant part, through borrowing. Some economists actually maintain that the elimination of deficit spending itself has recurrently brought on recessions (see Paget 1996).

Why, then, has the BBA, once considered a radical fringe idea, gained unanimous support among Republicans and picked up increasing support among Democrats? For many years, politicians (other than "true believers" intent on limiting government) thought that such a constitutional amendment would not stand a chance, yet found supporting it a convenient way to signal a desire for fiscal prudence. Others became more and more concerned about the federal budget as the policies of Ronald Reagan's era—supply-side tax cuts and a massive defense buildup—resulted in burgeoning deficits. Then Ross Perot made deficit spending the centerpiece of his 1992 presidential campaign, and suddenly talk of a BBA became more credible.

The 1980s deficit levels *were* excessive, exceeding the ratio of national debt to gross domestic product, the measure used by economists to gauge how serious indebtedness is. From the standpoint of the nation's economic health, President Bill Clinton's deficit-reduction strategies have been warranted and appropriate. But even though President Clinton and the Democrats in Congress, without any votes from Republicans, put the country on the road to a much more reasonable budgetary situation, insurgent conservative Republicans chose to endorse the Balanced Budget Amendment as a centerpiece in their 1994 Contract with America. This was a political much more than a fiscal move.

During 1995, Clinton's capitulation to the Republican demand for balancing the federal budget entirely and by a fixed date, the year 2002, stunned his administration's most ardent deficit hawks and helped to blur the boundaries between congressional fiscal prudence, which Clinton has always favored, and the constitutional BBA, which he opposes. For many Americans, the distinction between these two paths toward federal budget balancing becomes lost. If the goal of sudden balance is legitimate, why not enshrine it in the Constitution? Democratic House and Senate candidates, trying to avoid being called "tax and spend liberals," have mouthed support for the BBA as a way to signal a reformed, New Democrat identity to voters.

State legislatures have also played an important role in pushing for a BBA. The first serious attempt to introduce an amendment was during the 1970s, before the giant deficits of the Reagan-Bush era. Back then, more than thirty legislatures called for a constitutional convention for the express purpose of crafting a BBA. As the significance and possible consequences of calling a convention sank in, the remaining states got cold feet, and the movement was temporarily slowed. In the past few years, however, state legislatures have again passed resolutions urging Congress to launch the BBA and indicating their willingness to ratify it.

To underscore just how strong this state-level movement has become, before the BBA failed in Congress by only one vote in 1995, most analysts thought that ratification by the states would be highly likely. No state is currently in a sure "no" category, including the traditionally more liberal states of New York and Massachusetts. The *Wall Street Journal* made an assessment of battleground states in a recent article headlined "Balanced-Budget Battle Divides North and South" (Milbank 1996). Southern states all appeared ready to ratify. In the remaining states, Wisconsin was cited as a battleground state. Republican Scott Jensen, Wisconsin's majority leader, told the *Journal* that he didn't know which of Wisconsin's two competing traditions would "win out," should the ratification battle happen. Wisconsin's "progressive" and "fiscally conservative" traditions created a tension that could be resolved either way, he said.

These assessments are remarkable in light of the history of constitutional amendments, which have usually been notoriously difficult to get ratified by the states. The Equal Rights Amendment, for instance, was introduced first in 1923 but did not pass Congress until 1972. During a protracted ratification struggle, the amendment was ultimately defeated after passing thirty-five of the required thirty-eight states.

To understand the BBA's much better prospects for quick state-level ratification and to see just what progressives would face in a fifty-state ratification fight, one must turn the clock back a bit and trace the development of modern forces contending over fiscal issues in the United States.

Movements Against Taxes: States as Beachheads

For more than two decades, states have been the target of antitax efforts and of a much broader movement to shrink and hobble government in general. Tangible evidence of the success of such movements are the tax and spending limitations that have passed in over twenty-one states (McIntire 1996). Some states have multiple limits. The 1978 enactment of California's Proposition 13, a measure limiting the property taxes that can be levied, is usually considered the movement's first success. (Conceived during Reagan's reign as California's governor, an earlier initiative, Proposition 1, was rejected by voters in 1972.)

California now leads the way in the sheer number of voter-approved limitations on taxes. This state has constructed a fiscal straitjacket for itself, one as yet unparalleled among the other fifty states, although many seem to be following in the Golden State's footsteps. In addition to Proposition 13, Californians have enshrined rules that say only a supermajority of state legislators can raise taxes, and they have enacted spending limitations on the cities and the state budget. At the same time, Californians have mandated a "three strikes and you're out" criminal system, which requires extensive and expensive prison building (as many as fifteen new facilities will be needed over the next ten years). Other spending is being squeezed to death in California.

In November 1996, California voters approved a little-heralded initiative that limits the capacity of local governments to levy taxes by making all future taxes (including assessments and fees) subject to special popular votes. The initiative also requires retrospective votes on recently enacted taxes and gives property owners extra voting rights. This was yet another inspiration from Howard Jarvis's Taxpayers' Association, the sponsor of the original Proposition 13 initiative. Although there was nothing secret about this effort, it was subjected to little public scrutiny until late September, when the secretary of state certified that enough signatures had been gathered to place it on the ballot. Given the presence of numerous other propositions on the 1996 California ballot, the late visibility of this further effort to hobble government meant that opposition forces had little time to raise money or mobilize against the threat.

Called the Right to Vote on Taxes Act, this recently enacted California initiative constraining local taxation signals a new linkage of property ownership and voting rights. According to the director of the California Budget Project, Jean Ross (1996b), this new rule not only requires assessments to be voted upon but also changes the rules of the democratic polity as such.* The

*I would like to thank the following people, who shared with me their time and experiences in interviews and shared memos, newsletters, and other reports: Jean Ross, Jim McIntire, Iris Lav, Samantha Sanchez, Mel Duncan, Frank Mauro, Mike Ettlinger, Dianne Stewart, Jerry Stermer, Penelope Pi-sunyer, and Jeff Malachowsky.

new rule restricts voting rights to property owners. Owners of affected property get weighted votes, according to how much property they own. Ross uses the following example: If "one parcel would pay 40 percent of the total amount assessed, the ballot cast by the owner of that parcel would count as 40 percent of the total vote." The assessment fails if opposing votes exceed favorable ones. City officials will be required to calculate the exact amount of "special" benefit received by the property owner from "general benefits" and to assess only that amount. Renters, who may pay part of the cost of taxes through higher rents, have no votes. These provisions make Lani Guinier's most radical proposals look timid.

Jim McIntire, director of the Fiscal Policy Center at the University of Washington Institute for Public Policy and Management, has examined restrictions in twenty-one states. He calls attention to the interactive effects of tax and spending limitations, federal budget balancing through spending cuts, and the Balanced Budget Amendment. McIntire (1996) uses data applying to Washington State to illustrate some of these interactive effects. A spending limitation passed by that state's voters in 1993 restricts growth in expenditures to the rate of inflation plus population growth (omitting the important variable of growth in personal income or people's ability to pay).

The effect of this flawed formula is not only to limit spending in the state but actually to decrease what can be spent each year on current services. Thus a gap is created between what would be needed to maintain current services over the next five years and what can be spent. The gap is significantly widened when likely federal fiscal cuts are factored in, producing a gap estimated to be between $2.9 billion and $3.9 billion over the 1996–2002 period. According to McIntire, if Washington State's spending limit is not changed and if spending cuts are not offset by revenues, "by 2002 the relative size of Washington's general fund will shrink to a level it hasn't been at since the early 1970s—before it took on responsibility for fully funding basic K–12 education" (McIntire 1996, p. 23). In other words, state government's capacities will go backward several decades, even as public needs and population keep growing.

Iris Lav, associate director of the Center on Budget and Policy Priorities, calls Washington-style limitations "self-induced structural deficits," in which states guarantee that each year they will have less revenue to meet spending requirements. The situation in states without such measures is not much different. Many legislators either are sympathetic to or defer to antitax or antigovernment sentiment. This climate of opinion is often as effective as specific constitutional restrictions. Shrinking revenues, whether achieved via public sentiment or voter-approved limitations, have enormous political and organizing implications, as we shall soon see.

Samantha Sanchez, a tax-policy specialist with extensive experience in Washington, D.C., and who now lives in Helena, Montana, says that it has been "painful to watch this 'cap and cut' movement play out with no opposition." She cites a recent example in Montana, a state with no tax or expenditure limits but with referendum provisions. One angry Montana citizen gathered enough signatures to challenge a modest tax increase of $15 million that had been passed by the Republican legislature in a bipartisan vote. In the referendum that followed, the tax went down to defeat. Sanchez notes that the campaign was filled with "disinformation," but there was simply "no organization to counter it."

The receptivity of state legislatures and local governments to movements against taxes has been facilitated by a general shift of power to the suburbs. Nationally, suburban voters constituted a majority for the first time in the presidential election of 1992. While suburban shifts were evident much earlier, state legislatures controlled by Democrats were able to stave off the impact by controlling the redistricting process. After the 1990 census and the redistricting of 1992, suburban control was solidified. With Republican strength growing, state legislatures now are more evenly divided than they have been in thirty-six years. Several major consequences flow from this shift of power—away from the urban-rural Democratic alliances that formerly configured many legislatures.

First, the overall shift of voting strength to the suburbs has increased the fiscally conservative nature of most legislatures, regardless of party control. Partisan labels do not predict whether a legislature will support such measures as the Balanced Budget Amendment. For example, sufficient numbers of Democrat legislators support the BBA in Pennsylvania, Ohio, and Illinois— battleground states in presidential elections—to thrust these states into a "likely to ratify" column.

Second, interests and organizations that might be labeled progressive by and large do not have roots in the suburbs. Even progressive organizations that are nominally statewide generally have an urban, not suburban, base—although environmental organizations are an exception to this rule. Urban legislators, including the most progressive, find themselves increasingly without allies. In many western states, the old urban-rural Democratic alliance has been further splintered by a variety of environmental and property-rights issues, which have altered the partisan loyalty of rural constituencies, especially farmers and others whose employment depends upon timber and other natural-resources industries.

Third, for some years now, state legislatures have been the target of right-wing Republicans, who have gradually increased their power from the local school boards to state legislative offices. One longtime California legislative aide, now an elected assembly member, could identify only one moderate Republican in the assembly and only one in the senate after the 1996 elections, despite the fact that the Democrats won back the assembly and control the senate. This kind of ideological change in the Republican Party means that Republicans easily form coalitions with the more conservative Democrats. The converse is not true. With the decline of Republican moderates, moderate or liberal Democrats do not have an equivalent pool of legislators from which to seek support.

The Balanced Budget Amendment has a symbolic significance for the most conservative constituency, over and above its substantive effects on government spending. In a recent analysis of right-wing objectives, former Field Foundation director Richard Boone (1996) found evidence that the intent is to garner sufficient strength in state legislatures to amend the U.S. Constitution. This basic conservative objective, which might have been dismissed just a few years ago as pie-in-the-sky fantasizing, merits far more attention than it is currently given.

Tilted Playing Fields

The confluence of conservative fiscal ideology, the radical right, and business interests has been well documented. In *The Revolt of the Haves,* written shortly after California's Proposition 13 passed, Robert Kuttner described how a genuine populist movement against property taxes was coopted by business interests during the campaign and in the distribution of tax relief afterward. Proposition 13's success in California, moreover, spawned new national antitax organizations and reinvigorated older business coalitions. According to Kuttner, who was of course writing more than fifteen years ago, the "new wave of tax protest organizations overshadows a far more influential force for fiscal conservatism which has been part of the landscape since 1937—the Tax Foundation and its numerous affiliates at the state level" (1980, p. 287). He found thirty-three states in which business-financed foundations operated. Conversely, he identified only one state with a permanent progressive tax-reform lobby. Such foundations matter more than just numerically, Kuttner pointed out, because they affect the analytical balance of power on tax issues. In contrast to the situation in Washington, D.C., "in which dozens of public interest lobbies act to offset business influence, the tax foundations in the state capitals are usually considered *the* source of reliable data on tax matters."

A decade later, Tom Edsall and Mary Edsall argued in *Chain Reaction* that the strength of a center-right electoral coalition may be found in this populist-corporate alliance born during the tax revolt movement: "Working-class whites and corporate CEOs, once adversaries at the bargaining table, found common ideological ground in their shared hostility to expanding government intervention." The Edsalls see the tax revolt movement as "a major turning point in American politics. [It] opened up a new schism, . . . pitting taxpayers against tax recipients" (Edsall and Edsall 1992, p. 129).

Two of the more withering critics of the alliance between business and moderate taxpayers have been conservative insiders, Michael Lind (1996) and Kevin Phillips (1990, 1993). Lind believes that Republicans, now dominated by southerners, have joined with a multinational corporate elite to implement their vision of a "low-wage, low-tax, low-regulation economy in which economic segregation replaces formal legal segregation not merely in their native region but in the country as a whole" (Lind 1996, p. 136). Indeed, Lind believes that conservatives use cultural issues purposively to deflect attention from the fact that their program "is inimical to the middle class" (Lind 1996, p. 137). Phillips relies more on data than rhetoric in his books, but he makes many of the same points. He describes the 1983–89 period as "America's Third Capitalist Heyday," during which "a more ambitious new ideology was in development—in Europe as well as the United States—to shift burdens *towards* society's low- and middle-income users of products and services and *away* from capitalism's investors and other lions of the corporate veldt" (Phillips 1993, pp. 33–45).

Business strength at the state level is often manifest in a variety of tax breaks and subsidies. As Mel Duncan, director of the Minnesota Alliance for Progressive Action (MAPA), puts it: "Each session, the good guys visit the appropriations committee and try to get funding for a year or two; businesses visit the finance committee and get tax abatements forever." Massachusetts has given tax breaks estimated to be worth between $120 and $200 million a year to the defense contractor Raytheon. Alabama granted huge tax subsidies to attract the new Mercedes-Benz plant to its state. Corporations have been able to play one state off against another to get the best deal, despite the absence of economic analysis demonstrating that taxes play a significant role in corporate location decisions.

Legislators live in fear that their state will be seen as being antibusiness or that they will lose out on economic development opportunities, and they therefore frequently create broad-based subsidies for all businesses. While corporations and other businesses clearly do create jobs, the specific numbers of jobs that they frequently pledge are impossible to assess. Tax breaks for specific companies can be more easily assessed, but rarely are. State officials have few enforcement mechanisms to hold companies to their claims.

A new phrase, "corporate welfare," has emerged in the last few years, both at the national and at the state level, giving activists new impetus to examine questions of equity. In Minnesota, for instance, MAPA's Mel Duncan cites an analysis showing that in 1995 corporate subsidies amounted to $1.52 billion, while recipients of Aid to Families with Dependent Children received $116 million. Duncan, whose group has spearheaded legislation that would make corporations more accountable, says, "Every year the corporate lobby is there saying this will create X number of jobs. We're just saying, okay, prove it." Duncan notes that the 1997 legislative session continues to reflect the imbalance between who gets cut for the sake of budget balancing: while "the human social service committees are holding hearings to make excruciating choices in funding, over $1 billion worth of new corporate subsidies are being considered."

As states have emerged from the early 1990s recession, tax cuts are occupying an increasingly prominent place on legislative agendas. Not surprisingly, most tax relief is flowing to business and corporate interests, not to low- or middle-income taxpayers. For instance, in recent years, despite a deep recession and annual billion-dollar deficits, the California legislature gave businesses approximately $2.3 billion in tax relief. In his 1997 budget, California governor Pete Wilson proposed an additional reduction of 10 percent, worth $1.6 billion, in business and corporate taxes (Ross 1996a). By comparison, consumers are paying an additional $4 billion per year in increased sales taxes.

Even relief measures in the personal income tax are frequently skewed to benefit wealthy individuals. In New York, Governor George Pataki made tax cuts the center of his first administration. Despite the governor's claims that his tax relief would especially benefit the lowest-income taxpayers in the state, analysis showed otherwise. Frank Mauro (1995), head of New York's Fiscal Policy Institute, directed the analysis that showed "low and middle income families get little or no relief from Pataki's plan in 1995." He adds, "The wealthiest 5 percent of taxpayers got 40 percent of the income tax cut, while families earning $50,000 will save no more than $4.35 a week and many will get less." Mauro explains that the use of "average percent reductions" is misleading, because income tax makes up the majority of the tax burden for wealthier individuals, whereas for lower-income people, sales and property taxes are the greater burdens. Yet despite praise for the technical accuracy of the Fiscal Policy Institute's analysis, Mauro has found that penetrating the tax-cutting fervor is extremely difficult.

Constant battles against tax cuts or budget reductions drain the limited energy that does exist among progressive activists, leaving unattended more fundamental issues that affect the fairness and adequacy of most tax systems. Playing fields are not tipped only during specific fights; the ground itself is slanted. State tax systems are very regressive, resulting in tax burdens that fall disproportionately on low- and middle-income taxpayers. While a state income tax can be made highly progressive, falling least heavily on working families, in practice most states limit its progressivity. Perhaps one of the most extreme examples, apart from those states who have *no* income tax, is Illinois, whose constitution prohibits progressivity. Such unequal tax burdens legitimately fuel anger against taxation. In addition, most state tax systems not only lack equity but are often antiquated and inadequate, premised on an industrial base that no longer drives most state economies. This inadequacy virtually ensures that revenues rarely keep pace with spending needs and is the source of many states' chronic deficits.

These observations merely scratch the surface of issues that progressives will face as the action shifts to the states. On the budget side, in the absence of a ratification battle, cuts in federal aid required to balance the budget by 2002 and beyond will squeeze state budgets and increase competition over scarce dollars. The budget wars of 1995–96, especially the Republican-passed Balanced Budget Act of 1995, which was vetoed by President Clinton, gave Americans their first glimpse of how "balance" might translate into specific dollars. In order to balance by 2002 (a date driven strictly by political considerations, not economic ones), the budget act contained over $1 trillion in reductions. Who was hit the hardest? While spending on low-income programs composes roughly 21 percent of the federal budget, 67 percent of the cuts came from low-income programs.

States, counties, and cities have an enormous stake in these decisions. Individual states receive anywhere from 20 to 35 percent of their general-fund revenues from the federal government. In the past few years, defense, Social Security, and interest payments, which represent slightly over half of the federal budget, have been largely immune from budget cuts. Medicaid and Medicare cuts have proved politically risky to both parties. In practice, therefore, spending cuts have been taken disproportionately from non-defense discretionary spending—that portion of the budget from which states receive the bulk of their aid.

A perverse effect of the end of welfare guarantees is that many states received an initial windfall of funds. Payments to states were based on years when welfare rolls were up, due to the recession of the early 1990s. The full effects of balance will not be apparent for a few years, and long-range planning is virtually never on any legislative agenda.

Until recently, the capacity of progressives to confront tax and budget issues has been woefully limited, not only because progressives lack real political clout, but also because they have fewer analytical and organizational resources than their opponents do.

Building State-Level Analytical Capacities

For the most part, just two nonprofit organizations, Citizens for Tax Justice (CTJ) and the Center on Budget and Policy Priorities, have supplied activists with state-level tax and budget data, although labor unions have at times been another important source of data. Mike Ettlinger, tax policy director for CTJ, argues that, to date, progressives have lacked the power to initiate tax reform, although they sometimes make progress if "taxes are put into play." By and large, Ettlinger thinks, "good things have not been the result of progressive coalitions pulling together and affecting policies," but by "progressive legislators who have been effective in making good things happen."

The Center on Budget and Policy Priorities, founded in 1982 to focus on federal tax and budget issues, helped to make the case to several national foundations that the absence of analytical capacity in the states was a serious deterrent to leveling the playing field in those capitols. As Iris Lav, who directed the center's work with states and is now its associate director, told funders (Paget 1997, p. 3), "it is rare that anyone looks at overall state budget priorities and tax policy from the point of view of the needs of low- and moderate-income citizens and does so in a manner that can help shape the public policy debate at the state level." In 1993, the Ford, Annie E. Casey, and Charles Stewart Mott Foundations responded to the center's diagnosis and embarked on an unprecedented collaboration to strengthen state-level capacity. This program, known as the State Fiscal Analysis Initiative (SFAI), has funded twelve state organizations to assess tax and budget issues from the perspective of middle- and low-income individuals.

Dianne Stewart, director of the Center for Public Policy Priorities in Austin, Texas, and a SFAI grantee, says, "We have filled an incredible gap here—people didn't realize how great the gap was until we were here to fill it." According to Stewart, the Texas Association of Tax Payers Center, funded by business, has "always been viewed as *the* source of reliable information," even though the organization is a corporate front and "absolutely not independent." In three years, Stewart says, the Center for Public Policy Priorities has become a "credible, public interest voice on tax reform." Increasingly called upon to brief state officials and to give legislative testimony, the center was influential in getting an equity-note procedure adopted. An equity note requires the legislature to analyze the impact of all new tax measures. When Governor George W. Bush introduced his tax reform plan, the first-ever equity note revealed that, contrary to Bush's claims, his tax proposals "would make an already regressive system more regressive." Stewart agrees with Ettlinger of the Center for Tax Justice about how difficult it is to initiate action. "Without the momentum set in motion by the Governor's plan we couldn't have gone this far."

In a few short years, the SFAI program has yielded considerable analytical fruit. For instance, several SFAI-funded organizations have already been mentioned in this essay and include the Fiscal Policy Institute in New York, which analyzed the Pataki tax cuts; the California Budget Project, which analyzed the imbalance in tax relief between business and consumers; and the Fiscal Policy Center at the University of Washington, which demonstrated the flaws in that state's spending limitation. But while the SFAI program is a major addition to state-level fiscal infrastructure, its focus is on analysis, not organizing and advocacy. Whether or not analyses are effective instruments of change depends on other organizations that are able to lobby and mobilize constituencies and upon how broad or narrow their reach. Depending on the particular state, consumers of SFAI analysis range from broad-based coalitions to specialized program advocates.

The Challenge of Pulling Together

At least two nearly intractable organizing problems plague people in the states trying to put together coalitions to fight tax and fiscal battles. In the first place, program-created or related constituencies, by definition, are interested in increasing state spending in their program area, not someone else's. Scarce resources foster not only budget fights between constituencies (between, say, supporters of fighting crime and proponents of education) but also intra-segment fights (between, say, advocates for special education and those who look out for public education in general). New "welfare reforms" unleash lots of competition among advocates for specific sets of beneficiaries, be they legal immigrants, the disabled, single adults, and unmarried mothers. As Congress debates whether to restore any of the funds for legal immigrants, poor immigrants have been further subdivided into deserving and undeserving groups. Those who are elderly or physically or mentally disabled have the best chance of seeing their funds restored. The remainder have no federal safety net and no immediate prospect of obtaining one.

Federal cuts, block grants, and other forms of devolution—not to mention the BBA, should it be ratified—will intensify competition among traditional recipients. Had Medicaid been block-granted and capped, one could easily imagine a similar contest among the three main beneficiary groups of that federal-state program: the elderly, the disabled, and children. With resources generally tight, one program's increase is another's loss. Unless people can find ways to counter existing dynamics, this is a circumstance emphatically not conducive to coalition building or to mobilizing more broad-based voter support for public programs.

Another problem beyond the competitive divisions among programs bedevils those fighting cutbacks. Since not all beneficiaries or constituencies who seek government resources are equal in terms of political power, the constituencies with a broad base have tried to find ways to lock up their share of the state budgets. This strategy was used successfully by the education constituency in California. Voters approved an initiative that contained a formula guaranteeing a floor of funding for kindergarten through the first two years of college and that also allocated a percentage of any new state revenues to such spending.

A similar movement is afoot in the state of Washington. As voters in Washington have realized that their spending limitation does not keep pace with economic growth, the most popular corrective has been to split out the education budget rather than eliminate the limitation altogether or change its highly flawed formula. Michigan and Wisconsin are other states that have assumed huge general-fund increases for education expenditures, relieving local property-tax payers but effectively increasing competition among other claimants for general-fund monies. Since the sources of general state revenues, income and sales taxes, are less stable than property taxes during a recession, an economic downturn will squeeze other programs if a state maintains its commitment to education.

The single biggest challenge for progressives is to expand revenue streams or at least to keep them from shrinking further. Although the particulars vary by state, this is generally very difficult to do. Even apparent natural allies, such as social services and education constituencies, often find themselves at loggerheads.

Jerry Stermer, executive director of Voice for Illinois Children (VIC) and another SFAI grantee, has worked with both education and social services constituencies for years, and he says that his organization "rests comfortably in both camps." Since VIC's constituency is children and families, which cuts across both program areas, Stermer and others have tried to find ways to ease or negotiate tensions between the two groups. For example, in 1997 the education constituency has a chance for passing a tax increase in the Illinois legislature. Stermer says that the opportunity is "the first in the last ten years, and the last for the next ten years." With "unprecedented" unity on the education side—administrators, teachers, and PTA's have all coalesced—the task is to keep the effort from being derailed by the social services constituencies, which see any increase in the income tax as an opportunity to adjust the exemption for low-income families. While the education lobbyists' basic position is that "they are about school funding, not taxes," a tentative agreement has been reached: education's legislative backers will look "sympathetically on an amendment."

Would the education lobby in Illinois take on a fight against ratification of the Balanced Budget Amendment? Stermer isn't sure. On one hand, he reasons that education would benefit if there were room for revenue growth in both the federal and state budgets. On the other hand, he isn't sure that federal education funds—and the threat of their loss—are sufficiently large to mobilize this constituency. Since teacher's unions have considerable influence in state legislatures, much will ride on their decision to oppose the amendment and the resources they choose to mobilize.

One of the few organizations with long-term experience in trying to coalesce a wide range of constituencies (social services, education, housing, and so on) in order to expand revenues is New York City's AlterBudget, formerly known as the City Project. While AlterBudget operates at the city level only, New York City is so large that its political challenges mirror conflicts found in most states. Manhattan borough president Ruth Messinger helped to create this project over ten years ago, when she was on the New York City Council. Messinger knew that she would be branded as just another free-spending liberal if she didn't tackle the revenue side of the budget. Alter-Budget's director, Penelope Pi-sunyer, who has led the organization for over ten years, says that they have had "some success." Under AlterBudget's leadership, numerous organizations united in the mid-1980s to oppose J–51, a proposition that would provide city tax subsidies to landlords; they surprised almost everyone by defeating it.

Pi-sunyer said that when revenues were expanding, child care was an issue binding social service and education constituencies together. Each coalition member put an elaborate effort into crafting common budget proposals. They were careful not to rely exclusively on new revenues. Rather, proposal writers identified both budget cuts and tax loopholes as potential sources of funding. Shrinking resources in the 1990s essentially ended this kind of cooperative effort. Pi-sunyer said they have tried to "refocus on the revenue" side, but not with much success. In an it's-a-dirty-job-but-someone's-got-to-do-it tone of voice, Pi-sunyer adds, "If you don't do it, you have no prayer."

In California, proponents of child care elicited opposition, not support, from education constituencies when they sought more funding. In Montana, the teachers' union parted company with a progressive, statewide, multi-issue coalition over differences on taxes, a split that severely weakened a once-strong coalition. Desperate for resources, the education lobby supported a sales tax increase that the rest of the coalition argued was too regressive to support. These examples highlight that assorted constituencies of social programs do not easily and certainly not invariably work together.

What about public interest coalitions? Jeff Malachowsky, former director of the Western States Resource Center, which supports organizers and progressive forces in an eight-state region, has been visiting coalitions throughout the country in 1996 and 1997. When asked during an interview whether these coalitions would fight a balanced budget amendment, Malachowsky was skeptical: "These coalitions are perfectly appropriate vehicles for fighting the Balanced Budget Amendment, . . . but they are slow to take it on." Malachowsky cites a number of deterrents to waging such a battle, including a lack of preparation and education on the topic, the complexity of the balanced budget issue, and the paucity of funding for tax and budget analysis. Malachowsky also raised the "David and Goliath problem," describing several instances where either business interests have dictated the course of action or political leaders have betrayed public interest organizations after seeking their support. "The sheer naked power differential . . . [shows] how difficult it is to get reliable allies among public officials to check the power of the business community." He speculates that many of the progressive public-interest coalitions "may take a pass on leadership" in any ratification fight.

Whether any of these constituencies can transcend their particular concerns, all valid, to work together against BBA ratification or for greater tax and budget equity is unclear. What is clear is that the inability to fight tax battles over the last two decades has cost progressives tremendous ground. Neither "program" constituencies nor broader groups (such as unions and public-interest organizations) have been able take up the broader fiscal policy agenda. With a few exceptions, moreover, progressive funders have been notoriously reluctant to fund tax reform or state budget fights. And in the absence of such funding, activists have been reluctant to take on the challenges.

Despite these problems, a growing analytical and organizational infrastructure is developing, however unevenly, across the fifty states. Groups with some analytical and organizational capacity and with some willingness to work together are tentatively entering the state-level fiscal wars. And some of these state groups enjoy ties to national organizations. By these small steps may be built a shared body of knowledge about the role of good fiscal analysis in creating organizing strategies.

Turning Things Around

What seems crystal clear from even the briefest survey of various states is that, for progressives and others who care about a positive social role for government, fighting purely defensive battles in a fragmentary way is a certain losing strategy, one likely to foster continuous division and demoralization. Progressives must reframe many fiscal and tax issues, preparing to make a strong case for government.

In the short term, progressives will face one of two scenarios in their individual states. Either there will be an all-out ratification fight over the Balanced Budget Amendment, or there will be a slower, more fragmented, but equally important fight over the trickle-down effects flowing from congressional budget balancing and other devolution measures.

The progressive strategy for a ratification fight is relatively straightforward. Slowing down the amendment's support must be our imperative. The Republican governors have devised a "thirty-thirty" ratification strategy, calling for quick action by thirty states in thirty days. Several Republican governors used their State of the State speeches in January 1997 to announce a goal of being the first state to ratify, should Congress send the BBA to the states. Proponents know that speed is essential, because any considered airing of the amendment will not work in their favor. For BBA opponents, a critical task is to secure a commitment from the leadership in state legislatures to hold hearings—ideally not just in the state houses but also in numerous forums around the state. In such hearings, critics can loudly ask what happens during recessions should the BBA be ratified.

Progressives can then point to the extensive data on how much states have relied on federal funds during previous recessions. Maine, for example, is a relatively poor state with a high level of federal dependency, and during the last recession it received a 58 percent temporary increase in federal funds. For other states during the same period, increases of 30 percent or more in federal aid were not at all unusual. Such emergency federal recession assistance would be very much in jeopardy under the BBA. Proponents sometimes glibly assert that the BBA can be suspended in the case of a recession. Although the amendment does contain a murky suspension provision, in the event of a regional recession, an increasingly common situation, it would be hard to get the requisite third-fifths vote of all members of both houses of Congress. The BBA greatly privileges minorities opposed to using government to help particular groups or particular regions in recession.

An often overlooked reason that suspension provisions will not work has to do with the time lag between the growth of caseloads on state unemployment, food stamp, and welfare programs on one hand and the official identification of a recession on the other. It can take as long as two years before policymakers identify a recession, as they figure out whether caseload increases represent trends or blips. Consequently, no mechanism for Congress's suspending balanced budget rules could sufficiently protect areas of the country as they slipped into a recession. Indeed, any attempt by Congress—whether required by the BBA or not—to institute perfect budget balancing year by year creates a trap from which there can be no good escape hatch. Yet restricting federal aid to states in an economic downturn would necessitate denying food, health care, and unemployment insurance to individuals caught in hard times. This would be inhumane as well as economically foolish.

As progressives engage in these struggles—either all-out fights to prevent ratification of the BBA or step-by-step efforts to slow the erosion of government services for working families—activists should experiment with bold, new ways to frame fundamental tax and budget issues.

On the tax front, shifts in assistance to the very poor may spur fresh examinations of "corporate welfare." Mel Duncan of Minnesota's MAPA, for instance, has compared state subsidies that go to corporations with those that support welfare recipients. In 1995, Minnesotans spent $1.52 billion in corporate subsidies. They spent exactly $116 million for AFDC, the largest welfare program before the 1996 reform. The Minnesota coalition is now working on a series of accountability measures that would hold corporations to the promises they make when they gain such tax breaks.

On the budget front, progressives need to familiarize themselves with the cumulative effect that federal cuts will likely have for their state. Jim McIntire's work at the University of Washington's Fiscal Policy Center offers a fresh way to view state budgets. McIntire and his colleagues display Washington State's budget in three categories: education, economic support for working families, and "all other" expenditures. These budget categories suggest an organizing strategy that transcends specific program areas, helping average citizens to understand state budget priorities and see how they relate to daily life. This budget format reveals that in the important category of economic support for working families, 50 percent of funding comes from the federal government. No clearer indication of the interdependency of state and federal finance could be found.

The role of Voices for Illinois Children demonstrates the importance of defining an encompassing constituency, such as families and children, with claims cutting across the boundaries of particular public programs. VIC also became the first public-interest organization in Illinois to display the state's budget in terms of support for children and families. Until then, the Illinois budget had been displayed as a collection of departments and agencies or as a line-item budget, making it difficult for the ordinary citizen to see the bigger picture or to characterize funding priorities in terms of daily life.

Foundation resources will be critical to the development of state-level analytical and organizational strategies. Some funders appear to be having trouble responding to the new world of devolution. Finding it hard to sort through thousands of proposals from groups across fifty states, many foundations, even those with ample staff, prefer to deal with national organizations that in turn can credibly propose to serve state and local organizations. Another alternative to the daunting task of funding on fifty fronts is to strengthen regional efforts. In some parts of the country, coalitions and organizations have already formed across state lines. Some, such as Northeast Action, have years of experience and can provide models and guidance to other regional efforts.

Progressive legislators are a key part of these New England coalitions. In general, legislators need to be drawn into the development of a center-left strategy. A network of progressive state officials throughout the United States could also be developed, a counterpart to the network of conservative legislators managed by the corporate-funded American Legislative Exchange Council (ALEC). Fortunately, the Center for National Policy, an outgrowth of an older network of progressive state officials, is doing more with state legislators, particularly on budget issues. Wes Watkins, director of the center's leadership programs, disclaims direct competition with the conservative ALEC, but he is sensitive to the tilted playing field among state legislators. It "may be a free market place of ideas," he observes, "but there's only one guy selling."

Perhaps the tilt will begin to right itself a bit, as the devolution revolution chugs forward. Pressures to balance the federal budget, whether through an amendment or through statute, may turn out to have paradoxical effects. What began as an effort to dismantle public programs and liberal coalitions may end up providing progressives with opportunities to shift public debates from a focus on the size of government toward discussion of the purposes of government. When asked if they want to balance the budget, voters may quickly answer yes. But they often change their minds or suggest proceeding more slowly when consequences for such cherished programs as Social Security and Medicare are mentioned. People also care about safe airplanes, uncontaminated food, federal assistance in natural disasters, access to quality health care and educational opportunity, and a host of other government functions at national, state, and local levels. Far from scattering and dividing constituencies for progressive action, Gingrich-style devolution may afford openings to discuss the terms of a new social contract.

Notwithstanding all the obstacles discussed here, the Republican revolution in Congress may force us to pay attention to problems and challenges that progressives have neglected over the past generation. As we do new kinds of organizing and coalition building and as we learn to dramatize in human terms what is at stake in disputes over taxes and budgets, we can transform Newt Gingrich's "scramble to the states" into a new source of progressive energy and popular cohesion.

Championing Democracy Reforms

Miles S. Rapoport and Marc Caplan

As the challenge of shaping the future is engaged, progressives have the responsibility and a tremendous opportunity for championing a comprehensive Democracy Agenda to enhance and revitalize the nation's political process. Any progressive revival in America must include a full agenda of reforms, leading toward more citizen engagement, deeper democratic participation, increased accountability from powerful institutions, and a significantly reduced place for money and fund-raising in politics. Such reforms are just as important as the stands that progressives take on questions of economic and social policy, because a revitalized national democracy is vital to the improved quality of life that all of us want for us and our children.

The Democracy Agenda that we outline here addresses some of the most serious concerns that have crystallized in recent years about the health of America's democratic process. Consistent with the best traditions and heritage of the Democratic Party, the pursuit of these reforms offers party loyalists particularly and progressives generally an opportunity to enlarge the electorate, empower and motivate significant constituencies, win new adherents among existing voters, and achieve electoral success into the future.

Voters of varying allegiances are looking for leadership in achieving meaningful political reforms.

The Democracy Agenda includes four major elements: making democracy as fully participatory and inclusive as it can be by expanding the electorate and increasing engagement; fighting for campaign finance reform that frees our political process from domination by wealthy special interests; enhancing the accountability of key institutions that affect people's lives; and encouraging a true sense of community both in particular places and across the nation.

This agenda, let us emphasize, is one part of a larger progressive project for the years ahead. The pursuit of democratic reforms goes hand in hand with building support for a broader program. In order for good jobs and a clean environment to be achieved and for full access to health care and better family benefits to be ensured, all of these progressive objectives require countering the increasing domination of political decisions by powerful economic interests. At the same time, efforts to register and motivate voters will succeed only if potential participants are engaged by campaigns that address issues about which they care deeply. The Democracy Agenda is part of the larger New Majority project—both substantively and strategically.

Although we argue that reforms should be championed by Democrats, our agenda offers special opportunities for all progressive groups and coalitions. Community and issue organizations, civil rights groups, women's organizations, and the labor movement all have the chance to greatly expand their influence by promoting meaningful reforms in the political process. Every constituency that matters to popular progressive politics can benefit from a reduced role for money in politics and a fuller engagement of people in politics and civic life.

For that matter, there are opportunities for other groups and movements, too. The nation can only benefit if people across the political spectrum step forward and work for the revitalization of our shared democracy. Implicit in every part of our program are values central to a healthy democratic society, regardless of the political implications resulting from the endeavor. Fairness, justice, increasing people's sense of power over their own lives, and creating a stronger degree of civic engagement—these are values that matter for all Americans, quite apart from any policy or political outcome that they may prefer.

For a long time, the political process has mainly been the province of academic observers, democracy buffs, and starry-eyed reformers. "Serious" politicos have assumed that negative trends in participation are a given. They have taken it as a challenge to devise ways to win anyway, to get at least 50 percent of the vote, even if more and more people are dropping out, having been turned off by politics as usual. Activists have not wanted to seem naive, so they have concentrated on immediate victories in a shrunken and largely closed electorate, within a system awash in almost limitless spending.

But we don't have to settle for contests within a shrinking political universe. Those who want to build an energized, progressive Democratic Party can challenge current assumptions passing for political realism. The political terrain on which we contend can be enlarged by taking up the four elements of the following Democracy Agenda, as part of a broad popular program of economic justice and democratic renewal.

Expanding and Engaging the Electorate

A Democracy Agenda starts with working to ensure that people are engaged in the political and decision-making process, in the strongest possible way and at every turn. The involvement of every citizen in our society—in voting and in community life—is the most fundamental hallmark of a healthy democratic society and the strongest guarantee that public policy will indeed reflect people's needs and concerns. The narrowing of the electorate and the shrinking of people's involvement can only assist those who seek public policies not in the interests of the broadest majority of our citizens; and conversely, if progressives believe that our agenda holds far more promise for the future of our country and of each of its citizens than a conservative agenda does, then we should be relentless in our efforts to expand the involvement of people and to bring our message to them.

One essential component of this effort is to expand the electorate by registering large numbers of new voters and again involving former voters who have become disengaged and disenchanted with the system. This will guarantee that the voices and concerns of poor people, working families, citizens of every racial group, and young as well as old people will be counted in our political process. Expansion of the electorate opens up new possibilities of success for progressives and indeed for all Democrats willing to embrace a larger and more diverse electorate. It will also widen the framework of acceptable policy options, enlarging a public discussion that today so often seems sharply limited.

Democrats may have made headway in 1996, but from the standpoint of participation, that election was nothing to celebrate. Despite increased registration, turnout was down substantially from 1992. The 1996 election cycle did point the way to several important conclusions for progressive and democratic strategists. Stanley Greenberg's post-election survey shows that new voters in 1996 supported Clinton by 20 percentage points, or 54 to 34 percent. They also supported House Democratic candidates by 12 points. This corroborates the view that people who have not been part of the process are likely to support progressive and Democratic issues. In 1994, a survey by *USA Today, CNN,* and Gallup showed that Democrats represented just 32 percent of voters but 44 percent of nonvoters (cited in Greenberg 1996c, p. 264). Turning nonvoters into voters can expand our base, and less of the conversation will then need to be about wooing swing voters with a toned-down message, since a narrower swath of those voters will be needed in order to win. While this is not a new notion, it is astonishing how little the conversation and practice among the elites of politics, and of the Democratic Party, reflect it. We believe this is the case even as larger numbers of new voters are registering as unaffiliated voters. In Connecticut, for example, the number of unaffiliated voters soared past the number of registered Democrats for the first time in 1996, but Democrats scored impressive electoral gains, including retaking control of the state Senate.

There is another strong reason for moving voter registration efforts to front and center at this time. We have unprecedented new tools created by the National Voter Registration Act (NVRA, sometimes misleadingly dubbed Motor Voter). NVRA has three components: offering people opportunities to register to vote when they apply for motor vehicle licenses, offering the same opportunity at other public agencies, and facilitating voter registration by mail. Above all, mail-in voter registration in virtually every state provides an enormous opportunity for activists to develop a truly participatory program. But NVRA as a law is only the framework for voter registration efforts. There must also be an energized, comprehensive effort to reach out to new voters and bring them into the process.

This was done with great success in Connecticut in 1996, when an extraordinarily cooperative nonpartisan effort was coordinated by the office of the secretary of the state. Hundreds of businesses—banks, retailers, manu-facturers, supermarkets—offered registration cards to consumers and employ-ees alike. Community organizations, labor unions, civil rights organizations, churches, libraries, women's organizations, colleges, and people returning from the Million Man March distributed large quantities of cards. Half of the state's high schools used First Vote, a program sponsored by People for the American Way, to register seniors. Several of the state's newspapers, includ-ing the *Hartford Courant,* put voter registration inserts in their papers. The overall effort registered hundreds of thousands of new voters and laid a framework for ongoing efforts. In every state, Democratic elected officials and the party itself have the opportunity to provide similar leadership.

We believe that voter registration efforts should be widespread and across the board, and the value of them is enduring. But at the same time, there is special need and opportunity to target segments of the citizenry es-sential to the success of a progressive agenda.

One pivotal group of potential voters are eighteen- to twenty-five-year-olds. Young people have a specific set of concerns about politics, and for years they have provided a refreshing source of energy, idealism, and com-passion to the body politic. But now the political involvement of young people is at an all-time low. Only 28 percent of incoming freshman in 1995 thought that keeping up with political issues was important, according to a UCLA survey of students at eighty-eight schools (Jakes 1996). The survey also found that the number of students who considered themselves politically ac-tive had dropped from a high of 58 percent in 1966 to an all-time low of 38 percent in 1995. Low participation among the young is especially worrisome since habits of voting, political activism, and community involvement are formed early and can persist over a lifetime. If nothing is done to register and involve young people, then what is currently viewed as a dismal 50 percent voting rate may end up looking unusually participatory in the future.

The recent partisan identification and voting patterns of young people are revealing. Of the eighteen- to twenty-four-year-olds who voted in the 1996 election, according to a poll by Lake Research and Deardourff-The Media Center (1996, p. 2), 50 percent identified themselves as Democrats, 31 percent as Republicans, and 21 percent as independents. Young people aged eighteen to twenty-nine voted for Clinton by 53 to 34 percent, the high-est percentage that any Democratic candidate has received since eighteen-year-olds won the right to vote in 1971. They also voted for House Democratic candidates by a margin of 55 to 44 percent.

But exhorting young people to vote is not enough. A true Democracy Agenda must feature efforts to encourage young people to take first steps into civic life. Community service programs are increasing in high schools. Essay contests, debates, the inclusion of young people in important political events, and awards to students for community activities are all ways of beginning to engage students and others in the process. Democratic elected officials, progressive organizations, and local party organizations could build these activities into their agendas, and they should.

The Latino community in America is flexing its electoral muscles in new ways. A recent *New York Times* article reported that the "results of balloting around the country made clear that the Democratic-leaning Hispanic vote is becoming an ever larger factor in American politics" (Drummond 1996, p. A1). Latino votes, growing in each election cycle, helped the 1996 Democratic presidential candidate to carry Florida for the first time since 1976, and Arizona for the first time ever. The percentage of Latino voters supporting President Clinton was 72 to 21 percent.

The Republican Party has cast the Latino community aside, with its shortsighted and counterproductive policies on immigration, affirmative action, and other key issues. Even conservative Linda Chavez strongly chastised her own party for creating a "growing suspicion that the GOP is becoming the anti-immigrant party" (1996, p. A17). But all too often, the Democratic Party has also failed to properly represent and include the Latino community. A true commitment to inclusion cannot merely be a quick preelection blitz; it must be a sustained effort to draw the Latino community fully into the life of the party, including into consistent voter-registration efforts.

A similar opportunity exists among all new American citizens. Every citizenship ceremony conducted today by the Immigration and Naturalization Service (INS) includes people from a wonderful variety of countries and nationalities, all pledging allegiance to the flag. Local officials should work with the INS to include voter registration as an integral part of every swearing-in for new citizens. Recent experience indicates that over 90 percent of new citizens will register on the spot if offered the opportunity.

Studies have shown that the participation of African-Americans, especially African-American men, went up in 1996. This was in part the work of people returning from the Million Man March (voter registration was almost universally cited as one of the activities to be undertaken after the march) and of the ongoing efforts by Jesse Jackson and organizations in the black community that have long been engaged in voter registration and mobilization. Nevertheless, African-American communities remain underregistered by a significant margin. The debates in Congress and even state legislatures have paid very little serious attention to meeting the needs of urban residents. There continue to be racial overtones in the debate about welfare reform, and calls for jobs creation and human services investments have been conspicuous by their absence among the priorities of the Democratic party. Understandably, therefore, African-American leaders are often skeptical of last-minute efforts to get out the vote. A commitment to a true Democracy Agenda must have an inclusive view of racial diversity and involvement at all levels. We need a policy agenda that puts the issues of the cities, education, and the well-being of African-American and Latino communities at the fore. We need an ongoing commitment to programmatic inclusiveness as well as a serious effort to register and activate minority voters.

Unions and members of union households also took on a greatly renewed significance in the 1996 election. Studies show that the experience of union membership affects political activity and voting patterns, and a crucial part of Clinton's victory came from union households ("Portrait" 1996). Clinton split the nonunion household vote with Dole, 46 to 45 percent, but won union households, 59 to 30 percent. There was a 32 percent swing between how white male AFL-CIO members voted (Clinton, 55 to 34 percent) and how all white males (including union members) voted (Dole, 49 to 38 percent) The energetic efforts by the AFL-CIO and its member unions played a crucial role in bringing this about. But there are still large numbers of unregistered union members, and building voter registration into unions' membership mobilization efforts is extremely important.

Clearly, unionized workers are but a small portion of working families in America. A much larger pool of working households are not in unions. Working families, often non–college educated, also contributed significantly to Clinton's and other Democrats' victories in 1996 ("Portrait" 1996). Compared to upper-income adults, working-class adults are also less likely to be registered voters and less apt to vote if they are. We are heartened that the AFL-CIO is committing major resources to organizing these workers, and we believe that an energized, progressive Democratic Party should lend its efforts to assisting and coalescing with union efforts in these new venues. But it is also possible, through efforts at community colleges, workplaces, public events, and shopping malls, to help members of working families register to vote, even if they are not directly involved in union activities.

Voter registration and attempts to expand a progressive electorate are mutually complementary. On one hand, expanding the electorate and bringing new and previously disengaged voters into the process will provide popular support for issues like health care reform, fighting poverty, winning racial inclusion, maintaining a safety net, and fighting to raise the living standards of working families. On the other hand, a Democratic Party that has a program inspiring to ordinary people will attract new support at the polls. Voter registration should be ongoing, yet it should be integrated fully into issue advocacy and substantive campaigns.

Voter registration work should be accompanied by strong voter education and efforts to stimulate turnout. New voters who are encouraged into the process will need a reason to stay, a continuing set of invitations to do so. This multipronged approach will help not only to bring political success for progressives but also to strengthen our democracy, allowing people to participate in the decisions that affect their lives. Whatever the result of any particular election, such enhanced participation is a crucial component of a popular progressive project.

Winning with Campaign Finance Reform

Changing our campaign finance system is another crucial prong in the Democracy Agenda. Making people count more than money in elections and building popular confidence in the institutions of democracy are critical objectives for popular progressives.

By now, it is abundantly clear that both national parties have been engaged in a fund-raising race to the bottom—and alienating people from the political system in the process. We are all still reeling from revelations about fund-raising for the electoral contests of 1996. The allegations surrounding abuses in campaign fund-raising that surfaced during the final month of the presidential campaign contributed significantly to the sudden drop in President Clinton's margin, and they also hurt Democrats in close House and Senate races around the country. As Ellen S. Miller, executive director of

Public Campaign, summed it up: "The parties and the candidates operated as if there were no regulations whatsoever" (cited in Rosenbaum 1996). The result is a catastrophe for American politics and a huge obstacle to efforts for reenergizing the Democratic Party as a winning, progressive force.

Nothing has undermined people's faith in the system more than the spectacle of well-heeled, influential special interests drowning out the voices of ordinary citizens. Nothing undermines the sense that the Democratic Party is the party of the people more than the realization that it, too, along with the Republicans, is waist-deep in the muck of private-interest financing in politics.

The total amount of money spent on all federal races in 1996 was a staggering $3 billion. House candidates alone spent $477.8 million in 1996, up 18 percent from 1994 (Federal Election Commission 1996). The biggest story, however, was the explosion of soft money in the election process. The *New York Times* reported that the fifty largest donors alone—corporations, trade associations, and unions—together contributed over $63 million (Rosenbaum 1996). Ongoing revelations about foreign money in the Democratic campaign, the spectacle of White House coffees where millions of dollars were raised, and the selling of opportunities to go on outings with members of Congress from both parties—such revelations and more fuel public disdain and media inquiry. In the heady days of 1995, the Republican congressional leadership's blatantly shaking down and threatening lobbyists who didn't get on board was indeed a sorry sight.

Of course, we don't really need the spectacles of 1996 to know that change is necessary. Evidence of money's disproportionate role in politics has been abundant for years. Many qualified people refrain from contesting for public offices at all levels of government, because fund-raising has become such a daunting, distracting, and indeed sordid affair.

Money-raising threatens to become all consuming, making real contact with voters more and more difficult. "In New Jersey, Meeting the Voters Is a Luxury," announced the headline of a *New York Times* story on November 1, 1996; the article went on to recount how the two candidates in the state's U.S. Senate race spent almost no time with voters. As the *Times* reporter explained, voter contact "has been driven to extinction even in this geographically compact state by the real campaign: raising money for a barrage of television ads." Democratic candidate Robert Torricelli, we are told, actually left the state during the last week of the campaign to fly to California to "hob-nob with Hollywood donors" (MacFarguhar 1996, p. A1).

Any study of contributors reveals the fundamentally undemocratic nature of campaign finance. In Connecticut's 1994 gubernatorial campaign, for example, 75 percent of all campaign dollars came from one-fifth of 1 percent of the state's population (Connecticut Money and Politics Project, and Common Cause Connecticut 1994, p. 1). This pattern was also found in Maine, where only one-half of 1 percent of the population gave fifty dollars or more to candidates in 1994, and those giving five hundred dollars or more made up 70 percent of the money spent in the 1994 race for governor (Maine Citizen Leadership Fund 1995).

For progressives, the system is especially problematic, because financial imperatives drive politicians to the right and render out of bounds a whole series of policy options that a truly popular party must entertain and promote. At all levels, Democratic officials now lean over backward not to be—or appear to be—antibusiness. During 1996, for example, the Clinton administration responded favorably to aerospace industry lobbyists' urging that it pull back from doing a study requested by the machinists' union about the employment impact of foreign concessions by American companies (Gerth 1996). This is a reasonable democratic issue for a union to raise, but the administration apparently worried more about its image among business contributors.

Unsurprisingly, a wide variance separates the attitudes of large donors from the preferences of other members of the public. Using the findings of a Lake Research survey of one thousand donors in July 1996, Robert Borosage and Ruy Teixeira found that "those who pay for the parties differ with most Americans on what's wrong with the economy and what needs to be done to make things better. The voice of money is more supportive of free trade and big business and more opposed to government spending and regulation than the public." While Democratic donors are generally more conflicted about these issues than Republicans, the survey finds that "donors of both parties are more pro-business on all questions than the public at large" (1996, p. 21).

There can be little doubt about the subtext of much of the advice given to candidates and party officials. Contributors convey that the party should loosen its ties to its traditional allies among labor and the poor and look more closely at pro-business, entrepreneurial solutions to problems. That many

Democrats drift in such directions sometimes occurs for reasons of good policy but also often because officeholders and candidates are seeking to succeed in the corporate fund-raising race.

Progressives need to fight for campaign finance reform—first at the state and then at the national level—in order to free candidates from the need to court wealthy interests merely to mount competitive campaigns. It's that simple. The best way to do this and to thereby open the door to more popular influence in politics and government is to support reforms offering full public financing to candidates who give up private contributions and agree to observe strict spending limits during their campaigns. By a solid margin of 56 to 44 percent, Maine voters adopted just such a sweeping reform in November 1996. They approved an initiative that reduces campaign spending significantly, takes candidates almost entirely off the treadmill of private fundraising, provides public funding for candidates running for both the governor's office and the state legislature, and addresses the problem of independent expenditures by adjusting public funding to offset private money. As the *Boston Globe* appropriately editorialized on November 1, 1996, the Maine initiative is "a blueprint for national change, enabling Americans to take back their democracy." The Maine initiative was backed by a broad coalition called Maine Voters for Clean Elections (MVCE), which included the AFL-CIO, the Perot Maine Reform Party, the Natural Resources Council of Maine, the Maine People's Alliance, the American Association for Retired Persons (AARP), Peace Action Maine, the League of Women Voters, Common Cause, and the Dirigo Alliance (the state progressive alliance that was the driving force in organizing MVCE).

We are enthusiastic about the 1996 Maine reform, but we are skeptical about incremental proposals that single out political action committees as the major problem. Study after study has shown that the overwhelming problem of campaign contributions is attributable to wealthy individuals representing monied interests (Center for Responsive Politics 1990, 1992, 1994). This is the big problem that must be addressed. Of the $6.4 million that Newt Gingrich raised in his 1996 reelection campaign, for example, only $1.1 million was channeled through PACs.

Effective reforms are not politically impossible. Maine's experience shows that how the issue is framed is extremely important. A poll released by Maine's largest newspaper in September 1996, shortly before the election, reported 78 percent of Maine voters saying that they were opposed to "tax-payer funding" of state legislative campaigns ("Poll" 1996). Had the debate in Maine been framed as a question about using public funds to pay for political campaigns, the initiative certainly would have lost. But instead, MVCE succeeded in framing the referendum as a decision about whether special-interest money (and lots of it) should continue to dominate politics in Maine. Reform supporters did not hide the fact that public financing was a part of the solution. The Maine ballot read: "Do you want Maine to adopt new campaign finance laws and give public funding to candidates for state office who agree to spending limits?" But Maine reformers focused their literature, public comments, and paid advertising on the issue of what public financing would do, rather than what it was. Such funding, reformers argued, would set spending limits, cut private contributions, shorten campaigns, and level the political playing field. In sum, the effort in Maine put the spotlight on the need to cut the power of wealthy special interests in elections.

As Maine's experience suggests, voters are ready for a thoughtfully and forcefully articulated approach to tough campaign finance reform. The 1996 outcome in the Maine referendum challenges the conventional wisdom that people do not care about reforming the process, that they reserve their passion for other concerns. What is more, the signal from Maine is corroborated by recent polling done by the Mellman Group (1996, p. 13) and indicating that a solid majority of respondents nationwide favor a Maine-style public financing reform—dubbed The Clean Money Option—even when presented with the arguments of those opposing the reform. A CNN–USA Today–Gallup poll conducted in October 1996 found that 65 percent of the respondents favored full public financing for candidates who agree to give up private contributions, with only 27 percent opposing (p. 13). Gallup has been asking its question repeatedly since 1974, and these findings reflect the highest level of support for public funding since the days of Watergate. In addition, in twenty-four Massachusetts legislative districts in 1996, an overwhelming 89 percent of voters supported Maine-style reforms in advisory referenda (Commonwealth Education Project 1996).

Some people consider effective campaign finance reform a fruitless quest since recent U.S. Supreme Court decisions have reinforced *Buckley v. Valeo* (1976), which equated the endless spending of money in a campaign with constitutionally protected free speech. But we think that legally well-crafted challenges to the *Buckley* decision will result from successful efforts at reform in the years ahead. New challenges will come before courts that will have the advantage of documented patterns of spending and influence—evidence dwarfing anything available to the justices in 1976. Even in narrow legal terms, arguments about speech and campaign contributions may look different in the future, as overall public pressures for reform build.

Comprehensive campaign finance reform can have a major impact on creating a much more receptive climate for successful progressive politics in a number of ways. Perhaps most basically, campaign finance reforms can counter the alienation and cynicism that the public feels. Sharply cutting campaigns' access to private money is possibly the best way to assure the public that special interests will not subvert public policymaking.

Likewise, the Democratic Party can only improve its image with swing voters by championing tough finance reforms. Perot supporters, the quintessential swing voters, are certainly interested in campaign finance reforms along with other democracy issues. In at least two northeastern states—Connecticut and Maine—the Perot organization has participated in coalitions fighting for comprehensive campaign finance reform. The Perot phenomenon has often been cast as a middle-class revolt against big government, but Greenberg (1996c, p. 239) found that while most 1992 Perot voters (62 percent) voted for Reagan and Bush, a majority wanted to radically reform government but not reduce its size and scope. In fact, fully 59 percent of Perot's 1992 voters agreed with the statement "The government should be given back to the people, reducing the influence of special interests and lobbyists," while only 27 percent agreed with the statement "The government should be made smaller so it will cost and do less" (Greenberg 1996c, p. 256). Since reducing the influence of special interests and lobbyists is a central goal of our Democracy Agenda, pursuing it offers progressives a strong way of attracting support from the discontented "radical middle" (Greenberg 1996c, p. 255).

Campaign finance reform will make it easier for ordinary citizens and grassroots candidates to run for office. Potential candidates will know that they will not have to spend endless time raising money, which for many people is both distasteful and discouraging, especially if they face running against well-financed opponents. And having a wider array of people willing to run for office really matters. By observing firsthand the work of five statewide political coalitions in New England that encourage activists from progressive groups to run, we have learned how much new excitement in elections that can generate.

If meaningful campaign reform happens, then organized grassroots constituencies will matter more in politics. If candidates contend for office with relatively equal resources, then their ideas will matter more, along with their energy, their ability to communicate with voters, and the networks and organizations through which each candidate can mobilize people to help. Candidates from progressive or grassroots organizations will do well not only in winning Democratic Party nominations, as they often do now; given the renewed importance of field activities, they may gain a new edge in general elections as well. The obvious corollary is that conservative candidates who have a grassroots base will have an advantage on the Republican side.

In a reformed electoral environment, progressive organizations, particularly unions, would have new incentives to build up and educate their grassroots base. Over time, and once candidates have won offices, this could make moving forward with progressive agendas much easier. Because campaign dollars would be limited, less television advertising would be needed, thus permitting greater emphasis on grassroots education. Innovative ways of communicating with voters could develop, and greater efforts could go into building grassroots connections to stay in place across elections. The role of civic groups, particularly local party and political organizations, would likely grow.

Some progressives are worried that public financing could encourage a proliferation of narrowly focused candidates, fragmenting the progressive vote and exacerbating differences. In our view, this risk is no greater among progressives than for others in the political spectrum. Although fragmentation could happen in some places at first, we believe that progressive constituencies would learn to coalesce. A reformed environment, we expect, would enhance the value of statewide progressive coalitions, which already exist in about half the states. These electoral coalitions bring together unions, citizens' groups, women's groups, civil rights organizations, environmentalists, and others into a unified political force focused on helping progressives to win office and win policy victories. Such alliances also build democratic infrastructure over time, just by fostering new conversations and connections among the various constituencies.

Comprehensive campaign finance reform, in short, promises to encourage more participation and reward the development of grassroots political organization—rather than marginalizing such contributions to civic life and elections, as the present, money-driven electoral system does. Promoting genuine finance reforms must therefore be a priority for popular progressives.

Fighting for Democratization and Accountability

The third objective in the Democracy Agenda is extending democratic participation into more areas of society and social decision making. Government is not the only institution whose decisions affect people deeply, so more democratic accountability and participation must become the norm in other institutions as well.

Corporate accountability is one extremely important objective. While many corporations and businesses pay close attention to their communities and contribute significantly to the public welfare, many make decisions that adversely affect employees, communities, consumers, and the environment. The advance of deregulation and downsizing has taken more and more decision making out of the public domain and outside the influence of citizens. Abdications of public responsibility have spread during the past decade. Layoffs, mergers and megamergers, and industry transitions take place outside public view and without serious community dialogue. Mergers, downsizings, and the transfers of operations from state to state and country to country cost workers and communities good jobs. Such corporate adjustments frequently leave loyal workers with less pay, fewer benefits, and less job security or no jobs at all, and they are all too often undertaken by companies that previously received substantial public supports, whether through tax abatements or other subsidies. Adding insult to injury, the very business executives who make such decisions are getting paid much more than ever before, especially compared to their own employees.

According to many economists, productivity gains based on new information technologies will lead to higher growth and heftier profits in the years ahead. Clearly, on Wall Street and in business surveys, economic confidence is now high. This is good news in general, yet as new growth takes place, political leaders should raise fundamental questions about how the benefits are to be apportioned among all stakeholders in our national economy. Is it too much to ask that a true democratic discussion take place on these issues?

Working families have always been at the heart of the Democratic Party, and ensuring their economic security must continue to be a central goal.

Surface satisfaction about economic expansion only lightly masks the growing worries that working and middle-class Americans have about their place in the new global economy and about security and opportunity for their families. Discussion of such deep concerns cannot be relegated to the margins of political life—and surely Ralph Nader and Pat Buchanan shouldn't be the only ones debating these issues in a forceful way. By championing reasonable standards of corporate citizenship, the Democratic Party can respond to the deep concerns many Americans feel about their economic plight and the growing powerlessness that they experience when confronting the arbitrary decisions of corporate managers. The party must signal that it is on the side of average Americans. If Democrats are willing to stand up, we can restore some sense of sovereignty, showing that communities and the nation can be in control of our shared destiny. America need not be powerless to help our people within the new global economy.

The role of the labor movement is, of course, critical. We are heartened and delighted at the changes taking place in the AFL-CIO. Its commitment to reenergizing the membership and organizing the unorganized promises a return of hope and involvement for American workers. Increasing the number of union members should be a significant priority for Democrats and progressives.

Historically, union involvement has been an important step toward self-actualization and democratic participation for thousands of workers and their families. Not only were unions attacked and decimated during the Reagan years; they also collaborated in their own decline by failing to organize new workplaces and acquiescing in undemocratic internal procedures. Now the AFL-CIO and individual unions are turning these trends around, and it is crucial for progressives to support organizing efforts as they arise. We must also work for labor-law reforms to reduce the obstacles that union organizers and supporters often face. How can America have a vibrant civil society if people can be fired for supporting unions? New approaches to organizing are being developed that combine union and community organizing. Advancing this important new strategy as well as other ways of building coalitions that unite labor and nonlabor constituencies must be a significant priority for all who aim to build a progressive majority and just society.

Union and nonunion people can work together on campaigns to redress corporate practices that threaten the economic security of many Americans. Several efforts in New England provide good examples. In Connecticut, a community-labor coalition has supported legislation to require corporate responsibility to communities and workers during mergers and layoffs. The Massachusetts Campaign on Contingent Work is developing strategies to deal with the spread of impermanent, insecure jobs as corporate decision makers transform once full-time jobs with benefits into temporary jobs without benefits. But for campaigns like these to succeed in the long run, they must get support from lawmakers, party activists, and local opinion leaders. Building such support is something the Democratic Party should do.

Corporations are not the only institutions that can fail to be sufficiently accountable for decisions affecting many people. Decisions with significant impact are made every day in local governments and other public agencies— environmental quality councils, metropolitan or regional commissions, zoning boards, public utility commissions, school boards, and state boards of education. Where our children will go to school, whether a hospital will be run for profit or not for profit, how much say patients and providers will have in managed care, how much regional cooperation there will be in the provision of public services, and where the hazardous waste discovered under the local ball field will be placed—such choices and many more are made in a myriad of agencies. In each of these situations, progressives should be arguing for maximum public input and involvement, as a matter of principled defense of democracy. We must resist the elitist view that public participation is an irritant to efficient policy implementation. Public participation is not merely animated by a NIMBY (Not in My Back Yard) spirit; participation can lead toward compromise and more legitimate public choices. But the absence of real opportunities for a democratic voice can feed the belief—already held by many citizens—that government is out of reach and does not want or value citizen involvement.

Another area where citizen input and governmental accountability is necessary is in the devolution process. For some time to come, shifts of federal funding and decision making toward states and localities will highlight areas where democratic practice—or the lack of it—matters for real people. People at the grassroots level—whether students affected by education policies, social service agencies affected by changes in block grants, women and children affected by welfare reform, or municipalities affected by various distribution formulas—should be insisting that decisions about resource allocation be made with democratic input from those affected. Citizen-based organizations with a true ability to influence choices and help to implement decisions should be built in to the ongoing process of devolution. If this does not happen, progressives and popular constituencies will find themselves scrambling for crumbs in a shrinking public universe.

In fact, it is important to note that citizen organizations and community-based institutions *have* begun to contend, with substantial success, for more business and governmental accountability. Bright spots include the strong, multiracial, church-based organizations developed by the Industrial Areas Foundation; the feisty low- and moderate-income branches of the Association of Community Organizations for Reform Now (ACORN); statewide organizations affiliated with Citizen Action; regional networks of progressive coalitions that work on issues education and voter participation, such as Northeast Action and the Western States Center; and a host of localized organizations working for community improvement. Such progressive networks and organizations have been at the forefront of campaigns to combat redlining by banks and insurance companies, seek property-tax relief and reform, oppose higher electric utility rates, push for faster environmental cleanups, and win improvements in health care. Such groups and efforts have sprouted up, quite self-consciously, in the vacuum created by the withdrawal of Democratic Party organizations from community advocacy.

Unfortunately and too often, the most active and hopeful progressive efforts operate in isolation from and are unrecognized by supporters of political reform. If the Democratic Party is to indeed be an energized, progressive party, there must be new dialogues about how community organizations and political progressives can unite in pursuit of economic justice and expanded citizen and political participation. Only by working together, even if there must often be a division of labor, can community organizers and political reformers make the institutions that shape people's lives more accountable. Forging new conversations and connections will stretch party activists and the leaders of community-based efforts. But this is one important way for the community of all popular progressives to become more than the sum of our parts.

Creating a Sense of Community

The fourth major element of the Democracy Agenda calls for building community. The dominant agenda setters of the Republican Party have clearly embraced individualism, along with unfettered markets. With occasional gestures toward purely local communities, Republican leaders pursue policies that are likely to disconnect Americans more and more from one another, while circling the wagons against one or another set of invaders or infidels. Of course, individual liberty is important, and people have private sides to their lives. But there is also a very deep yearning for true community. People want America to work for everyone; they want to be able to join with others in many endeavors. And Americans possess a reservoir of compassion and caring that should not be ignored.

Often called cornerstones of civil society, voluntary community-based associations greatly enrich our societal life. While it is a shopworn truism by now that government can't solve all our problems, people do understand that community must be involved at the intersection of government and the market. There is every reason for progressives to be in the forefront of encouraging the growth and health of civil society. Engaging in the real, day-to-day work of democracy, creatively solving community problems, and having honest dialogue about issues that matter are all valuable from a progressive standpoint.

We do not believe that achieving a thin, purely formal civility should be the goal of any democratic agenda. Some are calling for more politeness to counter negative campaigning and the shrill name-calling that has muscled its way onto the airwaves and into the chat rooms. Although people should, of course, practice politics respectfully, we should not overestimate how far that alone could take us. Worse, some deliberately misuse the notion of civility to work against strong, substantive, and necessary debates about important issues. Clearly there are issues so fundamental that strong words and actions are absolutely critical for challenging powerful actors and institutions. Furthermore, America's recent history is replete with examples of crucial issues—such as civil rights for African-Americans—that came to the fore only through protest and confrontation. Recommending civility in public discourse should not be used to blunt efforts to address important issues.

At the same time, engaging people in meaningful discussion and activities—at the local, state, and national levels—is a crucial part of restoring a vibrant democratic process. Our Democracy Agenda should encourage community efforts and voluntarism. Robert Putnam (1995) has explained how such "social capital" can further both economic development and effective democratic government. In recent years, a growing body of efforts to encourage civil society and community dialogue have grown up. Connecticut College recently launched the Institute for Civil Society; the Study Circles Resource Center has created a national program for assisting people in thoughtful discussions of complex issues; and Pat Schroeder has announced that she will chair a major project sponsored by the Institute for a Civil Society (a research group and foundation based in Boston) to promote community dialogue across the country. In addition, some recent state legislation has established new venues for community input and dialogue.

The sense of community that we as progressives must nurture cannot be just localized and inward-looking. We must also nurture a larger sense of community, one that bridges divisions to join people and communities in a sense of higher purpose. Community must extend over geographic boundaries, racial divides, and class or economic gaps. Progressives support national as well as local community, and we aim to link civic involvement with democratic politics.

One issue that tests our resolve to promote a broad community is the challenge of creating desegregated schools of high quality. In Connecticut and other states where some cities' school districts are both segregated and disadvantaged, the courts have ruled current school patterns unconstitutional. The courts have returned the problem to the legislatures and the towns for solutions. Whether Connecticut—as a regional and state community—can find the reserves to deal with this dilemma constructively, and do so for everyone, will be a crucial question in the years to come. If "community" merely means withdrawing into affluent suburbs walled off from everyone else, there can be little progress toward desegregated, quality education for all. But if community can be defined as a multiracial, cooperating group of citizens, then there is indeed hope that tough policy problems can be worked out.

Building and rebuilding community must also be a national priority. In earlier times, the Peace Corps, VISTA, the Teacher Corps, and other volunteer programs called upon people to commit themselves for some period of time to serving others within a shared national community. These programs have largely been dismantled, and the defining experience of working together, which was enjoyed by so many of their volunteers and host communities, has faded. Restoring community service should be an important part of a progressive Democracy Agenda. The AmeriCorps program is a start, but it is far too small and constricted to be able to accomplish all that must be done. (The 1997 Volunteer Summit is a hope for a larger effort.) Progressives should argue for a major expansion of national community service. And we should put community service and civic education at the core of the offerings of our nation's schools and universities.

Many Americans are already engaged in the kinds of voluntarism and community-building activities that we are advocating here. People serve locally and without pay on boards and commissions. Tens of thousands volunteer through PTAS, soccer leagues, church social action committees, AIDS awareness groups, food banks, and similar community-based activities. These are building blocks. Participating in community activities often quietly builds support for progressive solutions to society's problems and lays the foundation for a positive role for government.

But it is important to view community efforts in a political context as well. Although the Democratic Party no longer seems to participate directly in community activities, that could and should change. Democratic public officials and Democratic activists need to get involved in community activities, connecting them to democratic processes and practices. Organizing youth activities and encouraging voluntarism among young people are important pieces. And why can't Democratic activists and officeholders sponsor recognition for young people and adults who do special work in their communities? More schools, both public and private, are requiring hours of community service. Should we advocate making this a mandatory requirement? How about participating as a party or organization in a local walkathon or in the Habitat for Humanity Day? All such undertakings and more should be explored so that the Democrats can visibly and actively take the side of community participation and of rebuilding social capital. In the process, we can become the party of community, addressing shared needs and filling a space in individual lives as well.

Building the Democratic Party

Pursuit of the Democracy Agenda can help the Democratic Party reclaim its role as a meaningful progressive force in American political life. It won't be easy. But let's face it. If we are to register large numbers of new voters, engage the energies of young people, find compelling new candidates, and lead principled fights for campaign finance reform and other vital objectives, the Democratic Party itself will have to change.

In all too many parts of America, Democratic structures are weak or downright atrophied. Small oligarchies who enjoy the power that nominating candidates can bring may view party arrangements as mere formalities, procedures and occasions to manipulate rather than opportunities to involve their fellow citizens. From the local through the state level to the national level, the Democratic Party must become more open and inviting for the new participants that democracy could attract into the process. In many instances, real programmatic work—from voter registration to environmental cleanup work to issue campaigns—will be vital, if the Democratic party is to tap people's energy in ways that are productive and beneficial. People cannot be asked just to send in a check and sit back to watch the advertisements and staged party events.

Fighting for and winning the reforms that we have outlined can help to create the very conditions for party revitalization. Expanding the electorate, for example, will enfranchise and empower millions of presently disempowered people and at the same time provide Democrats with a broader, more progressive, and more organized base. Winning comprehensive campaign finance reform will shrink the power of monied interests and increase that of grassroots organizations. That will make a difference, both in party decision making about candidates and in what party officeholders do about public policy.

While we do not underestimate the hard work and bold steps required to persuade Democrats to champion this agenda, the effort must be joined on the local, state, and national levels, with particular attention given to the state level. Many issues are taken up in Washington after a number of states have adopted policy changes, and the state level may therefore be exactly the right place to achieve initial changes in the Democratic Party. State parties are often more open to change.

At the same time, efforts need to be mounted to spur the national party to provide leadership in campaigns in order to enlarge the electorate. Resources should be committed to voter registration and other key initiatives. While state-level work on campaign finance reforms may be more immediately productive, the national party should be pushed to provide leadership here as well.

We hope that progressive organizations will see reinvigorating the Democratic Party in order to further the Democracy Agenda and other initiatives as an important matter to which energy and attention should be devoted. The AFL-CIO and other important segments of organized labor, progressive coalitions, issue organizations, and organizations of color should be brought together to fight for changes in the way things are done, both within the Democratic Party and in the broader political arena.

Constituency and issue groups should work with progressive Democratic elected officials and candidates to promote the democracy reforms we have outlined here. Community issue groups should not put electoral politics at arm's length; they should strive for dramatic election victories—especially where democracy issues are visibly important factors in the victory. Progressives should be looking to run candidates who will make democracy reforms a major part of their campaigns. And progressive Democratic officials and candidates should be leaders in this effort, because the Democracy Agenda can improve their chances to win elections, help them realize their values while in office, and increase their sway within the Democratic Party as a whole.

Moving Forward as Champions of Democracy

The Democracy Agenda is not simply a bunch of paper promises to be written into party platforms and then ignored. Lip service alone will not do. In many respects, this agenda cuts against the grain, seeking to reverse the direction in which party practitioners of realpolitik have been traveling for some time. A new commitment to democracy will require rethinking some accepted wisdom. There must be faith that serious campaign finance reform can win politically and then make a positive difference for the democratic process. Progressive activists must also believe that ordinary people—given realistic new opportunities for engagement—will respond and join the ranks of voters and civic participants. We must hold to this faith even at a time when many pundits foresee an inexorable downhill slide into apathy and privatistic disengagement.

We believe firmly that the progressive project of reshaping Democratic party politics and American public life must include a commitment to furthering the fullest, most vibrant citizen participation. We also think that there is a constituency waiting for an optimistic, inviting agenda that calls out the best in people—enhancing their sense of power, deepening their commitments to one another, allowing them to engage in the day-to-day work of democracy.

By championing the Democracy Agenda, we can also bring out the best in the Democratic Party and in the progressive community as a whole. This effort can be a strong component of a new popular progressive politics, and we are eager to work side by side with others toward a more democratic nation where our shared institutions will listen to all of us and make life better for all Americans.

part three

Building the New Majority

An Emerging Democratic Majority

Paul Starr

The 1994 election devastated the self-confidence of the Democratic Party, and 1996 only partially restored it. After narrowly escaping the "Republican revolution," many Democrats have lowered their expectations and become resigned to the prospect of center-right government even though the public has recoiled from the agenda of the far right.

Skepticism about progressive possibilities reflects not simply the latest voting returns, opinion polls, or signals from the White House. Most sympathetic observers do not see why the underlying trends in American society and politics should return the Democrats, much less liberals, to a majority position. Democrats themselves do not have a believable narrative of the future that explains how and why they can become the majority party again. My purpose here is not to predict a new majority, but to suggest why certain social and economic trends over the next thirty years could help Democrats to achieve one—if they can develop the ideas, strategies, and organization to capitalize on the opportunities that these trends represent.

Of course, new majorities are rare, while dreams and theories of new majorities are more common—and mostly illusory. Yet in recent decades, two theories of new political majorities have proved, if not exactly correct, at least substantially valid. Both were based not merely on a hope, a prayer, or a debatable historical lesson but on long-term changes in American society that could be the rational basis of new political strategies.

The first was the theory famously proposed by Kevin Phillips (1969) in what remains the single most brilliant recent work of political forecasting, *The Emerging Republican Majority*. Published when Republicans were far outnumbered in Congress and had just barely won the presidency after losing seven of the nine previous races, the book should ironically be an inspiration as well as a benchmark for Democrats today. Much of the analysis still stands up a quarter of a century later, even though the author's own views have evolved.

Phillips's original new majority formula was one part political realignment, one part geodemographic transition. The Democratic Party's embrace of black interests had opened the South to the Republicans, he argued, while rapid economic and population growth in the Sunbelt presaged a continuing shift of power toward the most reliably conservative region of the country. The analytical force of the book came from Phillips's command of patterns of ethnic settlement and county-level voting since the Civil War. Putting those data together with the growth of the Sunbelt, he correctly anticipated the sources of the Republican ascendancy that would make Ronald Reagan president and Newt Gingrich Speaker of the House. That ascendancy did not happen automatically; the Republican Party drew new leadership from the South and West and altered its policies to take strategic advantage of the opening that the Democrats had provided.

The second theory of a new majority, also originating in the late 1960s, was the conception of the New Politics, or new liberalism, that emphasized such issues as civil rights, consumer protection, broader political participation, openness in government, feminism, and the environment instead of traditional lunch-bucket concerns. This strategy also built on a long-run trend: surveys from the 1950s to the 1970s show that Americans did become more liberal on these issues (though not on economics, taxes, or crime) in a historic shift of opinion that has not been reversed (Smith 1990; Page and Shapiro 1992). The new liberalism also took advantage of the opening that the Republicans' Sunbelt strategy was giving Democrats in other regions. And while many analysts now hold this version of liberalism responsible for the decline of the Democratic Party, it provided new vitality (particularly in the form of hard-working, highly committed candidates) and helped Democrats to keep control of Congress and state legislatures for another quarter century after the 1968 election and Phillips's forecast, for a total run of sixty-two years, about twice the duration of typical party regimes.

But how can these two theories, with opposite implications, have both been right? As a result of the trends that they identified and strategies that they suggested, the parties have reached a position of rough parity in electoral strength, each with the capacity to form a new majority—that is, a majority different from the one it previously assembled. Republicans can now usually count on majorities among men; Democrats, on majorities among women. Republicans win majorities among whites; Democrats can sometimes assemble majorities from whites and other groups combined. The parties have exchanged regional bases, with the South trending toward Republicans, New England toward Democrats. The rough parity between the parties has produced a divided federal government in twenty-two of the past twenty-eight years. In 1996 the total vote for the House of Representatives was split almost evenly—49.0 percent for the Republicans, 48.7 percent for Democrats. The Republicans maintained control primarily because of the way in which the votes were distributed; they won the overwhelming majority of close races, while Democratic votes were clustered in districts where they won by lopsided margins. Even so, the Republican House majority in 1997 is the smallest in four decades.

Rough parity in electoral strength does not, however, mean parity in all respects. Rising to parity creates a different sense of direction from falling to the same point. Some years ago, after Harvard scored two touchdowns in the final minutes of the Harvard-Yale game, the *Harvard Crimson* ran a headline: "Harvard Beats Yale, 24–24." Like Yale, the Democrats seem to have been losing tie games. While many observers have talked of party decline and "dealignment" as if they afflicted both parties equally, the changes have been asymmetrical, as Robert Kuttner persuasively argued a decade ago in his book *The Life of the Party* (1987). It is the Democrats whose machinery has deteriorated most (the party as organization) and who have lost most in popular self-identification (the party in the electorate). Since 1994, Democrats have also surrendered much of their own agenda to stay politically competitive. They have had fewer resources and run into more trouble (and scandal) in scrambling to obtain them.

Financial scandals have decimated the leading parties of Italy and Japan in recent years, and they could also severely damage the Democrats in the wake of the 1996 campaign (if only by chilling donors in a system still dependent on private money). Yet if we look to the long term, there are more auspicious signs: demographic growth among groups of voters with Democratic affinities; economic trends likely to emphasize the importance of issues identified with the Democratic Party; historical shifts as Democrats finally shed some of the burdens that they have carried since the 1960s. These developments pose two related strategic and intellectual challenges: Are the Democrats capable of capitalizing on these emerging tendencies? And in the face of scandals and cynicism, can they revive themselves not just as a party but as a cause?

The Demographic Opportunity: Flipping the Sunbelt

The 1996 presidential election diverged in several ways from the patterns of political support that Phillips had predicted in 1969. Clinton did better, for example, among Catholics and in the Midwest. But most remarkably, he won a series of states across the southern rim of the United States—Florida, Louisiana, Arizona, New Mexico, and California—that were supposed to be anchors of the new Republican majority. What makes these results especially significant is that, except in Louisiana, Clinton and other Democrats received critical support from two groups whose numbers will increase dramatically in coming years—Hispanics and the elderly. Continued Democratic support from these groups certainly isn't guaranteed, but their growing numbers provide a historic opportunity for a flip of the lower, "Latinized" Sunbelt back to the Democrats.

Although 1996 was not generally a realigning election, it may have had something of that character for Hispanic voters. Realigning elections characteristically see both an increase in turnout and a swing in party support, and among Hispanics both took place in 1996. Nationally, the Hispanic vote rose an estimated 22 percent over 1992, and Hispanics cast 72 percent of their votes for Clinton, up from 55 percent four years earlier. In what may be a signal of future bloc voting, 78 percent of Hispanics under age thirty voted for Clinton. In Arizona, which no Democrat had won since 1948, Hispanics put Clinton over the top with 81 percent of their votes, as they did in New Mexico, where Clinton "merely" won 66 percent of Hispanics. Perhaps the single most electrifying results were in California, where Loretta Sanchez upset Robert Dornan in a congressional race in what used to be the conservative bastion of Orange County, and where the Democrats retook control of the state assembly and chose a Hispanic, Cruz Bustamente, as the new Speaker. Clinton won 75 percent of the California Hispanic vote; he even won half of the Hispanic vote in Florida, despite the long-time Republican strength among Cubans. (These and other 1996 exit poll data that I cite are from the Voter News Service exit poll [1996]. Some of these data were generated at the CNN–Time *All Politics* site on the World Wide Web [http://allpolitics.com].)

According to Census Bureau projections, Hispanics will represent an astounding 44 percent of net population growth in the United States through 2025 (U.S. Bureau of the Census 1996a, reflecting assumptions of the middle series of Census population projections). The source of this growth is not only continuing immigration but also Hispanics' relative youth and high fertility rate. The median age of Hispanics is twenty-six, compared to thirty-five for the overall U.S. population (U.S. Bureau of the Census 1996b); thus even if Hispanic women had children at the same rate as non-Hispanics, the Hispanic population would grow more rapidly. Census projections for 2025 show Hispanics growing to 18 percent of the population in the United States as a whole but to 32 percent in Arizona, 38 percent in Texas, and at least 43 percent in California (U.S. Bureau of the Census 1996a).

Moreover, among Hispanics, the slowest-growing group is the most Republican, the Cubans, with a median age of forty-one, while the most rapidly growing groups are those from Mexico and Central America, who tend to be more Democratic. Thus the internal dynamics of the Hispanic population augur stronger Democratic leanings.

To be sure, several things could go wrong with the projected population shifts. The Hispanic population will be smaller if immigration is sharply reduced or if Hispanic fertility rates converge more rapidly with the general population than Census assumes. Some critics, such as Ben Wattenberg, argue that Census forecasts of fertility are generally too high; but even if Wattenberg is right, the fertility rates of non-Hispanics might fall in parallel with that of Hispanics, leaving as large a differential. And tighter immigration laws might not halt the growth of the Hispanic population if, as Douglas Massey argues, greater economic integration between the United States and Mexico (and other Latin American countries) increases the flow of people along with goods regardless of immigration laws (Massey 1996; Massey and Espinosa 1997).

Hispanics also might not vote in numbers that reflect their share of the population. Today Hispanics represent a much smaller percentage of the electorate than of total population because of their low median age, the high proportion of noncitizens, and low turnout. Nationally, Hispanics made up 10.5 percent of the population in 1996 but only 4 percent of the electorate; as they rise to 18 percent of the population, they have the potential to double or triple their share of the vote. Whether they will close the gap in turnout with other groups is impossible to say; the spurt in 1996 could turn out to be a special case. But as their median age increases and a larger proportion become citizens because they have naturalized or were born here, the Hispanics' share of the electorate should grow faster than their share of the population.

The Hispanic turn toward the Democrats in 1996 could also prove ephemeral. Republicans might increasingly appeal to Hispanics on the basis of conservative cultural values or by running more Hispanic candidates, and Hispanics themselves might become more conservative as they advance socioeconomically. The history of other immigrant groups suggests, however, that early political identifications tend to be highly persistent; Irish Americans, for example, have maintained their identification with the Democratic Party long after its original basis disappeared. Of course, the Hispanic preference for Democrats in 1996 was well above prior levels because of the alarm created among Hispanics by Proposition 187 in California, the congressional cutoff of welfare benefits and other services to legal immigrants, and Republican support for making English the exclusive language of public business. Yet even if Republicans soften their stands, there is no mistaking which party will remain the home of both nativist sentiment and opposition to social programs that benefit groups with large numbers of poor working families. Family incomes among Hispanics, again except for the Cubans, continue to lag far behind those of non-Hispanic whites. Given recent trends toward growing income inequality and relatively slim gains among low-wage workers, Hispanics seem likely to remain predominantly working class in orientation and more favorable to the party that supports increases in the minimum wage and earned income tax credit and is more closely identified with unions, expanded educational opportunities, and broader access to health care.

The Demographic Opportunity: Aging and Gender

Nationally, voters over age sixty-five favored Clinton in 1996 by 51 percent to 42 percent for Dole. Although this 9-point margin was just above the average for all voters, it was significantly higher than among voters between the ages of fifty and sixty-four, who split for Clinton by only 46 percent to 44 percent. Except for the elderly, age was positively correlated with voting Republican; the deviation from this pattern among voters over sixty-five suggests some distinctive influence affecting those in retirement. The preferences of the elderly particularly mattered in Florida, where they favored Clinton by 56 percent to 40 percent and tipped the state to him, giving Democrats their first win in a presidential race in Florida since 1976.

In 1996, the elderly made up about 13 percent of the national population and 16 percent of voters; in 2025, they will make up one out of five Americans (U.S. Bureau of the Census 1996a) and perhaps about one-fourth of the electorate. As with Hispanics, the growing elderly population in coming years will be regionally concentrated; Census projections for 2025 show the elderly rising from 19 percent to 26 percent of Floridians (and probably close to one-third of voters). The regional concentration of Hispanic and elderly voters has particular relevance to presidential elections. During the 1980s, some observers spoke of a Republican lock on the electoral college in large part because the party's base in presidential elections seemed to include California, Texas, and Florida. By 2025, these states will be the nation's three most populous, and if the concentration of Hispanic and elderly voters gives Democrats an edge in those states as well as in traditionally Democratic New York (the fourth most populous in 2025), Democratic candidates may begin presidential races with a big electoral-college advantage.

Compared to the Democratic leanings of Hispanics, however, those of the elderly are much weaker to begin with and therefore more uncertain in the future. One key question here is whether their voting patterns mainly reflect formative political experiences earlier in life, their current economic interests (such as Social Security), or demographic factors (such as differences in mortality rates). Today's elderly came of age during the middle decades of the century, when there were high levels of unionization and Democratic partisan identification. The elderly of 2025 will be drawn mainly from today's middle-aged—the most Republican cohorts in 1996—who formed their views when unions and Democratic identification were declining. If such generational effects predominate, we might expect a shift among the elderly toward more conservative voting.

Some evidence does suggest generational differences between today's elderly and those just behind them, but the data from the 1996 presidential race are ambiguous. The generational effects should apply no less to men than to women, but men aged sixty-five and older gave Clinton about the same proportion of their votes (44 percent) as did men between the ages of fifty and sixty-four. Clinton's wider margin among the elderly than among the fifty- to sixty-four-year-olds was due entirely to a 4-point wider edge among elderly women and to the larger proportion of women among the elderly population because of their greater longevity. These patterns suggest that, at least in 1996, the Democratic margin among the elderly was related to the gender gap.

Voting patterns among women under age sixty-five, particularly differences by marital status, may offer a clue to future trends. Among the married middle-aged, there was no gender gap in presidential voting; married fifty- to sixty-four-year-old women voted for Dole by 51 percent to only 42 percent for Clinton, much as their husbands did. In contrast, unmarried fifty- to sixty-four-year-old women favored Clinton by 63 to 31 percent, displaying the same voting preferences as younger unmarried women, over 60 percent of whom also voted for Clinton. Single women might be more partial to Democrats for a variety of reasons: more experience in the workforce, a higher probability of depending on government programs, and, not least of all, less influence by men.

As the fifty- to sixty-four-year-old cohort ages, the proportion of women will increase, and more of these women will become single through divorce or widowhood (though the latter may have less impact on political attitudes). On the basis of these demographic factors alone, the elderly of 2025 will probably become more Democratic than they were in middle age.

And as the fifty- to sixty-four-year-old cohort retires, Social Security and Medicare should also become more salient issues for them. But how they construe their interests as beneficiaries may depend on whether these programs continue to exist in their current form. Extensive means testing, for example, could remove the more affluent elderly from the program and turn them into opponents of more generous benefits. Similarly, privatization of Social Security could expand the number of the elderly who see themselves as investors and reduce the number who see themselves as beneficiaries. This is precisely the objective of many who favor means testing and privatization. Even with some adjustments in Social Security, however, the most likely outcome is that the elderly will remain the age group most dependent on public social protection—and thus supportive of policies historically identified with the Democratic Party.

The Demographic Opportunity: A New Generation

In 1996, the age group that supported Clinton and the Democrats most strongly was actually not the elderly but the youngest voters. Those between the ages of eighteen and twenty-nine favored Clinton by 53 percent to 34 percent; first-time voters gave him an even higher margin, 58 percent to 40 percent; and surveys of high school students showed still stronger support (Greenberg 1996a; MCI 1996). This is a reversal from the pattern in the 1980s, when the young were more Republican; as Reagan tutored new voters then, so Clinton and Gore may be doing in the nineties. No doubt Dole's age cost the Republican ticket support among the young, a factor unlikely to be repeated. Clinton also did well among the young because of demographic characteristics, such as low income and unmarried status, that will become less pronounced as these young voters age.

But the Democratic leanings of the young may also herald a historical shift. Beginning in the late 1960s, Republicans were able to paint Democrats as being weak on crime, morality, and national defense and to win over much of their traditional white working- and middle-class base. Clinton's ability to reclaim these voters may stem not only from his personal success in reframing the social issues but also from the diminishing resonance of appeals rooted in the experiences of the 1960s and 1970s. The fading power of the past may be showing up first among younger voters, who have no memory of those years. And as time lifts that onus from the Democrats, the Christian Right is creating new burdens of the opposite kind for Republicans.

The swing among young voters may also be connected to economic issues that work in favor of Democrats. Stagnant earnings and cutbacks in fringe benefits have acutely affected workers in their twenties (Sum, Fogg, and Taggart 1996). New jobs, particularly in small firms and the service sector, often do not carry the health insurance and pensions, much less the job security, that were part of the standard employment package in the past. If younger workers and their families are going to receive health coverage and other benefits, they are almost certainly going to need government's help, either directly through public programs or indirectly through employer mandates. The Democratic Party is the only political vehicle available for such demands.

From Demography to Politics

Democrats certainly cannot take Hispanics, the elderly, the young, or any other group for granted. The trends only open up possibilities. Some of the trends even threaten to produce cleavages among the very groups that Democrats seek to unite. The aging of the population brings higher costs for Social Security and Medicare, but because total spending will likely be constrained, the politics of the budget could turn even uglier than in the past—in the nightmare scenario, into a civil war of the welfare state, with older whites on one side, younger Hispanics and blacks on the other. Support for public education has already eroded because of the disparity in racial and ethnic background between urban schoolchildren and taxpayers; given the rising share of Hispanics in the schools, white support for public education may erode even more. The growth of the Hispanic population may also further arouse anxieties among whites already evident in the vote for Proposition 187 and the English-only movement. Thus the same demographic trends that might benefit Democrats could also divide them.

To maintain support among these and other groups, however, Democrats do not need to be single-minded advocates for interests narrowly conceived; they have to be the responsible guardians for legitimate interests anchored in broadly shared values. Democrats need to make clear their fundamental concern for immigrants by strongly defending their civil rights and opposing the English-only movement, but they should be wary of supporting high volumes of legal immigration and thereby undercutting the economic position of low-wage workers. Democrats ought to be clear about protecting the integrity of social insurance programs and, for that very reason, willing to compromise on such measures as raising the age of eligibility; the current and soon-to-be elderly will likely accept a marginal reduction in benefits in exchange for the assured longevity and solvency of the programs. Democrats should similarly support expanded educational opportunities, a living wage, and other policies that benefit young workers and their families, but they do not need to develop separate programs that exacerbate racial and generational cleavages.

In 1996, the Republicans drove the elderly and Hispanics toward the Democratic Party by supporting measures inimical to their interests, and they alienated the young with a candidate who seemed to belong to another era; Republicans are unlikely to keep repeating the same mistake. But what happened in 1996 does reflect more than a casual Republican impulse. The Republican antagonism to government is likely to keep threatening those who need it. While the elderly depend on social insurance programs, Hispanics and African-Americans depend on public spending for education and other social services because they are disproportionately young and poor. The other demographic groups that supported Clinton—unmarried women of all ages and young men and women—tend to face more economic insecurity and have more need of government than older men and middle-aged married women do. The core of the Democrats' emerging majority consists, as it has since the New Deal, of the groups that are struggling hardest to take care of themselves and their families. Helping them to realize that aspiration is central to the purposes of the Democratic Party. The Democrats must appeal to these groups not merely because they make up a new majority but because their aspirations are a just and necessary cause.

The Party as a Cause

If the Democrats cannot take constituencies for granted, neither can those groups or anyone else assume that the Democratic Party will be able to deliver when they need it. For decades, during the heyday of the New Deal coalition and even during its subsequent New Politics permutation, liberals and progressives regarded the Democratic Party as the arena for pursuing their aims. They created new movements largely in the hope that the Democrats would respond to them. They had the luxury of pursuing issue-oriented activism instead of party-oriented activism because the Democrats could win elections, pass legislation, appoint judges, and thereby often translate their ideas into policy.

The shock of losing a sympathetic Congress in 1994 may have the positive effect of turning issue- and identity-oriented activists toward party activism, but the barriers are enormous. Many activists are not merely ambivalent about the Democratic Party but positively contemptuous of it. This dysfunctional relationship is another example of the asymmetrical condition of the major parties. The dominant conservative groups, publications, and writers have no doubt that the Republican Party is their vehicle. The Christian Coalition was created to support the Republican Party; in organizational terms, the party is the principal, the Christian Coalition the agent. The Democratic Party has supporters, but nothing like the Christian Coalition—an alliance created deliberately to mobilize support on the party's behalf.

There is a parallel in the relationships of the parties to the media. The *Wall Street Journal* and *Washington Times* editorial pages are far more concerned about the success of Republicans as a party than the *New York Times* or *Washington Post* editorial pages are concerned about the success of the Democrats. Rush Limbaugh is an unabashed advocate of the Republican cause in a way that no comparable figure on talk radio is an advocate for the Democrats. Conservatives often complain about the supposed liberal bias of the media—an especially weak charge when it comes to economic policy, and hard to prove from the direct evidence of reporting. My point, however, is about partisan advocacy, not ideology. Liberal publications and writers have a more distant and ambivalent relation to the Democratic Party. It is striking, for example, that no political weekly in the United States today wholeheartedly backs the Democrats. In the last election, the *Nation* urged its readers to vote against Dole, saying that it was fine if some voted for Nader and others for Clinton. According to tapes released in 1996, Richard Nixon at one point told his aides to try to induce a black candidate to run in 1972 to drain votes from the Democrats; in 1996 the *Nation* published an article by Tom Wicker urging blacks to desert the Democrats and do the same thing, and it later boosted the fractional left-wing New Party. The *New Republic* endorsed Clinton-Gore with the emphasis on Gore, repeatedly excoriating Clinton and the Democratic Party generally in both editorials and other articles. Most of the liberal columnists in the daily press seem to choke when it comes to explicit partisanship. No columnist in the major papers is as strategically partisan on behalf of the Democrats as William Safire is on behalf of the Republicans.

Liberals and progressives seem peculiarly afflicted by what might be thought of as the perils of high-mindedness. The old line that a liberal is someone who always sees the other guy's side of an argument is only slightly facetious. A long tradition of good-government advocacy disdains partisan-ship; an even older tradition, reaching back to the Founders, regards politi-cal parties as a scandal in public life. Political scientists have long argued persuasively that parties perform valuable functions in a democracy, but the pervasive view is that partisanship itself is corrupt. Virtue seems not to call people to parties but to warn them away. The campaign finance scandals (and nonscandals) of 1996 have reinforced this belief.

Then there are the institutional restraints on partisan expression that come from increased dependence on tax-exempt financing. Without popular movements to provide resources, activists turn to nonprofit organization, which legally limits political activity, as Newt Gingrich can explain. The hes-itancy to become engaged in the partisan arena even affects organizations that are not strictly barred from supporting policy proposals. The 1993–94 battle over health care reform provided a vivid illustration of the problem. Afraid to step into the partisan fray, key organizations that favored health care reform only enunciated general principles instead of endorsing a particular plan, or waited to make an endorsement until it was too late to use their influence effectively. Meanwhile, the opponents of reform had no such inhibitions in bashing the Clinton plan.

The prospects for Democratic Party renewal depend on the repair of these relationships. Party-movement relations fall into a number of general types, depending on whether a movement is inside or outside the party, whether its aim is to change or support the party (or both), and how closely tied the movement may be to particular candidates or issues.

External movements include the following types:

1. loose partnerships, where the movement and party are independent but generally allied with each other, as has been the case, for example, with labor unions and the Democrats, and where the movement both applies pressure and offers support;
2. principal-agent relationships, where the party is the directing force, the movement its instrument, as is the case with the Christian Coali-tion and the Republicans; and
3. third-party fusionists, where an independent party, such as New York's Liberals or today's New Party, tries to influence a major party by threatening to withhold its support and run alternate candidates.

Internal movements include:

4. candidate-centered movements inside parties, such as the McGovern or Buchanan campaigns;
5. other movements inside parties that transcend particular candidates, where the aim is to change the direction of the party, such as the Democratic reform clubs of the 1950s or the Democratic Leadership Council (DLC) today; and
6. parties themselves as movements.

Since the Democratic Party can use plenty of help, developing more than one among these possibilities might be productive. The external-movement models, however, suffer from the long-term decline of groups that might be the source of renewal. Many have lost membership and become little more than hollow shells—direct-mail organizations without much activist base at all (Judis 1992). If unions, women's groups, and environmental groups—to take three leading examples—call people to politics, it's not clear how many will come. The AFL-CIO provided valuable support to Democrats in 1996, but given the modest level of union membership and limited prospects for growth, the Democratic Party cannot expect to be carried to victory on labor's shoulders alone.

The third-party model is dangerous to the concerns that it claims to advance. If the New Party were to have any influence, it would have to demonstrate it could drain enough support from Democrats to defeat them—the very thing that Nixon was hoping to accomplish with a black candidate. And if the New Party were able to achieve that leverage over the Democratic Party, it might often put Democratic candidates in an untenable position: either accept an endorsement that would be the kiss of death, or reject it and lose. New York's Liberal Party, often cited as a precedent, has become a patronage machine for party leaders. The New Party is not likely to grow into a significant movement; the dynamics of the two-party system are simply too powerful, and the New Party itself is a throwback to the New Left of the 1960s. But given the rough parity of the major parties, even small diversions of progressive voters could be damaging.

What is bizarre about such third-party efforts is that the Democratic Party itself is so open to reform and innovation. Primaries are ubiquitous at every level—for federal, state, and local office. In fact, when one asks what organization could serve as an instrument of renewal, the most obvious answer is the Democratic Party itself. The party extends across the nation into virtually every county and town; its local, county, and state organizations, perhaps pale replicas of their former selves, still represent the strongest political structure available. The myriad local boards and councils that populate the landscape of American government remain, a century and a half after de Tocqueville, the single best schoolhouse of democratic politics—and the best places to give new grassroots vigor to the Democratic Party.

The image of the reformer as outsider is obsolete; in the aftermath of the party reforms of the 1970s, the relevant figure is, to use Kuttner's phrase, "the reformer as regular"—the committed activist who appreciates the critical importance of the partisan makeup of government. The dormant structure that the party represents has to be reawakened by all those who know that their causes are hopeless if the Democratic Party shrivels to secondary status. The party itself must become a cause.

Which Majority? Whose Story?

But of course, the Democratic Party is divided about what kind of cause it stands for, and each of the competing factions within the party has its own theory of a new majority. On the left, populists have a theory of a "sleeping" majority that requires stirring nonvoters from their political slumber. On the right, New Democrats posit a new Information Age and see a "centrist" majority that includes independents and moderate Republicans ready to ally with moderate Democrats.

The difficulty with the populist strategy is arousing enough nonvoters to win elections; people who tune out politics are inherently hard to reach. A hard-edged populism may also inadvertently mobilize opponents as well as supporters and thus have a negligible or even counterproductive impact. As a short-term proposition, the New Democrats' approach is more likely to succeed. Just as it is easier to sell a new brand to those who have bought another brand of the same product than to people who haven't bought any, so it is easier to sell a candidate or reformed image of a party to independents and moderates who vote than to nonvoters.

But while attracting independents and Republicans requires narrowing and blurring the differences between the parties, activating low- and moderate-income Americans could create an electorate more friendly to progressive ideas. In the long run, Democrats would be better off with an expanded electorate in which the median voter was closer to their position than with a smaller electorate in which they moved closer to Republicans—better off because even if they chose to make tactical moves toward the center, the electorate would be weighted further to their side.

The populist approach might also maximize the effect of the demographic trends that I have described. The growing Hispanic population turned out to vote in larger numbers in 1996, but it still lagged far behind the rest of the country. A politics addressing the needs of low-income workers may bring more of them into the electorate. Similarly, an inclusive, progressive approach to education and living standards is more likely to engage young people. The long-term interest of Democrats is to invest in a broader electorate, developing ideas and networks of organization to connect with the currently disengaged.

The New Democrats have not articulated a program that addresses, much less stirs, the politically disengaged and economically insecure. The vision of America favored by the DLC and its Progressive Policy Institute highlights the benefits of the information revolution and global economy but downplays the losses to those least capable of taking advantage of them. Like Newt Gingrich (1995), some of the New Democrats (Marshall 1997) have accepted the view, derived from Alvin Toffler, that the United States is entering a new technological era that dictates "demassification" of large institutions, including big public systems. In line with that view, the DLC's policy experts call for partial privatization of Social Security, Medicare, and public education. But the linkage here is tenuous; why the information revolution should favor privatizing these institutions is obscure. What is clear, however, is that privatization would aggravate inequalities in these spheres and undermine the already depleted sense of common social obligation in America. These policy prescriptions threaten to alienate groups vital to a new majority, drive a wedge through the Democratic Party, and give conservatives the necessary margin (and cover) to enact their agenda.

To their credit, the New Democrats and President Clinton have helped to reconstitute the moral authority of the Democratic Party by redefining the political middle ground on the social issues, such as crime and family values, that hurt the party badly in recent decades. The New Democrats' "tolerant traditionalism," as Bill Galston calls it, has more popular support than either the conservatives' intolerant traditionalism or what is perceived to be (and unfortunately sometimes is) the indiscriminate postmodernism of the left. Although often presented as a repudiation of liberalism, the New Democrats' views are not especially conservative on the issues championed by the new liberalism of the 1960s—civil rights, the role of women, environmentalism, openness in government. The divisions enflamed by the Vietnam War have now faded. However much they may vex each other, the right and left of the Democratic Party are much closer than they were during the long period when southern Democrats were bitterly opposed to the national party.

Each side of today's Democratic Party brings valuable assets to the task of building a new majority. Liberals and progressives are vital to party renewal, because a tolerant and popularly oriented progressive project has a greater capacity to inspire commitment to the party as a cause and a greater potential to expand its reach across the electorate. However defined, liberal Democrats are unlikely to make up a majority in the general population. But like conservatives among the Republicans, they can realistically aspire to be a majority within America's majority party. Managing this role requires a sense of both strengths and limitations. Progressive Democrats have a right to insist on their core role in setting the party's agenda. But their influence will often be less than their share of party activists might appear to warrant, because moderate voters (and, alas, donors) will continue to provide the additional votes and resources needed to win general elections. If the Democratic Party is to build a new majority, it needs energy and ideas from both liberals and New Democrats. The party won't fly without both of its wings.

Reversing Southern Republicanism

Ira Katznelson

The most significant shifts in the central tendencies of American politics in the past six decades—the New Deal, the civil rights revolution, and the sharp turn toward conservatism and Republicanism—all have had the South at their core.* From 1896 to the election of Franklin D. Roosevelt, the Democratic Party essentially was a southern party with a small number of urban-immigrant bastions. The Roosevelt realignment nationalized the Democratic Party and its coalition, but the South—with rock-solid Democratic majorities provided by white voters in an exclusionary and authoritarian electoral system—continued to provide the party with a stable, though not particularly salubrious, partisan foundation. The great normative gains made by the civil rights revolution dissolved the Democratic Party's southern electoral security and propelled a regional realignment.

Today, in spite of the region's Democratic heritage and its African-American electorate's massive support for the Democratic Party, the South ordinarily votes Republican in national elections. The South, not the nation,

*I owe warm thanks to John Lapinski for his research assistance and critical intelligence and to Guy Molyneux for saving me from the sin of exaggeration.

has realigned. The white South has taken up the Republican Party's auda-
cious offer to metamorphose into a racially conservative southern party. The
region, especially its rural areas, has become reliably Republican in presidential voting (though there have been deviating elections, to be sure, especially when the Democrats have run southern candidates) and is on the verge
of becoming expectedly Republican across the board.

As signified by the 1994 congressional elections—"very probably the
most consequential off-year election in [exactly] one hundred years," notes
Walter Dean Burnham (1996, p. 363) without hyperbole—and codified in
1996 largely as a result of the turnabout in southern voting behavior, there are
now both a strong pro-Republican bias in presidential elections and the
prospect of a long-term run for a Republican House and Senate undergirded
by a still-expanding southern regional base. Southern Republicans, moreover, compose the most reliably conservative members of Congress, regularly
scoring lowest on ADA and highest on ACU scores. This transformation has re-
called sectionalism to a pride of place in the polity. Differences between the
regions now are more important in shaping electoral outcomes than differences between other kinds of geographic units, such as those dividing cities
and suburbs (Archer 1988, pp. 111–25). The South, in short, has become
the instrument for the ascendance of conservative Republicanism in Congress and the source of a head start even for weak Republican presidential
candidates. Must these advantages for the Republican Party endure or even
deepen? I think not, and I shall explain why.

Thirty years ago, the country's leading analysts of southern political behavior downplayed the prospect of a thoroughgoing partisan realignment in
the region. "The Republican tide is sweeping over Dixie at glacial speed,"
Donald Matthews and James Prothro (1964, p. 105) observed in 1964; the
"Southern Democrat is still far from ready to receive Republicans with open
arms," Philip Converse (1966, p. 240) concluded in an article published two
years later. Writing during the peak years of civil rights agitation and legislative accomplishment, these scholars stressed the durability of partisan loyal-
ties, the breadth and depth of whites' attachments to the Democrats, and the
absence of an attractive Republican alternative. They expected southern politics to become more competitive but its essential features to prove durable.

Today, we are afflicted by a comparable myopia. Impressed by the striking gains that the Republican Party has made in the South, we are tempted to

think they constitute a law of nature. But there will be no New Majority, progressive or otherwise, for the Democratic Party unless a more even playing field is restored to the South. Is this renovation possible? I think it is. Given a strong black base (which must not be, as it too often has been, taken for granted), a shift of some 7 to 10 percent amongst white voters—an upper-level target—would match the South to the nation and retrieve a partisan mix tilting slightly to the Democrats. Yet even a smaller shift, one half this size and within reach, would make the South competitive and substantially enhance the chances for progressive presidential candidates to win nationwide and for Congress to return to Democratic hands.

The dimensions of this task are considerable but still manageable. The first big partisan shifts in the South came in presidential voting. By 1988, no southern state could be any longer classified as ordinarily Democratic in presidential elections; virtually all had become usually Republican, strongly tilting just under one-third of all electoral votes to give the GOP the kind of edge that once had belonged to the Democrats. To be sure, at the presidential level the parties had become more balanced during the Eisenhower-Kennedy era. Yet Republicans secured their recurring structural advantage only after the 1964 campaign by Barry Goldwater (who won 55 percent of southern votes while running against a popular southern president; his regional appeal can be traced to his pronouncement that "forced integration is just as wrong as forced segregation" and to his party's determined rejection of a strong civil rights platform plank at the Cow Palace convention), Lyndon Johnson's presidency (marked by the passage of the Civil Rights Act of 1964 and the Voting Rights Act of 1965), and the remarkable vote-getting of George Wallace (who garnered 40 percent of the South's vote in 1968, nearly twice Strom Thurmond's 23 percent for the Dixiecrats in 1948).

In 1988, Republicans outnumbered Democrats among southern white voters for the first time in American history; by that year, white voters in the South were voting Republican at a rate 10 percentage points higher—67 percent—than whites in the rest of the country. Four years later, in spite of the robust vote (18 percent) secured by third-party candidate Ross Perot in the South, President George Bush ran in the region nearly 12 points ahead of his white vote elsewhere. In 1996, a very good year for the Democrats at the presidential level in the South compared to their recent performance, Bill Clinton garnered 46 percent of the region's vote, not far off his 49 percent nationally. He carried Florida, Louisiana, Arkansas, Tennessee, and Kentucky and nearly won in Virginia and Georgia. Yet even in these favorable circumstances, the president trailed Dole amongst southern whites by a whopping 56–36 margin (southern blacks gave Clinton 87 percent of their votes, thus accounting for the Clinton-Dole tie in the region). In contrast, Clinton secured 51 percent of the white vote in the East, 45 percent in the Midwest, and 43 percent in the West (Voter News Service 1996, p. 28).

There has been a lag separating presidential and congressional partisanship. Between 1965 and 1985 the South gave over two-thirds of its votes to Republican presidential candidates but only about one-third to their candidates for the House and Senate, and it gave even less—24 percent and 14 percent, respectively—for Republicans running for governor and state legislative office. Today, two in three southerners still vote Republican in presidential elections, and, in a remarkable inversion of the party's social base, the only reliably Democratic counties in the South are the old Black Belt counties, Latino South Texas, and the big cities (Atlanta, Richmond, New Orleans) with large cohorts of African-American voters. The Republican Party also has a significant, if still smaller, head start in congressional races. In 1960, there were no southern Republican members of the Senate. By 1972, Republicans held one-third of the region's seats and secured fully half by 1980. Today, they command 60 percent. Democratic control of southern House seats proved more long-lasting; before the 1994 elections, they controlled just over 60 percent of the South's House seats. That year, as a central feature of the Republican sweep, the South went Republican for the first time since Reconstruction, by a 64–61 margin. Today's 71–54 Republican edge in the Old Confederacy virtually has reversed that held by the Democrats in 1992. The Republican Party's now stronger congressional hegemony in both houses is symbolized by the once unthinkable social geography of its congressional leadership.

All things being equal, moreover, there is little reason to believe that the realignment has entirely run its course. Though southern Democrats are now a minority in Congress, they are older and more likely than Republicans to vacate their seats in the next two or three electoral cycles, at just the moment when the power of Republican incumbency is likely to take root. But all things need not be equal. The South's near- and medium-term prospects are not foreordained. A fatalistic orientation to partisan trends in the South dominates current thinking amongst scholars, journalists, and politicians. I think that it is misplaced. My confidence rests both on an analysis of the re-making of partisanship in the South over the past three decades, which high-lights the importance of how the Republican Party played the race card to break the Democratic South, and on an assessment of the opportunity that Democrats now have to redefine issues of family, economy, and society, in-cluding those of race, in order to speak effectively to current circumstances in the region. In the short term, the trend toward southern Republicanism can be arrested; in the medium term, it can be reversed.

The Southern Realignment

Analysts of southern voting have long understood that electoral change in the region has been motored by two separate processes: the substitution of a per-ishing generation by new voters and an alteration in voting behavior by indi-vidual voters. It seems clear that before the mid-1960s what limited change had occurred in southern voting behavior had mainly been the result of gen-erational replacement. The passage of time inevitably deprived the Demo-cratic Party of its habitual electorate, substituting Jim Crow voters with those who entered the rolls either during the early civil rights era or after the tyranny of segregation was broken. Duration and death did their work. In 1952, eight in ten southern white Protestants born before the turn of the cen-tury identified as Democrats. This generation of stalwarts has been replaced by new voters with a slightly more Republican tilt than that of their counter-parts in the country as a whole (Green and Schickler 1996, p. 11). Given the history of southern apartheid and secure Democratic majorities, the passage of time has inevitably inclined toward a normalization of the southern white vote. Generational replacement could not but have worked against the Dem-ocrats. Viewed from the perspective of the health of American democracy, this transition to more ordinary patterns of partisanship was all to the good. It restored competitive elections and, later, reflected an end to formal racial barriers to voting.

Only about half of the partisan change characterizing the period from Eisenhower to Clinton can be explained this way. Over time, and in acceler-ating fashion in the past decade, a growing share of change in southern vot-ing behavior can be accounted for by shifts in individual partisan conversion at all levels of the electoral system (Miller 1991, pp. 557–78). These alterations are characterized by the movement, one voter at a time, from Democratic to Republican identification and voting habits. Such transfers in allegiance and behavior are more challenging to the Democrats than is the generational replacement of traditional solid Democrats in the electorate. But they also represent a considerable opportunity. The dead cannot vote, but proselytes can be induced to reconvert.

By the end of the tumultuous sixties, it was this second partisan process, the conversion of individuals one at a time, that had become increasingly significant. How are such individual-level modifications in white southern voting to be understood? Such transfers in allegiance have been produced by two distinctive but interrelated causes: individuals' quests for a party whose ideological views closely match their own, and political parties' strategic pursuit of voters in seeking to remake the electorate in their preferred image. Voters choose parties. Thus voting is explained in part by individual attributes, preferences, and choices. But, crucially, parties also choose voters; in so doing, they define, shape, and attract the electorate. "The voting behavior of individuals," as Adam Przeworski and John Sprague (1986, p. 9) argue, "is an effect of the activities of political parties." Parties comport themselves with greater or lesser success to reshape packages of appeals, offers, and inducements from which voters select.

The southern realignment has been shaped by these entwined elements. The Southern transition to democracy, from the mid-1960s to mid-1980s, freed voters who had been trapped inside a single party in spite of their very different ideological and policy preferences, enabling them to sort themselves into congenial partisan camps. Like generational replacement, this ideological reshuffling was both certain and necessary. For the past decade, however, how the major parties have chosen to woo prospective voters has become more important. Today, we shall see, white southerners cast Republican ballots in proportions that slightly exceed their conservative ideological preferences and significantly exceed their expressed allegiance to the Republican Party. We cannot properly understand the region's partisan recalibration as the result of voters pursuing ideological satisfaction without paying at least equal attention to the manner in which Republicans have chosen to activate southern voters and have thus reshaped southerners' ideological proclivities.

After the elimination of de facto segregation and the accession of a black electorate, Republicans conducted a self-conscious strategy to poach the white electorate across class lines, effectively exploiting the incorporation of African-Americans into political life as Democrats, an approach to party building that has taken on a successful life of its own and that has helped to fuel ideological adjustments in the electorate. In contrast, the Democrats, who were divided and demoralized by the turnabout in civil rights and who met the death of segregation and the Republican challenge with a combination of complacency and stunned incoherence, continue to be disarmed and presented no corresponding offer. For just these reasons, paradoxically, the Democrats have a favorable chance to recover lost ground. The ideological barriers to success that they face are not terribly high, and the scope for more effective party activity is marked.

It is not enough, I urge, to understand how the Republicans acted to reshape southern voting by skillfully using race to trump other clefts in the electorate. We also must come to see how they cultivated and developed strong candidates in order to take advantage of opportunities provided by the retirement of sitting members of Congress and how they mobilized voters by tapping into existing grassroots networks. To trace these party-centered factors, I scrutinize six congressional districts (one in Florida, one in Georgia, two in Tennessee, and two in Texas), five of which were durably Democratic before the 1990s. Today, only two of the seats remain in Democratic hands; one, a Latino district, is not close-run. By way of a look at these transitions and the single case where the Democrats have held on to a competitive seat, I try to delineate the dimensions of the party's electoral problems and the scope extant for its partisan recovery. I ask how a concerted effort sensitive to the variations among southern districts similar in form though not in content to the successful Republican endeavor of the past three decades might return the Democrats to a competitive position. Such a strategy requires modifications to the Democratic Party's rhetoric and substantive appeal, alterations to the bundle of issues that it projects as vital, direct talk without flinching about racial questions, augmentation to its cadre of engaging candidates, and attention to building an infrastructure of organizers and organizations in a region where such traditionally Democratic civil associations as trade unions are underrepresented. This challenging work may take a decade or longer. But we had better promptly begin. For without a more competitive South, a new majoritarian progressive politics will prove difficult, if not impossible.

Table 1. **Conservatism Among Whites by Region**

Year	Non-South (%)	South (%)
1972	36	58
1976	38	51
1980	44	49
1984	41	47

Source: Analysis of National Election Studies Surveys,
1952–1984, in Carmines and Stanley 1990, p. 23.

Voters Choose Parties

Under Jim Crow, the hegemony of the Democrats was secure. Ideological preferences dividing white voters were overridden in the "friends and neighbors" factional politics of the pro-segregation Democratic Party. Indeed, in the absence of a regional party system, political parties in the customary sense were absent. In this setting, voters could not pick parties, and parties were spared the task of selecting voters.

With the demise of this authoritarian political system, not only was a generational party shift certain; so, too, was an ideological realignment. Voters were compelled to choose parties differently as traditional group ties to the Democrats based on white solidarity yielded to a politics of partisanship and issues. In the aftermath of the civil rights revolution, white southerners were more likely than other Americans to identify as ideologically conservative (table 1). Given an option, many migrated to the Republicans. At a moment when the Democrats had moved to the left and Republicans to the right, southern conservatives acted to marry their votes to their views. In 1972, white southern conservatives were 11 points more Democratic than Republican; by 1984, they were 32 points more Republican. Moreover, though race clearly had precipitated this move, the ideological realignment came to be based on the full panoply of issues dividing liberals from conservatives (Carmines and Stanley 1990, pp. 21–33). As southerners increasingly identified as conservatives, they gravitated to the more conservative party; hence conservative Republican candidates were able to swim with the tide. As with generational replacement, there was more than a whiff of inevitability surrounding these developments since they put an end to an unusually

Table 2. Ideology by Region

	Non-South (%)			South (%)		
Year	Liberal	Moderate	Conservative	Liberal	Moderate	Conservative
1992	29	31	40	24	32	44
1994	21	34	45	19	33	48

Source: National Election Studies Surveys, 1992, 1994. Collapsed categories; unweighted results.

acute mismatch between patterns of belief and party preference. Painful as it has been for the national Democratic Party, the South's ideological realignment, like the substitution of age groups, has had a beneficial effect on democratic choice.

The Democratic Party, however, would have considerable difficulty in restoring a convergence between the nation and the South if white southerners today remain significantly more conservative than the rest of the country and if an ideological search by voters describes the primary component of present-day partisan change. In fact, current evidence suggests, the ideological mismatch characteristic of the South between the Johnson presidency and the election of Reagan has become less pronounced, in part because the rest of the country has shifted to the right and in part because the South's ideological transformation seems to have run its course. In spite of these developments, however, white southerners are voting for Republicans in considerably higher proportions than other Americans. Thus, it seems, the current electoral problem (and opportunity) for the Democrats must lie primarily elsewhere.

The present gap between Democratic and Republican voting in the South is difficult to explain by pointing to voters' ideological search alone. Regional opinion profiles do not differ very much across the country, but regional voting behavior varies quite a lot. The South is slightly, not dramatically, more conservative than the rest of America. In 1992, the National Election Survey found that 29 percent of Americans living outside the South designated themselves as liberal, 31 percent as moderate or middle of the road, and 40 percent as conservative; for the South, the identifications were 24 percent liberal, 32 percent moderate, and 44 percent conservative (table 2).

Table 3. Partisanship by Region

	Non-South (%)					South (%)				
				Likes	Dislikes				Likes	Dislikes
Year	Dem.	Ind.	Rep.	Dems.	Dems.	Dem.	Ind.	Rep.	Dems.	Dems.
1992	50	12	38	51	46	51	13	33	50	37
1994	47	10	42	43	52	49	08	41	40	47

Source: National Election Studies Surveys, 1992, 1994. Collapsed categories; un-weighted results; due to omitted categories and rounding error, some totals do not sum to 100%.

Two years later, the South had tilted rightward: now just 19 percent of polled southerners termed themselves liberal, virtually the same percentage, now 33, denominated as moderate, but 48 percent called their proclivity conservative. This movement, however, mirrored that taking place in the other regions of the country, which distributed liberal-moderate-conservative partisanship along a 21–34–45 split (the 1992 data is drawn from Miller et al. 1993 and Rosenstone et al. 1995). In short, the ideological differences distinguishing southern from nonsouthern electorates were narrowing just when the southern realignment hit full stride. Moreover, the modestly greater impetus to southern Republican voting for reasons of ideology might well have been offset by what remains of the traditional Democratic advantage in southern party identification. In 1992, 50 percent of the non-South thought of themselves as Democrats (including independents leaning toward the Democratic Party); two years later, this group had dropped to 47 percent (table 3). In the South in 1992, 51 percent identified as Democrats; 49 percent did so two years later. Moreover, though southerners liked the Democratic Party a bit less than nonsoutherners, as indicated by their replies to inquiries about whether they liked or disliked something about the Democratic Party, they also registered fewer dislikes.

These similarities and differences between the South and the rest of the country, moreover, are characteristic of both blacks and whites (see table 4). In 1992, southern blacks were 7 points more conservative and southern whites 6 points more conservative than respective members of these groups in all regions. By 1994, the gap among whites had narrowed to 4 points, well

Table 4. Partisanship by Race

	Whites (%)				Blacks (%)			
	Non-South 1992	South 1992	Non-South 1994	South 1994	Non-South 1992	South 1992	Non-South 1994	South 1994
Ideology								
Liberal	28	22	20	18	42	35	30	21
Moderate	31	31	34	31	38	38	50	52
Conservative	41	47	47	51	20	27	20	27
Partisanship								
Democrat	47	46	43	43	82	76	83	81
Independent	11	13	11	9	11	15	11	6
Republican	42	41	46	48	7	8	6	13
Likes Democrats	49	46	41	42	76	59	66	58

Source: National Election Studies Surveys, 1992 and 1994. Collapsed categories; unweighted results; due to omitted categories and rounding error, some totals do not sum to 100%.

under the divide distinguishing southern white voting from white voting patterns in the rest of the country. The sectional gap is nonexistent, moreover, with respect to party identification. A virtually identical number of whites—46 percent in the South versus 47 percent outside in 1992, and 43 percent in both regional categories in 1994—and high proportions of African-Americans in all regions (more so outside the South) called themselves Democrats. Similarly, there was little to choose between how whites liked the Democratic Party across regions (they liked it just a tad more in the South in 1994), though African-American enthusiasm in the South was more muted.

There also is little difference between the regions with respect to citizens' preferences about the role of the national government in issue and spending areas traditionally identified with the Democrats. In 1994, a peak year for conservatism, one-half of southern respondents wanted the federal government to spend less on food stamps and Aid to Families with Dependent Children; but these preferences, taken together, were quite similar to those voiced by citizens in the rest of the country (43 and 55 percent, respectively). Likewise, only 10 percent of southerners wanted to spend less on the environment, and just 14 percent wanted the federal AIDS research effort reduced, attitudes wholly consistent with the country's 11 and 14 percent, respectively. Indeed, with respect to support for the enhancement of federal programs, southerners proved more, not less, liberal than the country as a whole. In each of these issue areas both in 1992 and 1994 (with the sole exception of the environment in 1992), they favored enhanced federal spending more than nonsoutherners did. Clearly, something still remains of the receptivity to an activist national government that the South showed during the first half of this century.

Parties Choose Voters

If southerners actually voted in conformity with their expressed ideological predispositions, party identifications, and orientation to federal spending in diverse policy areas, the results would represent what probably is the best available outcome for the Democrats: a close convergence between the South and the rest of the country. The leading problem for the Democrats is that the South now votes Republican, ahead of these indicators of ideology and party preference.

The tilt toward the Republican Party currently makes the South's partisan realignment more pronounced than the ideological shift in the region toward conservatism. It is this interval—about 7 points in congressional elections and 10 points in presidential contests—that the Democrats must begin to close. I think we have reasons stronger than speculation but weaker than definitive evidence to believe that this gap is now mainly the result of party strategies. If such is the case—that is, if what has mattered most have been the actions that Republican Party leaders took to make their once illegitimate party in the South attractive and effective (as late as 1960, they failed to contest two in three races for the House of Representatives) and mirror-image failures by the Democratic Party—there is ample prospect the Democrats can correct the present out-of-kilter situation. There is no reason to let the prevailing partisan realignment simply run its course to the long-term detriment of the Democratic Party.

Thirty years ago, students of elections and voting behavior predicted that as a result of generational replacement and a drift to the Republican Party by ideologically conservative voters, southern politics would converge slowly to the national norm rather than realign as it in fact has. They understood that the kind of issue of great immediacy required for a more thoroughgoing electoral realignment did exist—the issue of race—but they believed that it would not be acted upon by a then-principled, pro–civil rights, Republican Party. In the absence of clear-cut partisan differences, they believed, race could not be a springboard for a southern realignment. For a realignment to occur, wrote Philip Converse (1966, p. 240),

> each of the antagonistic elements must be left in no doubt as to which party is the champion and which the enemy of its interests. This condition is clearly not fulfilled at present. . . . The southern wing of the Democratic Party has, in forty years, been obliged to temper slightly its rabid antagonism to the uplifting of the Negro. The national Democratic Party, in the same period, has moved from a position of occasional flashes of embarrassment about Southern Democrats to a position of increasing intransigence. What has not happened, of course, is that the Republicans have come forth to champion the Southern white. Instead, their gestures toward the Southern Negro have come close to matching those of the Northern

> Democrats. If we doubt that partisan realignment is likely to occur,
> it is to say we expect no dramatic change in this state of affairs.

Though this foretelling proved wrong, the terms of its analysis were right on target. It presciently implied that if the Republicans were to dare abandon their traditional endorsement of black rights, they would reap the benefits of a realignment.

So they have. Republican success with white southern voters has been the result of smart, if smarmy, politics. Since the Goldwater effort, the Republican Party has deployed race strategically to restructure southern politics and trump other cleavages in the electorate. It has worked hard, with considerable success, to identify the Democrats as the party of black officeholders and voters. Hence it has been glad to support hyper-minority districts not just to isolate black voters but to make the point that they define the heart of the Democratic coalition (Carmines and Stimson 1989). As Thomas Edsall and Mary Edsall (1991, pp. 259–60) have observed, the Republicans have self-consciously seized the opportunities that have come their way by the division of the South into a "politics of black and white": "The Republican Party, especially for the younger voters of the region, is becoming the political party of the white South. In some of the deep southern states, in turn, blacks are steadily moving toward majority status in Democratic primaries, and very few whites are prepared to be part of a coalition in which they are a minority." The Edsalls persuasively conclude that "these kinds of divisions are an open invitation to those seeking to build a political majority on the basis of racial polarization."

At the heart of the Republican effort to exploit this opportunity has been a usually soft but sometimes hard-edged version of proverbial appeals to white identity and implicit supremacy. No respectable Republican, to be sure, makes segregationist appeals. But even at their best, southern Republican politicians and strategists have largely abjured courtship of black votes, and they have failed to provide leadership on racial questions. In the main, they have signaled that they are the white persons' party by objecting not just to formal, employment-oriented, affirmative action but to other positive efforts at the state and national levels to smooth the skewed playing field of race and by utilizing "wedge" assaults on welfare spending and crime as a form of recognizable political cryptography (Carter 1992; Carter 1996).

They have effectively understood the political capacity of race to override other divisions and to facilitate the dispersion of the traditional Democratic electorate (Huckfeldt and Kohfeld 1989; Sniderman and Piazza 1993; Sniderman, Tetlock, and Carmines 1993; Kinder and Sanders 1996).

The Republicans, in short, have made electoral gains well in advance of the ideological gap between the two major parties by declaring themselves, in effect, to be a "southern party" by standing for and organizing voters on behalf of a cluster of assumptions about America's racial divide. Equipped as the white, and thus as the inherently and legitimately southern party, the Republicans have developed a rich crop of candidates ready to jump into contests over seats made vacant as a result of the retirement of long-sitting Democratic incumbents, and they have tapped successfully into the infrastructure of white civil society in the South to mobilize the electorate on us-versus-them terms. As a result, in pivotal elections they have often run the younger, more polished, more appealing candidates, who have campaigned against the ossified, complacent, status quo–oriented qualities of many local Democratic parties; and they have been able to tap the resources of the organized right, especially the religious right, in settings where traditional Democratic extra-party sources of mobilization, especially unions, are notably weak.

With fewer immigrants, Catholics, and Jews than any other region, the South also has had a distinctive Protestant subculture, one dominated by evangelicals. Traditionally, even fundamentalist evangelicals respected the traditional separation of church and state. No longer. Not just the advent of the Moral Majority or the Christian Coalition but significant transformations inside the region's dominant church, the Southern Baptist Convention, have signaled a new political involvement by religious activists in support of cultural conservatism and the Republican realignment. Complementing these church networks have been elaborate right-wing radio (and, more recently, Internet) networks, organizational legacies from the old days of battling against integration, conservative business associations, and single-issue grassroots campaigners, most notably the National Rifle Association, all of which have provided the Republican Party with access to politicized conservative elements of white civil society. In contrast, Democratic Party organizations in the region have withered, and the most important source of assets for Democrats nationally, labor-union organizational and media efforts and labor

PAC contributions, play only a muffled role in the South. Unions are weak, and their monies are mainly directed elsewhere.

In short, the Republicans successfully adopted a bold strategy characterized by three principal elements: first, an ideological component identifying their party as the keepers of acceptably modern versions of traditional sectional values, including those of states' rights and racial hierarchy; second, a candidate component geared, bottom up, to recruit attractive party leaders and activists by offering paths to successful political entrepreneurship that were relatively quick compared to those offered by the petrified structures of the Democrats; and third, a mobilizing component in which Republicans cultivated evangelical and other mass-based political networks and wooed business and professional groups who were put off by the Democrats' old-fashioned and often corrupt courthouse politics.

This bold party strategy, rather than ideological searching by voters, is the key to why the Democrats have stumbled so badly in the South in the 1990s. The question motivating this essay—Is a reversal of present trends possible?—thus transmutes into another: Can the Democratic Party mount an effective ideology- and issue-based, candidate-centered, and mobilizing strategic effort to recapture the portion of the white vote that it needs to be competitive in the South, and can it do so in the face of the Republican Party's offer to be the nation's southern party?

Into the Districts: Open-Seat Switchboards

Neither the distribution of ideological preferences nor the party identities of southern voters currently stand in the way of beginning to close the gap in white voting now distinguishing the South from the rest of the country. To the contrary, most recent changes in individual partisan behavior (as distinct from generational shifts) can be accounted for by a combination of strategic activity by the parties and the specific ways that they have or have not acted to exploit recent moments of relatively high partisan indeterminacy. As a step in the direction of coming to a more nuanced understanding of this admixture of elements, I have examined six southern congressional districts: one in Florida, one in Georgia, two in Tennessee, and two in Texas. Initially selected because these were the only southern districts sampled above a minimally acceptable threshold of respondents in the 1992 and 1994 National Election Studies, these districts suggestively capture important variations across the South and highlight the significance of party strategies and local situations. The experiences of these districts, joined to what we know about southern partisan and ideological proclivities, confirm the proposition that a concerted Democratic Party southern strategy is not only desirable but plausible.

It is important to remember that the realignment in southern congressional voting has come one district at a time. Four strategically germane aspects of recent partisan history in these districts are particularly noteworthy. First, incumbency has been important, as it is nationally. Each of the nineteen southern House seats lost to the Democrats in 1994 and 1996 was open. In 1996, a comeback year for the Democrats in the rest of the country, the party suffered a net loss of seven seats in the South. There were twenty-four open seats (one in a new district). Of the others, the Republicans kept their three, while the Democrats held on to thirteen but lost the other seven that the party had held, an attrition rate of 35 percent. Likewise, no sitting member was turned out in the 1980s or 1990s in any of the six districts. The closest election in each followed the voluntary retirement of its member of Congress, irrespective of party. Second, vote swings were astonishingly high in those pivotal switchboard elections, ranging from 22 to 42 points, well in excess of any national trend. Third, these changes in partisanship dwarf any short-term shifts in district-level ideology or partisan identification, which in every case were far more slight. Fourth, candidates made an important difference. The results when these elections were relatively close seem to have turned more on the qualities of the contending candidates than on other differences dividing the parties.

Two of the districts are safe seats, one Republican, the other Democratic. The Texas Fifteenth, in the lower Rio Grande, with most of its population living along the Mexican border, is three-fourths Latino and one-fourth white. Kika de la Garza represented the district from 1964 to 1994. He often ran unopposed but in his last two elections reliably garnered 60 percent of the vote in spite of being tarred by the House banking scandal and vulnerable to his state's pro-Republican surge. In 1996, the Democratic candidate, Ruben Hinojosa, improved on de la Garza's performance, gaining just over 62 percent. Tennessee's Second, which includes Knoxville (which was in Union hands during the Civil War) and the mountain counties to its south, is 97 percent white. It is one of the most dependably Republican districts in the country (ironically, it also is the home of the Tennessee Valley Authority, the great icon of New Deal resource planning). John Duncan, its member since 1988, holds the seat occupied by his father from 1964 until his death. John, Jr., won his first election with 57 percent of the vote; since then, his support has hovered between 70 and 90 percent. These safe districts are ideological exceptions: Texas's Fifteenth on the pro-government, liberal side (though even here "liberal" is something of a dirty name); Tennessee's Second on the side of Republican moderation, though not on issues of social policy.

The other districts, which might be called situational and contingent, deserve closer scrutiny. Florida's rural, noncoastal, historically Democratic Twelfth Congressional District (the slightly different Tenth extending to the Gulf of Mexico in the 1980s) was represented by Andy Ireland from 1976 to 1992. The district is primarily white (81 percent) but has notable black (13 percent) and Latino (6 percent) populations. Elected to his first four terms as a Democrat, Ireland switched parties in 1984, the first of what soon became a significant group of sitting Democratic representatives to move across the aisle. In 1988, Ireland commanded 74 percent of the vote. He ran unopposed in 1990 and retired in 1992. That year's election proved close. A moderate to liberal Democrat almost took the seat back. He led in the polls during most of the fall but fell just short, winning more than 48 percent of the vote. Two years later, the Republican victor, Charles Canady, was returned by a two-thirds' landslide. He was reelected in 1996 by a smaller but still wide margin, getting a vote of 62 percent.

Georgia's First Congressional District, in the southeast corner of the state, is 75 percent white and 23 percent black, with a smattering of Asians and Latinos. Combining deep rural poverty with a strong modernizing economic trend (especially in Savannah, much of which is in the district), it returned an incumbent Democrat, first elected in 1982, with 67 percent of the vote in 1988 and 71 percent in 1990. He retired in 1992. The Republicans ran Jack Kingston, a Savannah member of the Georgia House who had made a statewide reputation on insurance reform issues against a politically inexperienced rural school principal. Kingston was elected by a 58–42 margin. He garnered 77 percent in 1994 and 68 percent in 1996.

Tennessee's Fourth District, which is 96 percent white and 4 percent black, spans a century-old partisan fault line, incorporating the Tennessee Valley, which historically had had few slaves, and robust economic ties with the North and the slave farm country of middle Tennessee. The district was created for the 1982 election and was represented until 1994 by Jim Cooper, who ran unsuccessfully that year for the Senate. Cooper was unopposed in 1988 and won landslide victories, with 67 and 64 percent of the vote, in 1990 and 1992. In 1994, the Democratic candidate lost the general election by a 15-point margin to Van Hilleary, who in 1996 was reelected with 58 percent of the vote.

Texas's Eleventh—70 percent white, 16 percent black, 12 percent Latino, and 2 percent Asian—looks a good deal like Georgia's First before the Democratic incumbent retired, but it also contains lessons about survival and strong candidates. It is the only district of the four that the Democrats have managed to hold after a sitting Democrat retired. Located north of Austin but south of Dallas–Fort Worth in the heartland of the state, the district's main urban area is Waco, and the presence of Fort Hood, the second largest army fort in the country, makes military spending a key issue. Marvin Leath, the district's incumbent from 1978 to 1990, was a moderate in the House Budget Committee and a hawk on Armed Services. He was wildly popular, winning his last campaign in 1988 with 95 percent of the vote. When Leath stepped down, the Republican Party made a resolute run at the seat. An attractive state legislator who once had been a Mondale 1984 delegate before switching to the Republicans and who was strongly supported by Senator Phil Gramm, defeated two former mayors of Waco in the Republican Party, then fiercely attacked the Democratic candidate, Chet Edwards, for his moderate to liberal record in the Texas Senate and for his attendance at a gay and lesbian fund-raising event. Edwards proved an experienced and effective candidate. His vita included three years as a congressional staffer, a near victory at age twenty-seven in the primary that chose Phil Gramm (then still a Democrat) for a House seat, a Harvard MBA, and a visible state legislative career. He held the seat for the Democrats, but only by a 53–47 margin. Since then, he has garnered 67 percent in 1992, 59 percent in 1994, and 57 percent in 1996. He is now chief deputy whip for the Democrats in the House of Representatives.

In contrast, the Democrats ran weaker candidates in the switchboard elections in the other districts. Two, in Georgia and Florida, took place in 1992, quite a good year for the Democratic Party overall; the other, in Tennessee, in 1994. In part, the loss of Georgia's First District was the result of a redistricting that had removed Savannah's blacks to an adjacent black majority district. But even if the black voters had stayed put, the Democrats would have run at best even in a district that they had controlled with more than 70 percent of the vote in 1990. The Democratic primary split seven ways; the runoff was captured by a political novice who had to contend with a savvy, visible, relatively moderate state legislator from Savannah.

In Florida's Twelfth, the Democrats did run a more competent and experienced candidate (a two-term state legislator strongly backed by the state's teachers' union) than they had in Georgia; he faced an attractive, soft-spoken, experienced Florida House legislator who had first been elected as a Democrat in 1984 but who had switched parties in 1989. Unlike the Democrat, he did not have to face a tough primary.

When Jim Cooper chose to run for the Senate rather than for reelection in Tennessee's Fourth, the Democrats likewise produced a bruising primary, won by a thirty-four-year-old teacher of creative writing who had had considerable prior experience as a congressional staffer but who had never run for office. Two years earlier, his almost equally young Republican opponent, a lawyer who had run a large family business and who had served in the Persian Gulf War in the Air Force, had nearly ousted an eighteen-year incumbent in the Tennessee Senate. He campaigned as an antipolitician, preferring term limits and tough campaign finance restrictions. In contrast, his Democratic opponent ran to his right, favoring school vouchers, school prayer, and the death penalty.

Each of the pivotal elections, including the Democratic victory and three defeats, was characterized by noteworthy electoral shifts. In Texas, the Democrats lost 42 points in one fell swoop while holding their seat; in Georgia, 29 points; in Tennessee, 22 points. In Florida, the Republicans lost 22 points compared to the prior contested election in 1988. On the whole, these alterations were vastly out of kilter with the period's significant but more modest changes in individual-level partisanship and ideology.

We can see this disproportion if we examine the National Election Studies' district-level data for 1992 and 1994 (tables 5 and 6). In 1992, the Democrats scored generous victories in Texas's Eleventh and Tennessee's Fourth, lost a close election in Florida's Twelfth, and were dislodged by a considerable though not overwhelming margin in Georgia's First. In each instance, we have seen, the Republicans gained massively in 1994 (the smallest

Table 5. Attitudes in Four Contested Congressional Districts

	Florida Twelfth, 1992	Florida Twelfth, 1994	Georgia First, 1992	Georgia First, 1994	Tennessee Fourth, 1992	Tennessee Fourth, 1994	Texas Eleventh, 1992	Texas Eleventh, 1994
Ideology (%)								
Liberal	30	11	19	19	15	9	14	11
Moderate	26	26	33	24	41	36	32	37
Conservative	44	63	48	57	44	54	54	52
Partisanship (%)								
Democrat	40	34	43	41	56	46	54	58
Independent	19	9	20	12	20	18	15	7
Republican	40	57	36	46	24	36	31	35
Likes Democrats	40	38	38	22	51	48	65	39
Dislikes Democrats	29	49	29	41	49	52	35	62
Policy Spending (More–Same–Less)								
Food stamps	19-49-30	9-36-55	22-50-28	3-50-47	19-44-37	14-43-43	10-58-32	8-47-35
Welfare	20-35-46	12-41-47	21-45-43	5-32-62	16-38-46	19-43-38	11-55-34	8-47-45
AIDS research	55-41-4	42-36-21	61-32-7	61-21-18	59-37-4	30-50-20	82-16-3	59-27-14
Environment	47-51-2	41-50-9	49-49-2	31-55-13	66-32-2	55-41-5	61-37-2	33-53-14

Source: National Election Studies Surveys, 1992, 1994. Collapsed categories; unweighted results. Due to omitted categories and rounding error, some totals do not sum to 100%.

Table 6. Should Washington Help Blacks?

	Florida Twelfth, 1992	Florida Twelfth, 1994	Georgia First, 1992	Georgia First, 1994	Tennessee Fourth, 1992	Tennessee Fourth, 1994	Texas Eleventh, 1992	Texas Eleventh, 1994
Respondents who say federal government should help blacks (%)	13	9	25	15	2	4	19	30
Respondents who are neutral, choosing midpoint in scale (%)	31	18	26	30	18	23	19	23
Respondents who say blacks should help themselves (%)	56	73	50	55	79	73	63	47

Source: National Election Studies Surveys, 1992, 1994. Collapsed categories; unweighted results. Due to omitted categories and rounding error, some totals do not sum to 100%.

Note: Respondents were asked, "Some people feel that the government in Washington should make every effort to improve the social and economic position of blacks. Others feel that the government should not make any special effort to help blacks because they should help themselves. Where would you place yourself on this scale?" The respondents were offered a seven-point scale. I have collapsed the highest three and lowest three responses into the "should help" and "should help themselves" categories, respectively.

advance was an 8-point increase in Texas's Eleventh, held comfortably by the Democrats). Yet in three of the four districts, party identification and policy opinion changes were moderate by comparison, and there was no consistent pattern across the districts in the relationship of opinion and voting. The ideological and partisan profiles of the Texas district shifted only slightly; the main changes were sharp alterations to whether the Democratic Party was liked or disliked. In Tennessee and Georgia, the gains for conservatism and Republican identification were strong, but fell a good deal short of the electoral swing, and the like-versus-dislike shifts were inconsistent: tiny in Tennessee, quite considerable in Georgia. Only in Florida did the 13-point gain in Republican votes closely track alterations in opinion. It is also hard to credit shifts in racial attitudes for these short-term changes in voting behavior. In both years Tennessee's Fourth was very reticent about a federal role in helping blacks, and Florida's Twelfth displayed the largest shift toward a belief that blacks should "help themselves." Though Georgia's First turned slightly to the right on this issue, Texas's Eleventh, the only district held by the Democrats in 1994, tilted toward the left. In that year each of the three Republican districts was less inclined than the South as a whole to support a federal role to help blacks (22 percent in favor, 54 percent saying that blacks should help themselves, and 23 percent at the midpoint of the scale); only the respondents in Texas proved more liberal than this regional benchmark.

A Progressive South?

The Democrats will hold the line and possibly recover in the South only if they make a big offer to choose voters as the Republicans have since the 1960s. The Democrats cannot and should not counteroffer in order to become a "southern party." But the Democrats can adopt a bold strategy characterized by three elements: first, an ideological component that identifies their party as tolerant, open, and committed to strengthening families and building opportunity for everyone in an era of uncertainty; second, a candidate component that, bottom up, attracts new leaders to a party newly committed to winning in the South, particularly in the switchboard elections where members are retiring; and third, a mobilizing component that builds on the continued vitality of the black church and moderate evangelical ministries and a commitment to new union and school-based organizing efforts.

This is a period of change in the South, as it is in the rest of the country. In such circumstances, the Democratic Party might well be able to change the political conversation in the South in ways conducive to its success in the same manner in the rest of the country—not by running away from racial divisions and still sharp inequalities dividing blacks form whites, but by discovering fresh ways to address job insecurity, countervail the extraordinary policy capacities of business, advance the role of government in creating a workable economy, solve problems faced by families of diverse character, meet challenges of universal social protection (including health care), repair the country's inadequate infrastructure and broken-down cities, and confront unequal patterns of political participation. Concretely engaging issues of this kind can create new majorities in the country as a whole but especially in the South, which remains the least rich, least well-paid, least unionized American region with the least generous, least fiscally able state governments, at a time when they are being asked to assume greater and greater responsibilities.

Southern Democrats must learn not to run away from race questions, because in doing so they yield crucial rhetorical and substantive terrain to their opponents and thus come across as either cynical or fearful, neither of which is terribly attractive. In the South as in the rest of the country, tolerance and a commitment to build opportunity for everyone are important party principles. Democrats would do better if they addressed race head on, acknowledging its scars and pointing to the ways that the Republicans have sought to manipulate the issue in order to bust potential populist and progressive coalitions, while developing policy options that move in the direction of building transracial interests and coalitions. Unless the Democratic Party in the South stops running away from racial issues, other axes of political division that should work to its advantage—including the presentation of alternative models for economic modernization and formulas for grappling with the continuing unevenness of southern prosperity inside the region and compared to the rest of the country—will not effectively shape the political agenda.

The Democrats must gear up for the momentous election opportunities that come with retirements. There are now more Republicans in the House and Senate than Democrats; soon, though not immediately, they will begin to retire in at least comparable numbers. Unless the Democrats can learn to avoid wounding primaries and can recruit first-class candidates, their chances will be dim. State by state, district by district, it thus is essential to rebuild the party's organizational structure with substantial national strategic and financial assistance. These are no simple tasks. But the Republicans have managed such feats; why not the Democrats?

Last, a medium- to long-term mobilizing strategy is vital. Even in a media age, networks linking "friends and neighbors" continue to matter. In this respect, southern union weakness is particularly disabling. Union households gave 59 percent of their votes to Clinton and only 30 percent to Dole. Nationally, 17 percent of National Election Surveys respondents belong to a union household; yet this proportion is only 11 percent in the South as a whole, and it is even smaller in the Republican seats that I have examined (9 percent in Tennessee and Florida; just 3 percent in Georgia). There also are important community-organizing resources to be tapped, including liberal and moderate Protestant ministries disaffected with the conservative ascendancy among evangelical Christians. And there are the public schools in which a majority of blacks and whites achieve their education, where renewal remains central to building opportunity in this new era.

We might do worse than return to the concluding section of V. O. Key's *Southern Politics in State and Nation* (1949), written nearly a half century ago. Although so very much has changed in the South under the impact of the civil rights revolution, economic modernization, and changing demographic patterns, which include a good deal of in-migration from other regions, Key's analysis remains sharp and germane: "The presence of the black provides a ready instrument for the destruction of tendencies toward class division among the whites" (p. 655). Key understood at the time that three developments might portend a more decent, more progressive South. The first of these was the growing differentiation of the South between urban and rural, between economically advancing and stagnating, areas. Less and less was the South unitary. The new differences were creating political openings. Second, the movement of blacks into the electorate, he perceived, would be accompanied by a tandem movement of whites, and their votes, he thought, would be up for grabs. The third was a set of efforts then being mounted by the CIO and AFL to organize workers across racial lines. Key thought that their success, which he hoped for but did not anticipate, might transform the axis of southern politics to class issues, displacing race from its pride of place as the organizing principle of southern politics, and thus serve as a progressive basis for the incorporation of the new white and black electorate.

These labor efforts failed, of course, and race became secure as the region's hegemonic topic. But southern differentiation continued apace, and at a rate Key could not have imagined. At the moment, the South's economy, demography, built environment, gender and family patterns, and future prospects bear little relation to those he studied. Further, the results of the revolution in race and rights have been incorporated, albeit grudgingly, into southern life more auspiciously in many respects than in the country's other regions.

But Key also did not anticipate the transformative effects of the new global and information age that would challenge all U.S. families as never before. Just as the speeding marketization would change social relations everywhere, the South would find itself newly exposed and newly challenged.

At just this moment, the Republican regional and racialist strategy has become costly. Outside the South, the Republican Party is beginning to pay a price for its intolerance, regional provincialism, and ideological hostility to government and social support. Democrats, as a consequence, have won countervailing gains in the East and Pacific West. But the Republicans are also beginning to pay a price inside the South as well, as national Democrats have reemerged as competitive in Florida, Virginia, and Georgia.

The Democratic Party, in short, has ample reason to pursue a southern strategy of its own, but one integral to a renewed national purpose. Is a progressive South possible? Perhaps not in the imminent future. But a more competitive two-party South is within our grasp because the factors and hence the opportunities that matter—especially those centering on discourse and policy, organization and mobilization—now fall within the control of the Democratic Party.

Globalization, the Racial Divide, and a New Citizenship

Michael C. Dawson

L arge numbers of Americans believe that they are further from achieving the American dream than they were a decade ago, and the resulting economic anxiety is responsible for a good deal of the unease that people feel about their future. The globalization of the American economy has spurred new political conflicts and alliances, many of which are profoundly racialized. Globalization makes inequality worse, exacerbating the deprivation of many African-Americans, Latinos, and other less privileged Americans who have been in difficult circumstances all along. Immigration pressures also increase in a more globally integrated economy, and this can spark new or renewed tensions among groups already in the country.

A progressive politics will have to recognize that the globalization of the American economy is remaking the racial and ethnic map of the United States. If progressives ignore or minimize the racial realities and fail to further an inclusive kind of American citizenship, they doom any chance of achieving a broad alliance and risk stoking the fires of racial conflicts that could dominate politics well into the next century. On the other hand, if popularly oriented progressives can respond creatively to the economic anxiety that is gripping millions of people in the country, we have a chance to rebuild a strong multiracial alliance for a better America for all, an alliance of the sort that has not existed during the past several decades.

Globalization and Racial Politics

Globalization is creating economic anxiety among all Americans, but for many its impact is filtered through the lens of racial group interests and the racial order. Globalization has produced a racial effect and encouraged racialized political responses.

Global changes are undercutting the state and manufacturing sectors of the American economy and crushing the American labor movement. The economic devastation that has hit both the manufacturing and government sectors of the economy affects whites and people of color very differently. The latter are heavily concentrated in these sectors, which have historically provided relatively high-paying jobs to relatively low-skilled workers. The cities have been particularly hard hit by both white flight and the severe contraction of the urban tax base. Much of the nation's economic growth during the past ten years has occurred in suburban regions, like Oakland and Macomb counties in Michigan, while leaving neighboring jurisdictions, like Detroit, facing economic, social, and civil disaster. One-sided economic growth has shattered the organizational and institutional base of the inner-city black community.

Economic devastation has produced social and political isolation, with everyone inside the devastated urban communities becoming mistrustful of everyone outside (Cohen and Dawson 1993). The residents of the poorest black communities are even suspicious of labor unions, the black middle class, and other working people—those who might seem like natural allies. The partial collapse of the black left and the co-optation of black activists into electoral politics and the corporate world have led to a growing political vacuum in inner-city black communities.

Globalization, or what Sassen (1988) characterizes as the "internationalization" of production, has spurred immigration into the United States, producing new forms of racial conflict and intensifying the perceived threat to American workers at all wage levels. During the past couple of decades, those at the bottom of the economic ladder, particularly blacks, have come to believe that they are increasingly the victims of high rates of displacement due to immigrant labor. Many African-Americans think that immigrants, including black Haitian immigrants, should not be allowed to take American jobs until "real" Americans have their opportunity (Dawson 1996). One-fifth of whites think that increased Latino immigration is bad for the nation, and nearly one-fifth of blacks believe the same about increased Asian immigration (Brodie 1995). The large impact that globalization has had on black attitudes can be seen in the fact that 60 percent of blacks are worried about their economic future as opposed to "only" 38 percent of whites, 31 percent of Asian-Americans, and 43 percent of Latinos. While econometric studies suggest that more immigration has caused little or no displacement of low-skilled workers among blacks or other ethnic groups, the media and political rhetoric have fueled the politics of resentment to the point where many Americans believe that society *is* threatened by increased immigration (Card 1996).

The process of globalization and intensified international competitiveness has led to widespread downsizing by corporations. As employment becomes less secure, tensions increase among actual and would-be workers of different groups. Accompanying all of this have been massive attacks on taxes and the scope of state activities. Budget-slashing has produced endless fights over the redistribution of scarce governmental resources, with direct racial implications. The budget debates represent significant conflicts between urban and suburban groups who hold very different views on the size and scope of government.

At first blush these debates appear to be about dry budgetary issues. But more is at stake. Budgetary debates are also about the nature of the state and the nature of citizenship. If smaller and smaller groups of citizens are deemed worthy of citizenship, then there is less and less of a need for a strong central government. This is particularly the case if one believes that the domestic role of government is primarily centered on delivering benefits or services to morally undeserving members of society. An ever spiraling increase in the level of distrust toward government among the majority leads to the dismantling of the central state and the privatization of large swathes of governmental functions. Devolution of public functions proceeds until governmental institutions serve populations that are overwhelmingly homogeneous. As one Wisconsin doctor put it, "I want to make sure my tax money goes to people like me."

One, Two, Many Worlds

Because people experience the economic transformations of our era in different ways, to varying degrees, and from divergent vantage points, particular racial and ethnic groups of Americans are coming to see different worlds. Americans certainly share many values and concerns, as we shall consider later, but more striking now are the forces pushing blacks and whites in particular, but also Asian-Americans and Latinos, to call for radically different solutions to the nation's problems. America's racial groups sharply differ in their assessments of each other's social position, and they offer sharply different assessments of why racially disadvantaged groups remain in deprived circumstances. All these differences in turn encourage sharply contrasting views about the role of government—about what government has already done to help or hurt, and what it might do in the future.

Differing worldviews, then, are at the root of the corrosive silences that are poisoning American politics and the possibility of building a progressive new majority. Blacks and whites hold different views on a broad range of issues, from crime to macroeconomic policy, which are traceable to the two groups' distinct social realities. Basic perceptions of social reality are in fact so different that political debates between blacks and whites often leave participants from both sides completely baffled.

Blacks and whites by and large speak the same language (the controversy over Ebonics notwithstanding). But public opinion researchers constantly overestimate how much blacks and whites share the same media and information sources. Blacks and whites usually attend different, segregated churches, and churches are a critical source of political information for blacks; blacks tend to listen to talk shows whose politics are quite distinct from those of talk shows favored by whites. Black citizens are also exposed to a multitude of alternative but influential black news sources which are virtually invisible to white Americans (Dawson forthcoming). Further, while blacks and white espouse a shared set of values, they differ in their value priorities. Blacks tend to value equality more than liberty, whereas for whites, liberty has priority.

Blacks, whites, and Latinos are in different socioeconomic situations and offer very different economic assessments. Because they were forcibly brought to this country, many African-Americans believe, the nation's racial order and their own subjugation are rooted in economic hierarchy. African-Americans believe that they are doing considerably less well than whites, and this belief structures much of black public opinion (Dawson 1994a). Many whites, in contrast, believe that blacks are doing pretty well—and that where they are not, blacks themselves bear a great deal of the responsibility. Whites doubt that government can do much more to help, and even if it could, they are not sure that doing so is a proper role for government. Blacks disagree strenuously on every point.

Blacks and whites also disagree about the basic facts of economic status, as was evident in a national survey conducted in 1995 by the *Washington Post*, the Kaiser Family Foundation, and Harvard University. Although people in all groups understand that blacks and Latinos have high poverty rates, more than 30 percent of whites believed that black incomes are greater than or the same as white incomes. The reality is much closer to black perceptions: in 1992, median incomes for whites were over $32,000, whereas median incomes for blacks were below $19,000 (Brodie 1995). Even more amazingly, when it comes to jobs, 58 percent of whites (as opposed to 23 percent of blacks) believe that blacks are as well off as whites. In a land where blacks continue to be the last hired and the first fired, it should come as no surprise that in 1993, as in the past four decades, black unemployment rates continued to be twice as high as white unemployment levels. Frequent white misperceptions about black well-being are the norm across numerous other domains as well, ranging from health care to housing.

Such misperceptions of one another's status carry over into dramatically different black and white assessments of prospects for the future. While fewer than 45 percent of nonblack racial and ethnic groups are "very concerned" about their family and personal economic prospects over the next ten years, fully 60 percent of blacks are very worried. The disagreements extend to assessments of group economic attainment as well. Only 27 percent of blacks believe that blacks have achieved middle-class status, but a majority of all other groups think that most blacks belong to the middle class. Indeed, two-thirds of whites believe that blacks have achieved middle-class status.

The vast majority of blacks, who perceive their own economic circumstances relatively accurately, see racism as a major and continuing problem in American society. Meanwhile, substantial segments of other groups reject this proposition. In a survey conducted during the summer of 1995, individuals were asked whether they thought that racism in America was a big problem, somewhat of a problem, a small problem, or no problem at all: whereas only 33 percent of Asians, 38 percent of whites, and 49 percent of Hispanics thought that racism was a big problem, 70 percent of blacks did. The best predictors of a person's stance on whether racism is a major problem for society are therefore race (black or not) along with beliefs about whether blacks fare worse than whites when it comes to jobs. These remain the overriding predictors, even when controls are introduced for such factors as Latin or Asian ethnicity, age, income, gender, and ideology. Racial identities and interests, in short, powerfully shape Americans' views of society and its problems—including the problem of racism.

Government as Problem or Solution

Not surprisingly, sharply divergent views of problems are associated with equally divergent views about possible solutions to problems of racial disadvantage. Here the differences span matters ranging from how aggressively the federal government should pursue antidiscrimination efforts to issues of tax policy and government spending. Still, there are some new complexities and new twists in the responses of various racial groups to public policy questions. Whereas Latinos and Asian-Americans were closer to whites on assessments of economic position and racial disadvantages, on antidiscrimination policies they are closer to blacks. Even before one broaches the matter of affirmative action, massive group differences are evident in attitudes toward conventional antidiscrimination measures. Although fewer than one-half of whites agree that the federal government should enact "tougher anti-discrimination laws to reduce racial discrimination in the workplace" (Brodie 1995, p. 91), overwhelming majorities of other groups agree with this statement, ranging from 74 percent of Asian-Americans to 90 percent of blacks.

Whites are still less willing to help minorities if it means higher taxes. Asians are divided, but a small majority of Latinos and more than 75 percent of blacks are willing to pay higher taxes to help low-income minorities. White and Asian-American aversion to taxes extends generally to such trade-offs as more taxes for greater services, while Latinos are divided, and a substantial majority of blacks are willing to pay higher taxes in return for greater services.

Racial disagreements about the role of government are not confined to issues of taxation and spending. Blacks differ from every other racial and ethnic group in their conviction that, in areas of racial policymaking, devolving public authority to the states will hurt rather than help them. Most African-Americans, but only a minority of whites, think that only the federal government is capable of helping blacks. Blacks remain the group most skeptical of subnational government and the strongest supporters of a strong federal government.

White resistance to government efforts to improve the position of minorities in society seems attributable to the perception of many whites that they are the real losers under government racial policies. Although no racial group has a majority believing that fewer jobs or promotions for whites is a "bigger national problem" than discrimination against minorities, 40 percent of whites do think this, compared to 21 percent of Asian-Americans, 16 percent of Hispanics, and only 4 percent of blacks. Contrasting group perceptions on this issue hold up even after controlling for income, age, gender, and education.

In turn, people's perceptions about which group loses more—the majority or minorities—pattern attitudes toward such remedial racial policies as affirmative action. Even when controlling for ideology, party identification, and the degree to which one thinks racism a serious problem (in addition to the standard racial and demographic variables), a perception that whites lose turns people even more strongly against affirmative action. While Kinder and Sanders (1996) have shown that personal interests do not shape white preferences on racial policy, it is very much the case that perceptions of racial winners and losers influence the policy preferences of all Americans, not only blacks (see Dawson 1994a for more details).

Of course, there are important historical reasons for African-Americans' tendency to look toward a strong central state for remedies to social problems while other Americans may rely more on subnational governments or market openings. Historically, blacks have faced immense official and unofficial hostility from local authorities and white private citizens. The notion of states' rights is hardly politically innocent; it has been associated with the political disenfranchisement and economic dispossession of African-Americans.

Black skepticism about relying on market forces to correct social inequalities likewise has deep roots. African-Americans can remember at least a century's worth of instances where people were set back after clawing their way to a modicum of economic opportunity. Blacks amassed some land and started farming, only to be dispossessed; black laborers found themselves excluded from jobs in labor markets where they were prepared to compete. And there have also been very visible recent instances, such as the contemptuous actions toward black employees by the managers of Texaco Corporation. Experiences such as these have led blacks since the Civil War to believe that opportunities for them must be bolstered by federal regulations and initiatives.

Groups are in conflict about how to pursue the American dream. Progressives will have to wrestle with sharp differences about the relative importance of liberty and equality; the nature, rights, and obligations of citizenship; and the role of the state in the economy. For long-standing historical reasons, only blacks are strong supporters of a strong national government across all spheres, although Asians and Latinos believe that the state should play a role in redressing discrimination aimed at minorities. These days, many whites suspect that they have a lot to lose from government intervention in the economy on behalf of minorities and are therefore skeptical of any strong government measures. These are perplexing ambiguities for progressives today, because times of economic uncertainty create openings for building broad coalitions yet at the same time exacerbate the types of value conflicts that have historically destroyed progressive coalitions in this country.

Although all nonwhite groups are more supportive of government intervention than whites, then, only African-Americans champion strong governmental intervention across a variety of domains. Many other Americans believe that a strong state is of dubious value in winning the American dream, and some think that certain kinds of government action may hinder the access of some Americans to a better life. But the black experience has been that the national government must be on your side if you are to have a chance at the American dream. Generalizing from this experience, blacks favor government interventions in both the economy and race relations. Progressives, in short, will need to find ways to speak about government both to groups of Americans who are skeptical of strong public actions and to groups who feel a vital stake in such actions.

Black Anger and the Democratic Party

The economic and racial processes that I have described have led to very high levels of black dissatisfaction with all aspects of American society. This dissatisfaction has been growing steadily since 1988 (Dawson 1996) and has now reached the point where many blacks may no longer be reliable members of the Democratic Party base. Unless a convincing progressive counterweight is established in black communities and appeals effectively to black voters, nationalist or even demagogic appeals to African-Americans may be successful to a degree that we have not seen before in the twentieth century. Although the chance that blacks would defect to the Republicans is slight, many blacks might very well join an independent third party or withdraw from electoral politics altogether. These possibilities, all of which are certain to undercut popular progressive prospects in the Democratic Party, are strong and growing.

Black dissatisfaction is pushing African-Americans toward black nationalism (Dawson 1996, forthcoming). Nearly two-thirds of all blacks believe that racial equality will be achieved neither in their lifetime nor at any point in the history of the United States. These doubts about achieving racial equality are producing dramatic increases in support for independent politics. One-half of blacks now support the formation of an independent political party, a doubling of such supporters since 1988. A majority of blacks now believe that blacks should belong exclusively to black organizations—a belief that obviously poses an enormous challenge for those who seek to build multiracial coalitions.

The root of the problem is a corrosive dissatisfaction with American society as blacks experience it. Blacks continue to believe that they live in a country that is fundamentally racially unjust: 83 percent of blacks say that the legal system is not fair to blacks, 82 percent say the same about American society in general, and 74 percent say this about American corporations. An overwhelming 86 percent of blacks say that the American economic system is unfair to poor people. Significantly, large majorities see no prospect of an improving racial climate in the foreseeable future; indeed, a majority believe that the racial situation will get worse. This deep dissatisfaction and sense of exclusion challenge the ideal of an "American community." Over one-half of blacks believe that blacks constitute a nation within a nation, not just another ethnic group.

Doubts about participation in the American community go hand in hand with discontent about the Democratic Party in all sectors of the black community. The Democratic Party has had a historic contract with blacks, though its inclusive strategies were not always intended and were never fully effective. Blacks entered a Democratic Party that remained segregationist because the New Deal nevertheless expanded economic relief and recovery programs and made desperately needed aid somewhat open to African-Americans. New Deal programs were far from universal and were often administered by racists, but they still benefited large, impoverished sectors of the black community. Since the New Deal, all groups in the black community have supported the Democratic Party because it seemed committed to building a national state strong enough to advance a relatively egalitarian economic program.

But even as they have become intensely angry with and alarmed about Republicans, blacks have become increasingly discontented with Democrats since 1988. By 1994, the percentage of blacks believing that the Democrats work very hard on issues of concern to the black community had declined by 10 percent. During the same period, a growing percentage of blacks came to think that the Republicans are totally uninterested in supporting issues of importance to African-Americans. On economic as well as social issues, blacks oppose moves to the right by both parties. They are worried about the growth in both parties of antiurban sentiments, attacks on welfare programs, and highly punitive measures against criminals. Vociferous debates around affirmative action and immigration alarm many blacks. And blacks suspect that the Democratic Party in particular may be backing off from promoting racial equality as it seeks to win greater support from whites.

Rising black discontent with the two parties has led to growing volatility in black political opinion and politics. For example, over the course of one year, black assessments of George Bush went from the highest approval level for a modern Republican (61 percent) to the lowest such rating, as approval of Bush dipped lower than even the low approval rates for Ronald Reagan during a recession and for Nixon during Watergate (Dawson forthcoming). Black voter turnout has declined since the mid-1980s; and more blacks, according to time series data, are identifying as independents. This volatility reminds us of the 1950s and earlier in the twentieth century, when the perceived unfriendliness of both major parties also brought greater black electoral volatility.

During the 1980s, the racialized nature of the American political system was mirrored by Ronald Reagan and Jesse Jackson, each of whom anchored one end of the political spectrum and was viewed with approval by his racial group and with repugnance by the other. Again in the 1990s we see a similar racial duo helping to define the political spectrum. While neither Patrick Buchanan nor Louis Farrakhan are embraced as wholeheartedly by whites or blacks, respectively, as Reagan and Jackson were, both enjoy significant support in their racial group. In short, the racial politics of the 1990s is defined not only by group (mis)perceptions of exclusion and advantage but also by racial angers and recriminations so high among blacks and whites that a significant portion of each community is attracted to a truly extremist leader who rejects conventional talk of racial comity.

Wanted: A Convincing Progressive Strategy

In this globalized and racialized environment, blacks who are given the choice support politicians who call for public intervention in the economy, more government control over corporate decision making in areas ranging from plant location to employment policies, and an increase in spending for a wide range of domestic programs from urban initiatives to education. In the current environment of budget cutting and balancing, many black voters do not hear meaningful proposals from politicians. Blacks face a national politics full of silences. Political calculus encourages politicians to ignore the vast racial divisions in the country. Just as the Democrats want to attract white suburban votes while retaining their black base, Republicans need to hold on to a share of the Latino vote while strengthening white suburban support. Public silences about matters of concern to blacks are often the result—except when they are replaced by shrill calls for the political exclusion of one unpopular group or another.

What is missing is a serious national debate about full citizenship, the good society, and the proper role of active democratic government. These are at the heart of concerns about inclusion and the direction of the country that presently divide groups in American society. Popular progressives face a challenge and opportunity to promote government efforts to address particular and shared concerns as well as a more robust vision of the good society and a common citizenship.

The critical question, of course, is what progressives can do about festering racial divisions. Surely the starting point must be an open conversation among all citizens about the economy, the role of government, and our mutual obligations to one another. We must begin with an honest recognition

Table 7. Causes Cited as Roadblocks to the American Dream

	Whites (%)	Blacks (%)	Asians (%)	Latinos (%)
Discrimination		54		
Crime		57	55	58
Lack of jobs	54	72	53	67
High taxes	56	62		56
Rising cost of living	74	78	56	78

Source: Poll conducted by Harvard University, Kaiser Foundation, and the *Washington Post,* summer 1995. Only cells with 50 percent or greater support are displayed.

that blacks and whites, as well as Latinos, come to these challenges and questions from very different social realities, with different perceptions of the world and different value priorities. But members of all groups also share a common citizenship, even if that ideal often seems under attack. Americans of all groups also worry about realizing the American dream for themselves and their children during an era of globally driven economic transformations.

Widespread belief in the desirability of the American dream continues across racial and ethnic groups. Blacks are the most skeptical, with 30 percent professing that they do not believe in the American dream at all. But two-thirds of all blacks still do believe in the dream, and the percentages of believers are even higher among the other racial and ethnic groups. Except for Asian-Americans, however, majorities in every other group believe that people like themselves are further from achieving the dream than they were a decade ago: 55 percent of Hispanics, 58 percent of blacks, and 60 percent of whites all say that they have lost ground in the last ten years. Globalization and threats to wages and employment have increased worries about economic security and the future while sparking new (albeit racially differentiated) frustrations about what government has or has not done.

Blacks remain the most intensely dissatisfied, however. Blacks believe that they are being kept back by a big range of factors, above all by such economic ones as lack of jobs and a rising cost of living (table 7). Dissatisfaction is higher across the board for blacks than for any other racial and ethnic group. Not only are blacks the only group that has large numbers worried about discrimination and jobs, but blacks are also the group most dissatisfied with high taxes and the rising cost of living. Blacks are caught in the paradoxical situation of supporting the American dream but believing that virtually all of the key components of American life are seriously flawed.

Progressives will not be able to ignore the depth and scope of African-American discontent if they are to build an inclusive politics. Blacks have been crucial participants in progressive coalitions since the Civil War whenever they have been allowed to participate. African-Americans cannot be left out today if a new majority progressive coalition is to form. Not understanding, let alone addressing, the roots of black discontent can lead only to racially fractured, weak coalitions that are progressive in name only and incapable of defeating the right.

Jobs and Decent Communities for All

As popular progressives consider how to build bridges across the racial divide, it is important to highlight the importance of economic problems to blacks and whites alike in this period of global change. Economic hardships are the main obstacles that they face, say blacks. And whites, too, often focus on economic issues. As noted in table 7, nearly three-quarters of whites cite living standards as an impediment to realizing the American dream, and a comparable number of blacks agree. Problems with jobs are cited by 54 percent of whites; this is considerably below the percentage of blacks who express concerns about jobs, but it is a majority nonetheless. The overlapping economic worries of whites and blacks suggests possibilities for a broader progressive discourse relevant to people of both races.

Concern about group economic status underlies many of the concerns that blacks have about their racial status (Dawson 1994a). Throughout the 1980s and in survey after survey, large majorities of African-Americans listed jobs as the number one problem facing the nation. Even in the 1990s, despite growing concern with crime and drug problems in black communities, jobs and the economy remain the problems most often cited by blacks. In fact, black concern with the economy has been connected to a strong and stable majority view among blacks that the government should act to guarantee jobs to all Americans who want to work.

A frankly pragmatic view of U.S. politics has often led African-Americans to support political efforts featuring a progressive economic agenda, even if their racial agenda was either ignored or openly opposed. The original movement of blacks into the Democratic Party was not based on the New Deal's racial policies, which were in no way progressive. It was in response to the New Deal's progressive economic initiatives (Dawson 1994b; Lewis 1991). The modern relationship between black Americans and the Democratic Party is a pragmatic one, with blacks voting for Democrats on the understanding that Democrats would work for a strong federal government able and willing to shape a growing and inclusive national economy.

In this period of economic change, progressives must seriously agitate for an inclusive, job-centered economic program; a vigorous education program to revitalize the public education system throughout the country; and the type of strong health care and child care systems that allow adults to work while children thrive. This core economic program can be similar to the one that was beginning to garner a significant number of nonblack votes for Jesse Jackson, even in the face of widespread distrust of Jackson in nonblack communities.

A progressive program should be centered around job security and protection of the rights of unions to organize and strike. The programs should rally those who are fighting governors and national leaders intent on jeopardizing the eight-hour work day. At the center should be a guarantee of work for all those who desire to work. And the moral core of the new progressivism should be these twin principles: all able-bodied citizens are expected to work, and in return all are assured decent wages and benefits for honest work. The program must feature educational and health care reforms to ensure that American adults can both secure work and earn decent incomes.

A progressive program also needs to include rebuilding the quality of life in this country. Progressives must argue that the country cannot afford to write off the cities or entire groups of cities. It is not only dangerous to do so but immoral. Only in an environment where *all* residents of civil society have decent opportunities to earn a living and safe and happy lives for their families can we have the type of mutual trust that is vital for a good America. People in all areas of this nation—cities, suburbs, and rural areas—can, after all, find common cause in providing decent environments for our children and grandchildren. Many of the most sinister environmental problems occur in the cities, but there are problems everywhere that need to be addressed through shared or similar measures. As with concerns about jobs and economic opportunity, concerns about family and community can, if tackled cooperatively, build mutual trust and strengthen intergroup alliances.

A New Citizenship

To build real trust, progressives must defend the rights of every group to prosper within the shared social contract and within national boundaries. Progressives must defend legal immigrants and attack anti-immigration appeals often based on racial chauvinism, while supporting trade and foreign policies that make it more possible for workers in other countries also to earn a safe and decent living.

In these troubled times, shared citizenship is a fundamental mechanism for making and enforcing claims and acknowledging mutual obligations. Will we, at this point in history, continue along the difficult path forged by W. E. B. Du Bois and Martin Luther King, Jr., fighting for an inclusive polity that embraces active citizens with equal rights and dignity? Or will we embrace the dark and retrograde notions of Peter Brimelow (1995) and Richard J. Herrnstein and Charles Murray (1994), who propose a retreat from egalitarianism on the grounds that some groups will never be fit for democratic citizenship? Our choice will determine the shape of American politics for much of the next century.

Any progressive movement that remains silent in the face of division over who should belong to America, that does not discuss what shape the nation needs to take in order to include everyone, is bound to fail, as so many progressive movements have already failed in America's past. Today, the challenges posed by racial division are not exactly the same as those faced by earlier generations of progressives, and there are new potentials for building a multiracial progressive movement as well. But the need to face up to racial divisions and inequities remains as pressing as ever, and progressives will be measured by how well they promote the causes of a common citizenship and justice for all in our time.

Popularizing Progressive Politics

Stanley B. Greenberg

T he two national political parties have fought to a draw and nearly to exhaustion.* In 1996, they split the national vote for the Congress right down the middle and did the same at state level. But this photo finish was actually a race to the bottom, because Americans now look on the two major parties with similar disdain. Approval ratings for both parties now rank at the lowest levels in three decades of such record keeping (Greenberg 1997). Americans see a political world torn by unresolvable conflicts, where no one is ascendant and no one seems to speak for them.

No wonder politicians are looking for a bipartisan middle way to escape the party impasse—or are hurling charges at one another in endless ethics scandals. A Democratic president declares that the "era of big government is over" and says that a balanced budget is the chief goal for his second term. No longer wanting to be seen in public cutting popular programs like

*This essay could not have been written without the generosity of a number of organizations who sponsored research and then allowed their findings to be disseminated and published here. I want to thank Citizen Action, the Campaign for America's Future, and EMILY's List, whose commitment to a progressive politics is matched by their commitment to quality research.

Medicare, Social Security, and education, Republicans have turned to quiet legislative maneuvers to pursue the goal of shrinking government.

But the flirtation with bipartisanship and the endless scandals are symptoms of exhausted parties and leaders who are failing to take up the challenges facing America's families. Ordinary citizens have lost interest in politics and parties that have failed to articulate a dominant story that makes sense of the current era. People know that leaders in Washington are discussing and proposing little that would help badly strapped families maneuver their way through this period of change. By contrast, as this book argues, popularly oriented progressives *do* have a powerful story to tell about families in a time of social and economic change—a story that can transcend the partisan and ideological stalemate, bridge the racial divide, and reconnect people to politics.

Combined with aggressive organization, a popular progressive story and programmatic initiatives can change the political calculus in the country. A popular progressive Democratic Party can win support among working families—including northern Catholics, white southerners, and married women, who had nearly given up on the Democrats. It can forge renewed bonds between white and African-American and Latino voters, who bear the brunt of today's uncertainties and deepening inequalities. It can solidify the massive Democratic gains with single women, who, more than anyone else, face these uncertainties on their own. It can build enduring support with a younger generation in the front lines of family and economic change, while keeping faith with older people determined to achieve a secure retirement.

Popular progressive politics is not a series of tactical maneuvers and disconnected popular-sounding policies. It offers a story about what is happening in America today and explains what can be done to build a better future for all families. It creates opportunities to forge a new and enduring Democratic majority.

The Appeal of Family-Centered Progressive Politics

As Jeff Faux has argued time and again, the conservatives have won over broad segments of the electorate, including many workers and traditional women, because they have had a story to tell. It was a story, above all, about villainous government—about unnecessary, destructive, and expensive public programs that overspent and overtaxed and hampered business and economic growth. According to this story, "morning in America"—economic growth and a better life for ordinary people—would come again if Americans had the will to dismantle the bureaucratic state and "free" businesses and individuals to prosper. In early 1997, my colleagues and I at Greenberg Research tested this conservative-Republican story and others in a national survey conducted for Citizen Action. We presented respondents with the following rendition of the conservative story.

> Republicans believe that big government costs too much and limits people's freedom. Government regulation and taxes are a burden on business and individuals. People should have more of their own money to spend as they wish. If we place our hopes on the individual, expanded individual choice, and markets, we will be richer as a people and richer as a country. In this new period of rapid change, we should cut back inflexible and centralized government and give people the freedom to succeed on their own.

A respectable bloc of the electorate (30 percent) found the message very convincing, and many more overall (63 percent) found it very or somewhat convincing. In a period of stagnant incomes and government corruption, it should not be a surprise that working people view taxes as a burden that holds them down (Greenberg 1997). Attacks on government and taxes resonate precisely because they are embedded in a larger conservative story, one that claims to honor the individual and responsibility, one that stresses effort and enterprise. This story also responds to people's resentment of "corrupt" government and politicians who waste their hard-earned money. This story has helped conservatives to win power in recent years—especially since progressive Democrats have not told a compelling story of their own.

But with the pressures on families growing and with the Republican Congress's assaults on education spending and Medicare mounting, voters have begun to question the conservative story. Will a dismantling of federal programs really make it easier for families to maneuver their way to a better life? The conservative story makes a virtue of self-sufficiency and aloneness, since it puts the spotlight on the liberated individual able to make choices. But many working people have trouble seeing the virtue of being on their own when they find themselves beset with the challenges of family decay, social disorder, and economic uncertainty.

Facing growing popular skepticism about their story and policies, conservative political leaders have lately gone silent—to the dismay of conservative activists who fear their party may be adrift and abandoning principle (Glassman 1997).

People today, as it turns out, are much more intrigued with a progressive, family-centered story that makes sense of the current period of change and shows how government can help ordinary families achieve a better life. Progressive Democrats do have a story to tell, as set out by the Citizen Action survey (Greenberg 1997).

> The Democrats say this is a period of change, but for working middle-class families, it is also a struggle. People are working longer hours, rarely getting real raises and can't keep up. Democrats want to help families succeed in this period of change. We should ensure expanded access to education and college. We should help parents keep their kids safe and help with family leave and flextime. We should ensure that people have adequate health insurance and a secure retirement. In this period of change, families need somebody on their side.

Nearly three-quarters of the electorate (74 percent) finds this a very or somewhat convincing story—11 percentage points higher than we found earlier for the conservative Republican story. In fact, 38 percent find the progressive story very convincing. People are responding, above all, to a straightforward but powerful identification with the heroic struggle of working middle-class families facing change and tall odds—working longer hours and not being able to keep up. But they are also responding to the specifics of the story—a government that helps people to educate their children, that helps to ensure that people have health insurance, and that helps parents to keep their children safe while balancing work and family responsibilities.

A progressive story centered on the struggle of families is more compelling than a populist, antibusiness story that centers on corporate excesses, cheap labor overseas, and the need for international trade agreements that place a high priority on the prosperity of American workers. That story was also tested in the Citizen Action survey, as follows.

America faces big changes and people are on their own. Corporations move jobs overseas. CEOs take gigantic bonuses, while downsizing and laying off workers. Foreign countries like China use slave labor and undercut American businesses and jobs. America must compete in this new world, but not as suckers. American workers need more power to bargain for good wages and corporations must be accountable to their communities. Trade agreements must be fair and equal. Our first priority is prosperity at home for working middle-class families.

Over two-thirds of the electorate (68 percent) find this story very or somewhat convincing, including one-third (34 percent) who say that it is very convincing. Significantly, the populist story has greater strength than the conservative one that we presented and tested earlier. But while the focus on corporate and workplace practices forms an important chapter in the progressive story, it is only a chapter and not the whole story. The stronger progressive story underscores the loneliness and heroism of the family and the social support that makes it possible for families to succeed.

The Death of the Reagan Democrats

That Americans today are intrigued by a family-centered progressive story is an important measure of the changed political landscape on which Democrats will have to compete in order to win their new majority. Potentially, Democrats now have a story to tell about what is happening to working Americans and their families, but that is spectacularly new. For two decades, Democrats—the so-called party of working people—have downplayed broad popular concerns and lost touch with millions of working middle-class voters.

These working people pulled back from the Democratic Party as it grappled with the aftershocks of the civil rights revolution and the internal party struggle over the Vietnam War. When the party nominated George McGovern in 1972, Richard Nixon received an astonishing 60 percent of the union vote. Over the next fifteen years, conservatives and Ronald Reagan reached down to these working-class voters and built a more positive identification for the Republicans, promoting pro-growth, low-tax economics and proclaiming respect for religion and family values. The Democrats, meanwhile, built up support in minority and urban communities *and* among better-educated voters. But Democrats lost ground among many working blue- and white-collar families whose parents had been mainstays of the New Deal coalition.

Reagan Democrats were not so much a specific set of voters but a new electoral phenomenon—working-class voters supporting the party of business. In 1980, Reagan carried high school graduates as well as those with some post–high school education, and that remained true for Republican presidential candidates right through to George Bush in 1988. Democratic presidential candidates got slaughtered among the post–high school graduates in every one of these elections, losing by 15 points in their best year (1988) and 23 in their worst (1984) (Voter News Service 1996).

Among the lower-income segment, those earning from $15,000 to $30,000 per year, Jimmy Carter ran ahead in 1976, but Reagan carried them handily in both 1980 and 1984, and George Bush split them evenly in 1988. The story of lower-middle-income voters, those earning from $30,000 to $50,000, is even more disastrous for Democrats. Democrats lost them in every election for which exit-poll data is available, from 1976 to 1988. Dukakis lost this so-called swing middle-income group by 13 points.

But Bill Clinton's presidential campaigns of 1992 and 1996 won back the Reagan Democrats. The 1996 Clinton campaign may have aspired to win upscale suburban voters and lay the basis for a conservative, "new Democrat" politics. But that is just not what happened at the polls. In fact, in 1996 college-educated voters shifted marginally toward the Republicans by 2 points, while working and working middle-class Americans voted more Democratic by 4 points. As a result, Clinton nearly doubled his margin of 1992 and brought his total vote close to 50 percent in a three-way contest. The new Clinton voters of 1996—the bloc that raised Clinton's support from 43 to 49 percent of the vote—were overwhelmingly downscale. They were from lower- and middle-income families: almost three-quarters had family incomes under $50,000. They were non-college-educated voters: over three-quarters had not earned a four-year college degree (Greenberg 1996d).

Bill Clinton's campaigns in 1992 and 1996 together restored the idea that Democrats can have a broad popular base. Consider these striking contrasts.

- Democratic presidential candidates lost voters with only a high school degree in every election during the 1980s, but Clinton won these voters by 7 points in 1992 and 16 points in 1996.
- Democrats lost decisively among those with some post–high school education in every election during the 1980s, but Clinton carried them by 4 points in 1992 and by 8 points in 1996.
- Although lower-income voters with annual incomes of $15,000 to $30,000 supported Reagan in 1980 and 1984 and split evenly in 1988, they are now voting overwhelmingly Democratic: in 1992 Clinton won this voting bloc by 10 points and in 1996 by 17 points.
- Lower-middle-income voters ($30,000 to $50,000) were part of the Republican base in the 1980s, giving Republican presidential candidates overwhelming majorities, but no longer: Clinton carried them by 3 and 8 points, respectively, in the 1990s.

In the end, the recent Republican nominees, George Bush and Bob Dole, averaged only 39 percent of the vote among middle-income voters. That is 20 points below the level achieved by Ronald Reagan.

These shifts conclude a story that I have told elsewhere about Macomb County—the working-class, unionized home of Reagan Democrats in suburban Detroit (Greenberg 1996c). In 1960 and 1964, Macomb was the most Democratic suburban county in America. Then all hell broke loose. In 1984, Ronald Reagan took two-thirds of the vote, and thus were born the Reagan Democrats. All the presidential candidates in every national election since have gone to Macomb to pay homage; Dukakis even mounted a tank there. But in 1992, Clinton closed the Republican margin to 5 points, and in 1996, he won Macomb outright by 9 points (49 to 40 percent).

The Reagan era, however, also created a number of electoral legacies closely related to the Reagan Democratic phenomenon but broader than it. Reagan, for example, reached into working-class communities by reaching into the American family. He showed respect for religious expression and paid homage to family values. Those gestures were rewarded with the votes of married people, who became very reliable Republican voters. In 1984, Reagan won married women by 18 points (59 to 41 percent). In the 1980s, single women were voting increasingly Democratic, to be sure, but the gender gap could never prove decisive for Democrats as long as married women—especially married mothers, non-college-educated wives, and southern white women—were so ensconced in the Reagan-Republican coalition. While college-educated women were voting for Carter in 1980, Dukakis in 1988, and Clinton in 1992, non-college-educated women were an important mainstay in the national Republican coalition. They voted heavily for Reagan both times (by 10 points in 1980 and 17 points in 1984) and supported Bush in 1988 (by 5 points).

The 1996 election, however, ended the Reagan hold on the American family. Married women voted for Clinton by 4 points, while married mothers supported him by 6 points. Dole ran ahead of Clinton among southern white women, but only by 3 points (EMILY's List, 1996). And the most dramatic change came among non-college-educated women, who were once so critical to the Republican majorities. Clinton carried these women in 1996 by a near landslide of 18 points. When combined with the votes of single women who were now increasingly and overwhelmingly Democratic—supporting Clinton by 22 points in 1992 and by 34 points in 1996—Democrats had clearly found a formula for a new national Democratic majority.

Finally, one of the most enduring legacies of the Reagan era was the "Reagan generation" of younger voters. Voters who were fifteen or sixteen when Reagan took office and those in their twenties who voted in 1980 and 1984 are now people mostly in their thirties. In national surveys conducted after the 1996 election, the Reagan generation persisted as the most Republican in their party identification (Greenberg 1996d; EMILY's List 1996). In 1984, the under-thirty voters supported Reagan over Walter Mondale by 60 to 40 percent, and they carried their youthful sentiments into adulthood.

But now there may be a Clinton generation following after the maturing Reagan generation. Among all age groups in 1996, Clinton achieved his biggest electoral margin over Dole among voters under thirty. He won them by a quite astonishing 19 points, 53 to 34 percent, more than twice his margin for the electorate as a whole and comparable to the margin that Reagan achieved over Mondale a decade earlier. In 1992, Clinton carried young voters by 9 points (43 to 34 percent). The young were Clinton's second strongest age group after seniors (and, again, with a margin twice that for the whole electorate). After two national elections where young voters have emerged as the strongest voting group for Clinton, it is appropriate to ask, Are we seeing a distinctive cohort that has learned about public life under the tutelage of Bill Clinton (and Newt Gingrich)? There is good reason to think that the youth vote for Clinton has real depth to it—with Clinton's margin widening among voters under twenty-five and with would-be voters in high school (Greenberg 1996b; MCI 1996). The scale of Clinton's win among young voters was also made possible by the overwhelming backing of young women, who supported Clinton by 28 points. But Clinton carried young men as well (by 9 points), suggesting the prospects of a generational phenomenon of potentially considerable durability.

In short, the politics of the 1990s has closed the Reagan era and signaled the passing of a number of Reagan electoral legacies that had shaped the party fortunes. Now there are new political openings for Democrats among working families, women, and young people—all of whom may be prepared to listen to a new kind of progressive story.

New Openings to Working America

The Democratic Party forged during the 1960s and marginalized during the 1980s was understood by many—after years of caricature by the Republicans—as a "tax and spend" party that was indulgent toward criminals and "welfare cheats" and indifferent toward the needs of the hardworking middle class. In other words, Democrats found themselves on the dark side of the conservative story. This allowed the Republicans to play the race card and bash liberals in election after election, right up to George Bush's use of the infamous Willie Horton commercials. But in 1996, the Republicans sought to play the same cards to little effect. They called Clinton "liberal, liberal, liberal," promised to cut taxes, and bashed welfare and affirmative action, but the charges and the promises just sounded stale and artificial. The old conservative story was losing its hold on people.

Dole's charges were met with indifference partly because the Clinton presidency had laid to rest many of the lingering doubts of the sixties. Clinton proved that a Democratic leader could be tough on crime and a public champion of the concerns of ordinary American families. That is a major accomplishment for the Democratic Party—and it is an accomplishment that progressives should take into account and build upon. Many working middle-class people, married women, and young voters were able to turn toward the Democrats in 1996 because the party was now accessible to them. It seemed to reflect their values and speak to their concerns.

During the 1980s, the Republicans enjoyed overwhelming advantages on their version of the social issues. On taxes, voters preferred the Republicans over Democrats by 21 percentage points; on crime, the Republicans had a 19-point advantage—comparable to the Democrats' current strong standing on education and Medicare. But today the Republicans no longer own the social issues. Among all voters, Republicans have only single-digit advantages on issues like crime, drugs, welfare, and the family; they have no advantage at all on tax cuts for the middle class (EMILY's List 1996). Among women as a whole, the Republican identification with social issues has evaporated. In fact, among non-college-educated women—even the younger white non-college-educated women who were the special object of Reagan's appeal on values—Democrats have taken the lead on fighting crime, reforming welfare, and cutting middle-class taxes.

The 1994 congressional debacle should be a reminder of what happens when Democrats lose touch with the lives of working people. Bill Clinton's election was accompanied by great hopes in the country, but over the next two years those hopes turned to disappointment. On the eve of the off-year elections, Clinton seemed like a culturally liberal president who in the end could not deliver on his investment and health care agenda and who could not impose order on his own congressional party. The 1994 election was a disaster produced by a downscale, working-class revolt against the Democrats. Support for congressional Democrats among high school graduates dropped 12 points to only 46 percent. Among white male high school graduates, support for the Democrats fell off a cliff, careening 20 points downward to just 37 percent. College-educated voters, meanwhile, remained quite stable in their voting preferences (Teixeira and Rogers 1995). The election and the judgments of 1994, however, faded as the president stepped forward to stop the Republican Congress from doing harm to people and began once again to stress family concerns.

The issue facing progressives now and in future years is how to view Clinton's war on the demons of the 1960s. Some will want to ignore it because they find some of Clinton's social positions ideologically distasteful (though I suspect that even these people will not ignore the new openings now possible with many culturally moderate working people). Most, however, may come to see the Clinton project, whatever its shortcomings, as having created new opportunities for progressives to engage *all* working Americans. A Democratic Party now seen to be concerned with families has the legitimacy to address the challenges facing working America.

But the interest of today's working middle-class voters in the family-centered story that I tested in early 1997 is not just about the banishing of past doubts. The new popular interest stems from a changing economy and worrisome social circumstances that leave people looking for new kinds of explanations and new ways of making things better. Today, as Michael Dawson shows in his essay in this book, working Americans of all stripes are struggling to realize the promise of America: 60 percent of whites, 58 percent of blacks, and 55 percent of Latinos say that, compared to ten years ago, they are now farther away from attaining the American dream.

These shared challenges facing the family create an audience for a new family-centered, progressive story that has the potential to challenge the conservative story we presented earlier. Although married men remain skeptical, the new progressive story certainly captures the attention of married women: 51 percent find the story very convincing, compared to only 25 percent who feel that way about the conservative story. The new progressive story also proves more persuasive for women under age fifty (54 to 26 percent) and, most important, for non-college-educated women (50 to 21 percent), who had made the Reagan era possible. Not surprisingly, union households are more drawn to the progressive story (40 to 23 percent), but so are important swing blocs like Catholics (45 to 26 percent) and self-identified moderates (43 to 19 percent).

Although less compelling to respondents overall, the anticorporate, workplace-centered story was more persuasive to a range of groups that will be important to a future progressive coalition. People from union households and blue-collar, non-college-educated men found this version of events to be more credible. What is more, the populist story is the stronger one for alienated voters who think neither party can be trusted with the country's fate and for Perot voters who have already walked away from the two major parties. In sum, the heroism of American families will have to be the central story of progressives, but our story will have to acknowledge skepticism about private power that too readily sacrifices the interests of ordinary people. That formulation opens up a very large window to working America and offers the prospect of a popular, progressive majority.

Social and Family Support

The new openness to the Democratic Party among working Americans has occurred because people sense the end of old issues *and* because they are increasingly concerned with new and gritty dilemmas. In the 1990s people are living with real-life struggles that pose new problems and challenges and that cry out for new responses, including ones from government. Closing the book on old popular worries about the Democrats—Are they soft on crime? Are they too preoccupied with elite fashions? Will they waste my money?— allows average Americans to wonder about new problems to which a party committed to families and social support might offer some answers.

Ordinary Americans today work in an economy short on raises. They face the challenges of market-driven changes and the fading of predictable careers and necessary supports. More and more, people fear that they must face this new, uncertain world fundamentally alone. They sense a world in which parties and government are corrupt, companies lack loyalty, communities are beleaguered, and, above all, families are in trouble and young people confront uncertain futures. While the new Information Age is the source of considerable excitement in some quarters, for most ordinary Americans, ours is a time of a simultaneous squeeze on economic and family lives.

The realities of economic and family changes that leave many Americans feeling beset and insecure were already becoming evident in 1996, despite the strong economic recovery, and are bound to become more politically central in the years ahead. If progressives understand this new era, addressing people's economic and family concerns will be a central part of the progressive popular political resurgence.

The starting point for this popular narrative and political program is Americans' struggle to support themselves, to protect their families, and to find opportunities for a better future. This means devising ways to provide genuine and not just symbolic support for working men and women. It means giving people the tools to manage change.

When two-parent families become more scarce and more fragile, people are left more on their own, and just when the pressures from outside are growing. To restore the family is not just about flextime and quality child care, though these would help a lot. It is also about supporting parental authority and helping people to get married and stay married. The family values discourse, therefore, is not just about old political battles; it is also about the struggle of working people in this new era.

As we are all coming to appreciate, marriage and two-parent families are in trouble, and people know it. That both parents now work as a matter of course, even when they have young children, is just a mundane part of the problem. "Americans of all ages," Kristin Luker writes, "are retreating from marriage" (1996, p. 90). Society-wide in 1992, six of every ten families were single-parent families, and most were headed by mothers who were never married. The number of people who have never married reached one-third of the adult population in 1991 and has more than doubled in just eleven years. One-half of all marriages now end in divorce, and only one-half of divorced men make the payments that are due to their children and former wives. And if current trends carry forward, one-half of all children will spend at least part of their childhood in a single-parent household. The problem may be growing worse in blue-collar and lower-income areas, where women seem less willing to cope with the traditional marriage relations and where men are less able to contribute financially (Luker 1996, pp. 95–97, 103–05, 136, 159, 166–68).

The changes in marriage have been accompanied by extraordinary changes in work and family responsibilities, which compound the problems facing the average family. The proportion of women working has increased in every decade since the 1940s, accelerating from the 1970s onward. Two-thirds of high school–educated women now work, compared to a little more than one-third in 1950; over one-half of women with young children also work, doubling in two decades. While workplace participation is up dramatically, most working women continue to do all of the household work (and three-quarters, all or most of it). At the same time, women are assuming rising responsibilities for the care of older relatives. In the past decade, such caregiving has increased threefold; almost three-quarters of those caring for the elderly are women, two-thirds of whom work outside the home (Juhn 1996, pp. 15, 21; Center for Policy Alternatives 1996; Levine 1997).

The combination of economic and family changes leaves people deeply worried about their ability to provide for their families and achieve a better future. This is why ordinary Americans are starting to demand a serious debate about social and family support, even as the country's elites are pressing ahead with a long-term bipartisan agenda centered on deficit reduction, entitlement reform, and free trade.

In the 1996 election, the people looked past all the political bickering and cast their votes to defend the system of social support that allows people to pursue their strategies for success and survival in this period. Reassurances on spending and crime were no doubt important and help to explain the growing openness to Democrats among some voters. The state of the economy also lowered disaffection and raised confidence in the administration. But when asked why they voted for Clinton in 1966, these voters cited as their main reasons his defense of education and retirement security and his support for family values and parents—key themes about social and family support that are also central to our dominant progressive story (see table 8). People were looking for support in this period of change, and they thought that the Democrats and Clinton were more likely to be there for them.

Elites can now be heard urging the politicians to make the tough decisions and cut indulgent entitlement spending for greedy seniors and government subsidies for a spoiled middle class. Columnist and author Robert Samuelson is probably the most blunt on the issue, but he well represents the establishment's impatience with popular social programs. Somehow, Samuelson writes, Americans have gotten it in their head that everyone "ought to have opportunity to go to college, own a house, and enjoy a good retirement—not just a period of vegetating before death but a time ('the golden years') to reap the fruits of their labor" (1995, pp. 15, 47). As a result of such undisciplined "strivings," entitlement spending is exploding, Samuelson claims. And he sees this as the chief pathology in public life today. With such dire warnings ringing across the capital, politicians have taken up the tough task of "saving" Medicare and Social Security from the bloated expectations of the beneficiaries.

Conservative leaders in both parties have urged the country to reject big-government solutions and place greater faith in privatization, the markets, and choice. In that spirit, conservatives on the Republican side have urged the adoption of medical savings accounts (MSAs) so that people can manage their own health care, and they have called for *higher* campaign contribution and spending limits, combined with disclosure, to enlarge the "marketplace of ideas." Conservatives on the Democratic side propose independent char-

Table 8. Respondents' Reasons for Voting for Bill Clinton

Clinton's Support for Social and Family Issues (%)	
Education	30
Medicare and seniors	26
Family values and parents	16
Clinton's Moderate Politics	
He's a moderate—not too liberal or too conservative	11
He supports welfare reform	9
He supports a balanced budget and lower spending	7
He supports anticrime measures	6
Clinton on the Economy	
His approach to the economy	13
His vision for the future	13

Note: Multiple responses were allowed.

ter schools to promote competition, expanded use of managed care to reduce government health care spending, and privatization of Social Security to give people more control over their retirement savings (Marshall 1997).

Whether or not any particular reform could achieve its technical purpose, the larger message and prospective story are problematic. Conservative Democrats are saying, again and again, that markets and competition are the only way to advance the public interest and further the welfare of families. They would take us in a direction of market-driven uncertainty that perhaps other conservatives are more honest about. The revival of markets, Samuelson concludes, gets us away from the idea that we can "completely control our economic, social and political surroundings" and gets us back to our forebears, who "understood that life was full of chance and uncertainty" (1995, pp. xvi, 5). But for ordinary Americans, common sense says that such freewheeling marketization will only exacerbate the uncertainties and inequalities that already make life so problematic for families today. People are quite receptive to expanding choice in many areas, but in some very important areas of their lives, most people are looking for greater stability and assurance, for the restoration of standards and rules, and for more support as they care for their families and help their children to succeed.

In some areas, such desires imply more, not less, government. People may support public initiatives, despite well-founded skepticism about inefficient and wasteful government and about politicians who take care of themselves instead of the public. We are living in a period when people are increasingly demanding that government support their efforts, despite a political atmosphere so poisonous that it should doom anybody's interest in politics. Over the past two years, while the federal government was under assault and while national politicians were awash in special-interest money, overall confidence in government rose by 7 to 10 percentage points, depending on the level of government. Confidence was not very high, but still, 38 percent of national poll respondents report that government programs already help their families to achieve the American dream—up 7 points over 1995. More important, three-quarters of the public say that they would have increased confidence if the government had "programs that benefit all Americans rather than particular groups" (Council for Excellence in Government 1997; National Opinion Research Center 1997, pp. 2–5). The economic and family realities of late twentieth-century America, along with the conservative attacks on public supports that people value, seem to make people, however cautiously, more open to discussion of what government can positively do.

That is why, we suspect, voters today are much more inclined to support a progressive Democratic set of policy priorities than a conservative Republican agenda. In the Citizen Action national survey, respondents were presented with eleven policy ideas for each party and allowed to select the three that would be most important for their lives. The top three Democratic agenda items—protecting retirement security (45 percent), guaranteeing health care coverage (35 percent), and expanding support for education (33 percent)—scored as high or higher than any of the Republican policy priorities. The defense of retirement security—the defense of the golden years—is clearly the centerpiece of the Democratic agenda, because people understand a decent retirement as the final chapter of their own life stories.

Democrats also have an opportunity to champion bold initiatives on education. Although conservatives in both parties have responded to worries about schools with proposals for charter and independent schools, market vouchers, and increased school choice, the public expresses only a passing interest in such ideas, which score at the bottom of its priorities for education. People are much more interested in seeing higher national education standards. They want a greater national investment in modernizing school buildings and expanding young people's access to computers. They want to see preschool children get expanded access to Head Start programs and older children to have expanded access to college loans (Citizen Action 1997). The public is prepared to support leaders and a party that will use government to universalize educational opportunity, making it possible for all families to do better in a period of accelerating change.

Democrats also have an affirmative opportunity to, once again, champion universal health care coverage. The idea is nearly an orphan these days, but ordinary people refuse to let it go. They understand all too well that families are a first casualty in the battle for business competitiveness. Family health coverage and pensions cannot be counted upon in today's workplace. That is why people say their biggest economic worry is being unable to afford necessary health care when a family member gets sick (Greenberg 1996d). Elites and political leaders have responded to these concerns cautiously, but the electorate wants something bigger and more dependable. Three-quarters of the electorate want our country to require that employers provide health insurance to their employees and families (Greenberg 1997).

Finally, the public is looking for the renewal of civic order so that families and parents can find the space to raise children safely and teach them the right skills and values needed to succeed in life. That is why voters responded to Clinton's rhetorical support for parenting and are now strongly supportive of tough Democratic initiatives on crime. A Democratic focus on punishing and preventing crime brings increased Democratic support in the South, among older non-college-educated voters, and among African-Americans (Greenberg 1997). Popular progressives should realize that this focus should be part of the larger family-centered narrative in which Democrats can emerge as the primary champions of social and family support.

The New Majority

By focusing single-mindedly on the bold project of helping working and middle-class families to improve their lives in this new, uncertain period, a popularly oriented progressive Democratic Party can come to dominate America's politics again. Right now, with public airwaves dominated by financial controversies, partisan skirmishes, and even bipartisan deal making, that hardly seems likely. With the Republicans ensconced on Capitol Hill and the Democrats in the White House, no party seems poised to achieve ascendancy. Yet, as the authors of this book make clear, the Democrats have an opportunity to dominate our era if they take up the historic project proposed here.

With the weight of old issues lifted from their backs, Democrats are able to stand and speak forcefully about this new period and to champion the interests of the ordinary citizen. With working people confronting growing pressures on their economic and family lives, they are newly attentive to the Democrats who would not leave them to face alone all the uncertainties of this changing world. Republicans, on the other hand, are clearly intent on destroying the critical social supports provided by government. They would champion aloneness as a virtue, at a time when people are looking to community and government to buttress their individual efforts. In any case, working people are less and less attentive to the Republicans, who, unlike the Democrats, are still hopelessly weighed down and divided by their old issues.

Though there is broad interest in the Democrats' family-centered narrative and broad support for bold Democratic initiatives on education, health care, and civic order, we should not underestimate the enormous political challenge of bringing together the diverse elements of a popularly oriented progressive coalition. African-Americans, for example, are experiencing the downside of global and competitive economic changes in especially severe ways, even as the country loses interest in affirmative action and targeted welfare programs. Black discontent is on the rise, as is black resentment toward Latino immigration, the public schools, and other institutions central to progressive politics. The Democratic Party will have to find ways to affirm its inclusiveness and to break down discriminatory barriers, even as it embarks on a new course. Similarly, Democrats will have to build support among union members and industrial workers, even as Democrats give increasing priority to a family-centered agenda. There will be no new Democratic majority without the enthusiastic support of union households across America, and they are looking for a fairer trade regime and greater corporate accountability. A popular progressive politics will have to expose and fight policies and groups that would enrich the privileged while increasing the uncertainty and odds facing working families.

These critical groups will be won over to the primacy of a program of support for all families because, ultimately, it has a universalizing quality that makes coalition building both possible and promising. African-Americans are the voters most supportive of a strong governmental role, yet moderate and conservative Democrats—mostly non-college-educated, older people and women—are the ones most protective of government retirement programs and most supportive of universal health insurance (Greenberg 1996d; Greenberg 1997). More than others, members of union households and many blue-collar men have grown resentful of corporations that compete globally at the expense of their own workers, yet these voters also strongly favor expanded support for the family, from education to retirement. Blue-collar white men, married women, and southern white voters tended to feel that the Democrats had abandoned them on social issues (as such issues were defined) back in the 1970s and 1980s. But today these same groups are listening to a family-centered story about fighting crime, protecting retirement security, expanding health care, and reinforcing parental authority and family integrity. This is very similar to the family-centered story about what government should do that has such a strong following in the black community.

From the 1960s through the 1980s, the Democratic coalition was built from the top among the best-educated and those most committed to expanding individual rights, and it was built from the bottom among those with the lowest incomes and disadvantaged minority voters who faced widespread discrimination. That pattern of support for Democrats reflected the historic and difficult tasks that the Democratic Party sought to complete on behalf of the country. The new popular progressive majority will be built broadly among working middle-class families, shaped by the new task of helping people of ordinary luck to achieve a better life in a world of unimagined changes and of growing economic and family pressures. Democrats should expect to build up strong majorities with all families earning under $50,000 per year and with all those struggling to succeed without benefit of a four-year college degree—huge groups that together make up perhaps two-thirds of the country's voting population. That emerging pattern of support and the new task should establish the character of this popular progressive party.

At the same time, Democrats will remain the overwhelming choice of single women, college-educated women, African-Americans, and union members, who will want to support an inclusive party committed to creating affirmative opportunity and helping families. With wages falling and anti-immigrant sentiment rising, Latino voters may also begin to find their home here. Young voters and retirees as well as Roman Catholics may be ready to give consistent support to a Democratic Party respectful of family and committed to defending government's unique role in providing social supports in education and health care.

Finally, if Democrats devote themselves to the historic project of securing the integrity of the family in this period of economic and civic decay, then Democrats will earn the chance to compete for the votes of married women and voters across the South, particularly southern white women. The new majority, then, will start with a newly competitive South, gain speed in a more than competitive Midwest, and charge ahead in the growing Democratic strongholds on the East and West Coasts.

In the short term, we may witness none of this. The Republicans, who are virtually silent about their antigovernment agenda but still able to exploit the perquisites of incumbency and the vast financial resources of the business community, may be able to maintain their small majorities in the Congress. The diminished, bipartisan agenda of the White House and endless stories about scandal may leave the Democrats diminished as well. But recognition of the sheer scale of the changes in the economy and in the lives of families will not long be suppressed. Nor will our politics long be able to ignore the fundamental question posed by these changes: How do citizens of ordinary luck prosper in this new era? If a popular progressive Democratic Party devotes itself to answering and addressing that question, it will build a new majority in the country.

References

Adams, Paul, and Gary L. Dominick. 1995. "The Old, the Young, and the Welfare State." *Generations* 19(3): 38–42.

Addams, Jane. 1907. *Democracy and Social Ethics*. New York: Macmillan.

Advisory Commission on Intergovernmental Relations. 1986. *The Transformation in American Politics: Implications for Federalism*.

Aldrich, John H. 1995. *Why Parties? The Origin and Transformation of Party Politics in America*. Chicago: University of Chicago Press.

Amenta, Edwin, Bruce G. Carruthers, and Yvonne Zylan. 1992. "A Hero for the Aged? The Townsend Movement, the Political Mediation Model, and U.S. Old-Age Policy, 1934–1950." *American Journal of Sociology* 98 (September): 308–39.

Archer, J. Clark. 1988. "Macrogeographical Versus Microgeographical Cleavages in American Presidential Elections, 1940–1984." *Political Geography Quarterly* 7:111–25.

Arnesen, Eric. 1994. "'Like Banquo's Ghost, I Will Not Down': The Race Question and the American Railroad Brotherhoods, 1889–1920." *American Historical Review* 99:1601–33.

Balz, Dan, and Ronald Brownstein. 1996. *Storming the Gates: Protest Politics and the Republican Renewal*. Boston: Little, Brown.

Bellah, Robert N., Richard Madsen, William Sullivan, Ann Swidler, and Steven Tipton. 1991. *The Good Society*. New York: Knopf.

Bennett, William J. 1995. "Reflections on the Moynihan Report Thirty Years Later." *American Enterprise* 6 (January–February).

Bernstein, Michael A. 1987. *The Great Depression: Delayed Recovery and Economic Change in America, 1929–1939*. Cambridge: Cambridge University Press.

Bibby, John. 1994. "State-Party Organization: Coping and Adapting." In *The Parties Respond: Changes in American Parties and Campaigns*, ed. L. Sandy Maisel. Boulder, Colo.: Westview Press.

Blank, Rebecca M. 1997. *It Takes a Nation: A New Agenda for Fighting Poverty*. Princeton: Princeton University Press.

Bloch, Farrell. 1994. *Antidiscrimination Law and Minority Employment: Recruitment Practices and Regulatory Constraints*. Chicago: University of Chicago Press.

Bobo, Lawrence, and James R. Kluegel. 1993. "Opposition to Race Targeting: Self-Interest, Stratification Ideology, or Racial Attitudes?" *American Sociological Review* 58:443–64.

Bobo, Lawrence, and Ryan A. Smith. 1994. "Antipoverty Politics, Affirmative Action, and Racial Attitudes." Pp. 365–95 in *Confronting Poverty: Prescriptions for Change,* ed. Sheldon H. Danziger, Gary D. Sandefur, and Daniel H. Weinberg. Cambridge: Harvard University Press.

Boone, Richard. 1996. "The New Right and a Progressive Response." Paper prepared for the Albert A. List Foundation. Washington, D.C.: Communications Consortium, December.

Borosage, Robert, and Ruy Teixeira. 1996. "The Politics of Money." *The Nation,* October 21, p. 21.

Bradley, Bill. 1995. Address to the National Press Club, Washington, D.C., February 9.

Brandeis, Louis D. 1915. "Testimony Before the United States Commission on Industrial Relations," reprinted in *The Curse of Bigness: Miscellaneous Papers of Louis D. Brandeis,* ed. Osmond K. Fraenkel. New York: Viking Press, 1935.

Brimelow, Peter. 1995. *Alien Nation.* New York: Random House.

Brinkley, Alan. 1993. "Liberals and Public Investment: Recovering a Lost Legacy." *American Prospect,* pp. 81–86.

———. 1995. *The End of Reform: New Deal Liberalism in Recession and War.* New York: Knopf.

Brodie, Mollyann. 1995. The Four Americas: Government and Social Policy Through the Eyes of America's Multiracial and Multiethnic Society: A Report of the *Washington Post*-Kaiser Foundation–Harvard Survey Project.

Bronfenbrenner, Urie, Peter McClelland, Elaine Wethington, Phyllis Moen, and Stephen J. Ceci. 1996. *The State of Americans: This Generation and the Next.* New York: Free Press.

Buchanan, Constance H. 1996. "The Religious Roots of Civic Engagement: Lessons from the Nineteenth-Century Women's Movement." Paper presented at the Social Science History Association, October 12.

Burnham, Walter Dean. 1996. "Realignment Lives: The 1994 Earthquake and Its Implications." In *The Clinton Presidency: First Appraisals,* ed. Colin Campbell and Bert A. Rockman. Chatham, N.J.: Chatham House.

Butler, Stuart, and Peter Germanis. 1983. "Achieving Leninist Strategy." *Cato Journal* 3 (fall): 547–61.

Califano, Joseph A., Jr. 1988. "Tough Talk for Democrats." *New York Times Magazine,* January 8.

Campaign for America's Future. 1996. "Taking Back Our Future: It Is Time to Make America Work for Working Americans." Washington, D.C.: Campaign for America's Future, July.

Card, David. 1996. Immigration Inflows, Native Outflows, and the Local Labor Market Impacts of Higher Immigration. Working Paper no. 368, Industrial Relations Section, Princeton University.

Carmines, Edward G., and Harold W. Stanley. 1990. "Ideological Realignment in the Contemporary South: Where Have All the Conservatives Gone?" In *The Disappearing South? Studies in Regional Change and Continuity,* ed. Robert P. Steed et al. Tuscaloosa: University of Alabama Press.

Carmines, Edward G., and James A. Stimson. 1989. *Issue Evolution: Race and the Transformation of American Politics.* Princeton: Princeton University Press.

Carter, Dan T. 1992. *George Wallace, Richard Nixon, and the Transformation of American Politics.* Charles Edmonson Historical Lectures. Waco, Tex.: Markham Press Fund.

———. 1996. *From George Wallace to Newt Gingrich: Race in the Conservative Counterrevolution, 1963–1994.* Baton Rouge: Louisiana State University Press.

Center for Policy Alternatives. 1996. "Women's Voices '96." National survey conducted by Lake Research, American Viewpoint, and Buffalo Qualitative Research, September.

Center for Responsive Politics. 1990. Open Secrets Report.

———. 1992. Open Secrets Report.

———. 1994. Open Secrets Report.

Chavez, Linda. 1996. "The Hispanic Political Tide." *New York Times,* November 18, p. A17.

Children's Defense Fund. 1994. *Wasting America's Future: The Children's Defense Fund Report on the Costs of Child Poverty.* Boston: Beacon Press.

Clark, Kenneth B. 1967. "The Present Dilemma of the Negro." Paper presented at the annual meeting of the Southern Regional Council, November 2, Atlanta.

Clinton, William Jefferson. 1993. "Remarks to the Convocation of the Church of God in Christ in Memphis," November 13.

———. 1994. "Address Before a Joint Session of Congress on the State of the Union," January 25.

———. 1996. "State of the Union Message," January.

CNN–*USA Today*–Gallup Poll. 1996. October 29–30.

Cohen, Cathy J., and Michael C. Dawson. 1993. "Neighborhood Politics and African-American Politics." *American Political Science Review* 87:286–302.

Commission on Family and Medical Leave. 1996. *A Workable Balance: Report to Congress on Family and Medical Leave Policies.* Washington, D.C.: U.S. Department of Labor, Women's Bureau.

Commonwealth Education Project. 1996. Money and Politics Project, Summary of Public Policy Questions, November.

Connecticut Money and Politics Project, and Common Cause Connecticut. 1994. *Governing Interest, Part II: An Examination of 1994 Gubernatorial Campaign Contributions.*

Converse, Philip E. 1966. "On the Possibility of Major Political Realignment in the South." In *Elections and the Political Order,* ed. Angus Campbell, Philip E. Converse, Warren E. Miller, and Donald E. Stokes. New York: John Wiley.

Cotter, Cornelius P., James L. Gibson, John R. Bibby, and Robert J. Huckshorn. 1984. *Party Organization in American Politics.* New York: Praeger.

Council for Excellence in Government. 1997. "Findings from a Research Project About Attitudes Toward Government." March.

Covotsos, Louis J. 1976. "Child Welfare and Social Progress: A History of the United States Children's Bureau, 1912–1935." Ph.D. diss., University of Chicago.

Croly, Herbert. 1965 [1909]. *The Promise of American Life.* Indianapolis, Ind.: Bobbs-Merrill.

Danziger, Sheldon, and Peter Gottschalk. 1995. *America Unequal.* Cambridge: Harvard University Press; New York: Russell Sage Foundation.

Dawson, Michael C. 1994a. *Behind the Mule: Race and Class in African-American Politics.* Princeton: Princeton University Press.

———. 1994b. "A Black Counterpublic? Economic Earthquakes, Racial Agenda(s), and Black Politics." *Public Culture* 71:195–223.

———. 1996. "Structure and Ideology: The Shaping of African-American Public Opinion." Unpublished manuscript.

———. Forthcoming. *Black Visions: The Roots of Contemporary African-American Political Ideologies.* Chicago: University of Chicago Press.

———. Forthcoming. "The Reagan-Bush Regime and Volatility in African-American Public Opinion." In *African-American Politics and Power,* ed. Hanes Walton, Jr. New York: Columbia University Press.

Democratic Congressional Campaign. 1996. "Families First Agenda: Fighting for America's Working Families."

Democratic Leadership Council. 1996. "The New Progressive Declaration: A Political Philosophy for the Information Age." Washington, D.C.: Progressive Foundation, July.

Derthick, Martha. 1979. *Policymaking for Social Security.* Washington, D.C.: Brookings Institution.

Dietz, Mary G. 1991. "Hannah Arendt and Feminist Politics." Pp. 232–52 in *Feminist Interpretations in Political Theory,* ed. Mary Lyndon Shanley and Carole Pateman. University Park: Pennsylvania State University Press.

Dionne, E. J. 1996. *They Only Look Dead: Why Progressives Will Dominate the Next Political Era*. New York: Simon and Schuster.

Drew, Elizabeth. 1996. *Showdown*. New York: Simon and Schuster.

Drummond, Ayres B., Jr. 1996. "The Expanding Hispanic Vote Shakes Republican Strongholds." *New York Times,* November 10, p. A1.

Edsall, Thomas Byrne, and Mary D. Edsall. 1991. *Chain Reaction: The Impact of Race, Rights, and Taxes on American Politics*. New York: W. W. Norton.

Ehrenhalt, Alan. 1991. *The United States of Ambition*. New York: Times Books.

EMILY's List. 1996. Post-election national survey. Washington, D.C.

Emirbayer, Mustafa. 1992. "The Shaping of a Virtuous Citizenry: Educational Reform in Massachusetts, 1830–1860." *Studies in American Political Development* 6 (fall): 391–419.

Erie, Steven. 1988. *Rainbow's End: Irish Americans and the Dilemmas of Urban Machine Politics, 1840–1985*. Berkeley: University of California Press.

Erlanger, Steven, and David E. Sanger. 1996. "The Clinton Record." *New York Times,* July 29.

Faux, Jeff. 1996. *The Party's Not Over: A New Vision for the Democrats*. New York: Basic Books.

Featherman, David L., and Robert M. Hauser. 1978. *Opportunity and Change*. New York: Academic Press.

Fishkin, James S. 1983. *Justice, Equal Opportunity, and the Family*. New Haven: Yale University Press.

Frank, Robert H., and Philip J. Cook. 1995. *The Winner-Take-All Society*. New York: Free Press.

Fraser, Nancy. 1989. "Rethinking the Public Sphere: A Contribution to the Critique of Actually Existing Democracy." Pp. 109–42 in *Habermas and the Public Sphere,* ed. Craig Calhoun. Cambridge: MIT Press.

Freeman, Richard B., and Lawrence F. Katz. 1994. "Rising Wage Inequality: The United States Versus Other Advanced Countries." In *Working Under Different Rules,* ed. Freeman. New York: Russell Sage Foundation.

Friedman, Milton. 1962. *Capitalism and Freedom*. Chicago: University of Chicago Press.

Friedman, Thomas L. 1994. "World's Big Economies Turn to the Jobs Issue." *New York Times,* March 14, pp. D1, D6.

From, Al. 1996. "Push Bipartisanship, Entitlement Reform," *USA Today,* November 7.

Galbraith, John Kenneth. 1958. *The Affluent Society*. Boston: Houghton Mifflin.

Galston, William A. 1997. "A Progressive Family Policy for the Twenty-First Century." Pp. 149–62 in *Building the Bridge,* ed. Will Marshall. Lanham, Md.: Rowman and Littlefield.

Ganz, Marshall. 1994. "Voters in the Cross-Hairs: How Technology and the Market Are Destroying Politics." *American Prospect* 16 (winter): 100–109.

Garbarino, James. 1995. *Raising Children in a Socially Toxic Environment*. San Francisco: Jossey-Bass.

Garraty, John A. 1986. *The Great Depression*. New York: Harcourt Brace Jovanovich.

Gephardt, Richard A. 1996. "The Families First Agenda: Toward a New Practical Politics." Remarks by House Democratic Leader Richard A. Gephardt at the National Press Club, Washington D.C., June 28.

Gerth, Jeff. 1996. "Business Gains with Democrats." *New York Times,* December 25, p. B7.

Gingrich, Newt. 1984. *Window of Opportunity: A Blueprint for the Future*. New York: Tom Doherty Associates and St. Martin's Press.

———. 1995. *To Renew America*. New York: HarperCollins.

Ginsberg, Benjamin, and Martin Shefter. 1990. *Politics by Other Means*. New York: Basic Books.

Glaser, James M. 1996. *Race, Campaign Politics, and the Realignment in the South*. New Haven: Yale University Press.

Glassman, James K. 1997. "Gingrich Must Go." *Washington Post,* March 25.

Goldwater, Barry. 1990 [1960]. *The Conscience of a Conservative*. Washington, D.C.: Regency Gateway.

Green, Donald P., and Eric Schickler. 1996. "The Grim Reaper, the Stork, and Partisan Change in the North and South, 1952–1994." Paper presented at the annual meeting of the Midwest Political Science Association.

Green, John C. 1995. "The Christian Right and the 1994 Elections: An Overview." In *God at the Grass Roots: The Christian Right in the 1994 Elections*. Lanham, Md.: Rowman and Littlefield.

Greenberg, Stanley B. 1996a. "The Clinton Generation? A Survey of Youth Voters." A post-election study of Minnesota voters. Washington, D.C.: Democratic Leadership Council.

———. 1996b. "The Economy Project." Washington, D.C.: Greenberg Research, January 16.

———. 1996c. *Middle-Class Dreams: The Politics and Power of the New American Majority*. Rev. ed. New Haven: Yale University Press.

———. 1996d. "The Popular Mandate of 1996." Post-election national survey for the Campaign for America's Future. Washington, D.C.: Greenberg Research, November 12.

———. 1996e. "Private Heroism and Public Purpose." *American Prospect* 28 (September–October): 34–40.

————. 1997. "Agenda for Progressives." National survey, Citizen Action. Washington, D.C.: Greenberg Research, February 12.

Greenstone, David J. 1977. *Labor in American Politics*. Chicago: University of Chicago Press.

Guthman, Edwin O., and C. Richard Allen, eds. 1993. *RFK: Collected Speeches*. New York: Viking.

Habermas, Jürgen. 1994. "Three Normative Models of Democracy." *Constellations* 28:1–10.

Harris Poll. 1996, September 26–30.

Heckman, James J. 1995. "Review of *The Bell Curve: Intelligence and Class Structure in American Life*." Paper presented at the Meritocracy and Equality Seminar Series, Chicago, February 2.

Heclo, Hugh. 1986. "The Political Foundations of Antipoverty Policy." Pp. 312–40 in *Fighting Poverty: What Works and What Doesn't,* ed. Sheldon H. Danziger and Daniel H. Weinberg. Cambridge: Harvard University Press.

————. Forthcoming. "Values Underpinnings of Poverty Programs for Children." *The Future of Children,* a periodical publication of the Center for the Future of Children, the David and Lucille Packard Foundation.

Heidenheimer, Arnold J. 1981. "Education and Social Security Entitlements in Europe and America." Pp. 269–304 in *The Development of Welfare States in Europe and America,* ed. Peter Flora and Arnold J. Heidenheimer. New Brunswick, N.J.: Transaction Books.

Henderson, Vivian. 1975. "Race, Economics, and Public Policy." *Crisis* 83 (fall): 50–55.

Herrnstein, Richard J., and Charles Murray. 1994. *The Bell Curve: Intelligence and Class Structure in American Life*. New York: Free Press.

Hewlett, Sylvia Ann. 1991. *When the Bough Breaks: The Cost of Neglecting Our Children*. New York: HarperCollins.

Hochschild, Jennifer L. 1995. *Facing Up to the American Dream: Race, Class, and the Soul of the Nation*. Princeton: Princeton University Press.

Hodgson, Godfrey. 1996. *The World Turned Right Side Up: A History of the Conservative Ascendancy in America*. Boston: Houghton Mifflin.

Hollinger, David A. 1993. "How Wide the Circle of the 'We': American Intellectuals and the Problem of the Ethnos Since World War II." *American Historical Review* 98:317–37.

Holtzman, Abraham. 1963. *The Townsend Movement: A Political Study*. New York: Bookman.

Hout, Michael. 1984. "Occupational Mobility of Black Men, 1962 to 1973." *American Sociological Review* 49:308–22.

Huckfeldt, Robert, and Carol Weitzel Kohfeld. 1989. *Race and the Decline of Class in American Politics*. Urbana: University of Illinois Press.

Jakes, Lara. 1996. "Campuses Cooling as Hotbeds of Activism." *Albany Times Union*, March 1, p. B1.

Jefferson, Thomas. 1787. *Notes on the State of Virginia*, reprinted in *Jefferson Writings*, ed. Merrill D. Peterson. New York: Library of America, 1984.

Johnson, Lyndon B. 1964. "Remarks Before the National Convention (August 27, 1964)." Pp. 1012–13 in *Public Papers of the Presidents of the United States: Lyndon B. Johnson, 1963–1964*, vol. 2. Washington, D.C.: U.S. Government Printing Office, 1965.

Judis, John B. 1992. "The Pressure Elite: Inside the Narrow World of Advocacy Group Politics," *American Prospect* 9 (spring): 15–29.

Juhn, Chinhui. 1996. *Relative Wage Trends, Women's Work, and Family Income*. Washington, D.C.: American Enterprise Institute Press.

Kahlenberg, Richard. 1995. "Class, Not Race." *New Republic* (April 3): 21–27.

Kamarck, Elaine Ciulla, and William A. Galston. 1993. "A Progressive Family Policy for the 1990s." Pp. 153–78 in *Mandate for Change*, ed. Will Marshall and Martin Schram. New York: Berkeley Books.

Katznelson, Ira, and Margaret Weir. 1985. *Schooling for All: Class, Race, and the Decline of the Democratic Ideal*. New York: Basic Books.

Kennedy, John F. 1961. "Inaugural Address," January 20. Pp. 1–3 in *Public Papers of the Presidents of the United States: John F. Kennedy, 1961*. Washington, D.C.: U.S. Government Printing Office, 1962.

———. 1962. "Commencement Address at Yale University." In *Public Papers of the Presidents of the United States: John F. Kennedy, 1962*. Washington, D.C.: U.S. Government Printing Office, 1963.

Kernell, Samuel. 1986. *Going Public: New Strategies of Presidential Leadership*. Washington, D.C.: Congressional Quarterly Press.

Key, V. O., Jr. 1949. *Southern Politics in State and Nation*. New York: Knopf.

Kinder, Donald R., and Lynn M. Sanders. 1987. "Pluralistic Foundation of American Opinion and Race." Paper presented at the annual meeting of the American Political Science Association, September 3–6, Chicago.

———. 1996. *Divided by Color: Racial Politics and Democratic Ideals*. Chicago: University of Chicago Press.

King, Martin Luther, Jr. 1967. *Where Do We Go from Here: Chaos or Community?* Boston: Beacon Hill Press.

Kingson, Eric R., Barbara A. Hirshorn, and John M. Cornman. 1986. *Ties That Bind: The Interdependence of Generations*. Washington, D.C.: Seven Locks Press.

Kluegel, James R., and Eliot R. Smith. 1986. *Beliefs About Inequality: Americans' Views of What Is and What Ought to Be.* New York: Aldine de Gruyter.

Kristol, William. 1996. Interview on C-SPAN, October 26.

Kuttner, Robert. 1980. *The Revolt of the Haves.* New York: Simon and Schuster.

———. 1987. *The Life of the Party: Democratic Prospects in 1988 and Beyond.* New York: Viking.

Ladd-Taylor, Molly. 1986. *Raising a Baby the Government Way: Mothers' Letters to the Children's Bureau, 1915–1932.* New Brunswick, N.J.: Rutgers University Press.

Lake Research and Deardourff–The Media Center. 1996. *Survey of Voter Attitudes Among Young Adults.* Washington, D.C.: Heinz Family Foundation.

Lake Research and the Tarrance Group. 1997. "Great Expectations: How American Voters View Children's Issues." Washington, D.C.: Coalition for America's Children.

Landy, Marc K., Mark J. Roberts, and Stephen R. Thomas. 1990. *The Environmental Protection Agency: Asking the Wrong Questions.* New York: Oxford University Press.

Lawton, Leora, Merrill Silverstein, and Vern L. Bengston. 1994. "Solidarity Between Generations in Families." In *Intergenerational Linkages,* ed. Vern L. Bengston and Robert A. Harootyan. New York: Springer.

Leca, Jean. 1992. "Questions on Citizenship." Pp. 17–32 in *Dimensions of Radical Democracy: Pluralism, Citizenship, Community,* ed. Chantal Mouffe. London: Verso.

Leff, Mark. 1973. "Consensus for Reform: The Mothers'-Pension Movement in the Progressive Era." *Social Service Review* 47(3) (September).

Leone, Richard C. 1997. "Why Boomers Don't Spell Bust." *American Prospect* 30 (January–February): 68–71.

Leuchtenburg, William, ed. 1961. *The New Nationalism.* Englewood Cliffs, N.J.: Prentice-Hall.

Levine, Susan. 1997. "One in Four U.S. Families Cares for Aging Relative." *Washington Post,* March 24.

Lewis, Earl. 1991. *In Their Own Interests: Race, Class, and Power in Twentieth-Century Norfolk, Virginia.* Berkeley: University of California Press.

Lind, Michael. 1996. *Up from Conservatism.* New York: Free Press.

Lipset, Seymour Martin, and William Schneider. 1978. "The Bakke Case: How Would It Be Decided at the Bar of Public Opinion?" *Public Opinion* (March–April): 38–48.

Loury, Glenn C. 1984. "On the Need for Moral Leadership in the Black Community." Paper presented at the University of Chicago, sponsored by the Center for the Study of Industrial Societies and the John M. Olin Center, Chicago.

———. 1995. *One by One from the Inside Out: Essays and Reviews on Race and Responsibility in America*. New York: Free Press.

Luker, Kristin. 1996. *Dubious Conception: The Politics of Teenage Pregnancy*. Cambridge: Harvard University Press.

MacFarguhar, Neil. 1996. "In New Jersey, Meeting the Voters Is a Luxury." *New York Times,* November 1, p. A1.

Maine Citizen Leadership Fund. 1995. "Elections or Auctions? Who Paid for Maine's Gubernatorial Election," Money and Politics Project, February.

Mansbridge, Jane J. 1986. *Why We Lost the ERA*. Chicago: University of Chicago Press.

Maraniss, David, and Michael Weisskopf. 1996. *Tell Newt to Shut Up*. New York: Free Press.

Marmor, Theodore R. 1973. *The Politics of Medicare*. Chicago: Aldine de Gruyter.

Marmor, Theodore R., Jerry L. Mashaw, and Philip Harvey. 1992. *America's Misunderstood Welfare State: Persistent Myths, Continuing Realities*. New York: Basic Books.

Marshall, Ray. 1996. "Work Organization." Pp. 101–23 in *Reclaiming Prosperity*, ed. Todd Schafer and Jeff Faux. Armonk, N.Y.: M. E. Sharpe.

Marshall, Will, ed. 1997. *Building the Bridge: Ten Big Ideas to Transform America*. Lanham, Md.: Rowman and Littlefield.

Massey, Douglas S. 1996. "Immigration, Policy, and Social Fragmentation in the United States." Paper presented at the Conference on Social Fragmentation in America, Princeton University, December 5.

Massey, Douglas S., and Kristin E. Espinosa. 1997. "What's Driving Mexico–U.S. Migration? A Theoretical, Empirical, and Policy Analysis." *American Journal of Sociology* 102:939–99.

Matthews, Donald R., and James W. Prothro. 1964. "Southern Images of Political Parties: An Analysis of White and Negro Attitudes." In *The American South in the 1960s,* ed. Avery Leiserson. New York: Praeger.

Mauro, Frank. 1995. "The Production and Use of Fiscal Analysis by Non-Governmental Organizations in the American States: The Case of New York's Fiscal Policy Institute and the Distributional Impact of Governor George Pataki's Tax Reduction Plan." New York: Fiscal Policy Institute.

Mayhew, David. 1986. *Placing Parties in American Politics: Organization, Electoral Settings, and Government Activity in the Twentieth Century*. Princeton: Princeton University Press.

McClure, Kirstie. 1992. "On the Subject of Rights: Pluralism, Plurality, and Political Identity." Pp. 108–27 in *Dimensions of Radical Democracy: Pluralism, Citizenship, Community,* ed. Chantal Mouffe. London: Verso.

McConnell, Stuart Charles. 1992. *Glorious Contentment: The Grand Army of the Republic, 1865–1900*. Baltimore: Johns Hopkins University Press.

MCI. 1996. "NetVote '96." Washington, D.C.

McIntire, James L. 1996. "The Federal Fiscal Revolution: Federal Budget Cuts and Their Impact on Washington State." Seattle: Fiscal Policy Center, September.

———. n.d. "The Balanced Budget Amendment: Impacts for States with Fiscal Constraints." Paper prepared for the Association of Public Policy Analysis and Management.

McLanahan, Sara, and Gary Sandefur. 1994. *Growing Up with a Single Parent: What Hurts, What Helps*. Cambridge: Harvard University Press.

Mellman Group. 1996. Poll Conducted for the Center for Responsive Politics, Washington, D.C., August 18–22.

Meyerson, Harold. 1997. "Dead Center." *American Prospect* 30 (January–February): 60–67.

Milbank, Dana. 1996. *Wall Street Journal,* November 22, 1996.

Miller, Warren E. 1991. "Party Identification, Realignment, and Party Voting: Back to the Basics." *American Political Science Review* 85:557–68.

Miller, Warren E., Donald R. Kinder, Steven J. Rosenstone, and the National Election Studies. 1993. *American National Election Study, 1992: Pre- and Post-Election Survey* (CPS Early Release Version, Computer File). Distributed by Inter-Varsity Consortium for Political and Social Research, Ann Arbor, Mich.

Mishel, Lawrence, Jared Bernstein, and John Schmitt. 1997. *The State of Working America, 1996–1997*. Armonk, N.Y.: M. E. Sharpe; Washington, D.C.: Economic Policy Institute.

Morehouse, Sarah McCally. 1980. "The Effect of Preprimary Endorsements on State Party Strength." Paper presented at the annual meeting of the American Political Science Association, August 28–31, Washington, D.C.

Morris, Charles R. 1996. *The AARP*. New York: Times Books.

Mosch, Theodore R. 1975. *The GI Bill: A Breakthrough in Educational and Social Policy in the United States*. Hicksville, N.Y.: Exposition Press.

Mouffe, Chantal. 1992a. "Democratic Citizenship and the Political Community." Pp. 225–39 in *Dimensions of Radical Democracy: Pluralism, Citizenship, Community,* ed. Mouffe. London: Verso.

———. 1992b. "Preface: Democratic Politics Today." Pp. 1–14 in *Dimensions of Radical Democracy: Pluralism, Citizenship, Community,* ed. Mouffe. London: Verso.

National Opinion Research Center. 1997. "Series on Confidence in Leaders of National Institutions." *Public Perspective* (February–March).

Neal, Derek A., and William R. Johnson. 1995. "The Role of Pre-Market Factors in Black-White Wage Differences." Paper presented at the Meritocracy and Equality Seminar Series, January 19, Chicago.

New York Times Poll. 1996. *New York Times,* March 6.

Oliver, Melvin, and Tom Shapiro. 1995. *Black Wealth/White Wealth: A New Perspective on Racial Inequality.* New York: Routledge.

Olson, Keith W. 1974. *The GI Bill, the Veterans, and the Colleges.* Lexington: University Press of Kentucky.

Page, Benjamin I., and Robert Y. Shapiro. 1992. *The Rational Public: Fifty Years of Trends in Americans' Policy Preferences.* Chicago: University of Chicago Press.

Paget, Karen M. 1990. "Citizen Organizing: Many Movements, No Majority." *American Prospect* 2 (summer): 115–28.

———. 1996. "The Balanced Budget Trap." *American Prospect* (November–December): 21–29.

———. 1997. "The State Fiscal Analysis Initiative." Washington, D.C.: Center on Budget and Policy Priorities.

Pateman, Carole. 1988. *The Sexual Contract.* Stanford: Stanford University Press.

Patterson, James T. 1981. *America's Struggle Against Poverty, 1900–1980.* Cambridge: Harvard University Press.

Pencak, William. 1989. *For God and Country: The American Legion, 1919–1941.* Boston: Northeastern University Press.

Penn-Schoen Associates. 1996. "What Families Really Value: The Action Agenda of America's Parents." New York: National Parenting Association.

Peterson, Peter G. 1993. *Facing Up: How to Rescue the Economy from Crushing Debt and Restore the American Dream.* New York: Simon and Schuster.

Phillips, Kevin. 1969. *The Emerging Republican Majority.* New Rochelle, N.Y.: Arlington House.

———. 1990. *The Politics of Rich and Poor.* New York: Random House.

———. 1993. *Boiling Point.* New York: Random House.

"Poll." 1996. *Maine Telegram,* September 29, p. 1.

Polsby, Nelson. 1983. *Consequences of Party Reform.* New York: Oxford University Press.

"Portrait of the Electorate." 1996. *New York Times,* November 10, p. 28.

Przeworski, Adam, and John Sprague. 1986. *Paper Stones: A History of Electoral Socialism.* Chicago: University of Chicago Press.

Putnam, Robert D. 1995. "Bowling Alone: America's Declining Social Capital." *Journal of Democracy* 6:65–79.

————. 1996. "The Strange Disappearance of Civic America." *American Prospect* 24 (winter): 34–48.

Rakove, Milton. 1979. *We Don't Want Nobody Nobody Sent: An Oral History of the Daley Years*. Bloomington: Indiana University Press.

Reich, Robert B. 1991. *The Work of Nations*. New York: Knopf.

————. 1997. "Rebuilding America's Broken Social Compact." *Boston Globe*, January 19, p. E7.

Reichley, James A. 1992. *The Life of the Parties: A History of American Political Parties*. New York: Macmillan.

Rich, Frank. 1995. "The L.A. Schock Treatment." *New York Times*, October 4, p. A21.

Riemer, David R. 1996. "Welfare Recipients Need Wages, Not Workfare." *New York Times*, December 30, p. A15.

Rorty, Richard. 1991. "On Ethnocentrism." In Rorty, *Objectivity, Relativism, and Truth: Philosophical Papers*, vol. 1. Cambridge: Cambridge University Press.

Rosenbaum, David E. 1996. "In Political Money Game, the Year of the Big Loopholes." *New York Times*, December 26, p. D9.

Rosenstone, Steven J., Warren E. Miller, Donald R. Kinder, and the National Election Studies. 1995. *American National Election Study, 1994: Post-Election Survey*. Ann Arbor, Mich.: Center for Political Studies.

Ross, Davis R. B. 1969. *Preparing for Ulysses: Politics and Veterans During World War II*. New York: Columbia University Press.

Ross, Jean. 1996a. "Balanced Budget Would Open Pandora's Box." *Los Angeles Times*, December 11.

————. 1996b. "What Would Proposition 218 Mean for California?" *Budget Brief*. Sacramento: California Budget Project.

Rozell, Mark J., and Clyde Wilcox. 1996. "Second Coming: The Strategies of the New Christian Right." *Political Science Quarterly* 111(2) (summer).

Rubin, Lillian B. 1994. *Families on the Fault Line*. New York: HarperCollins.

Samuelson, Robert J. 1995. *The Good Life and Its Discontents: The American Dream in the Age of Entitlement, 1945–1995*. New York: Times Books.

Sandel, Michael J. 1996. *Democracy's Discontent: America in Search of a Public Philosophy*. Cambridge: Belknap Press of Harvard University Press.

Sanders, Lynn M. 1996. "Race and the Perception of Economic Facts." Paper presented at the annual meeting of the American Political Science Association, August, San Francisco.

Sassen, Saskia. 1988. *The Mobility of Labor and Capital: A Study in International Investment and Labor Flow*. New York: Cambridge University Press.

Schuman, Howard, Charlotte Steeh, and Lawrence Bobo. 1985. *Racial Attitudes in America: Trends and Interpretations.* Cambridge: Harvard University Press.

Schwarz, Jordan A. 1993. *The New Dealers: Power Politics in the Age of Roosevelt.* New York: Knopf.

Sewell, William H., Jr. 1992. "A Theory of Structure: Duality, Agency, and Transformation." *American Journal of Sociology* 98:1–29.

Sexton, George E. 1995. *Work in American Prisons.* Washington, D.C.: U.S. Department of Justice, November.

Shapiro, Robert J. 1997. "A New Deal on Social Security." Pp. 39–55 in *Building the Bridge,* ed. Will Marshall. Lanham, Md.: Rowman and Littlefield.

Shellenbarger, Sue. 1996. "Family Leave Is Law, but Climate Is Poor for Actually Taking It." *Wall Street Journal,* October 30, p. B1.

Shklar, Judith N. 1991. *American Citizenship: The Quest for Inclusion.* Cambridge: Harvard University Press.

Skerry, Peter. 1997. "The Strange Politics of Affirmative Action." *Wilson Quarterly* (winter).

Skinner, Quentin. 1992. "On Justice, the Common Good, and the Priority of Liberty." Pp. 211–24 in *Dimensions of Radical Democracy: Pluralism, Citizenship, Community,* ed. Chantal Mouffe. London: Verso.

Skocpol, Theda. 1992. *Protecting Soldiers and Mothers: The Political Origins of Social Policy in the United States.* Cambridge: Belknap Press of Harvard University Press.

———. 1996a. *Boomerang: Clinton's Health Security Effort and the Turn Against Government in U.S. Politics.* New York: W. W. Norton.

———. 1996b. "Delivering for Young Families: The Resonance of the GI Bill." *American Prospect* 28 (September–October): 66–72.

———. 1996c. "The Tocqueville Problem: Civic Engagement in American Democracy." Presidential address at the twenty-first annual meeting of the Social Science History Association, October 12, New Orleans.

———. 1997a. "Civic Engagement in American Democracy." Testimony prepared for the National Commission on Civic Renewal, January 25, Washington, D.C.

———. 1997b. "Democrats at the Crossroads." *Mother Jones* (January–February): 54–59.

———. 1997c. "The GI Bill and U.S. Social Policy, Past and Future." *Social Philosophy and Policy* 14(2) (summer): 95–115.

Smith, Rogers M. 1988. "The 'American Creed' and American Identity: The Limits of Liberal Citizenship in the United States." *Western Political Quarterly* 41:225–51.

Smith, Tom W. 1990. "Liberal and Conservative Trends in the United States Since World War II." *Public Opinion Quarterly* 54:479–507.

Sniderman, Paul M., and Thomas Piazza. 1993. *The Scar of Race.* Cambridge: Harvard University Press.

Sniderman, Paul M., Philip E. Tetlock, and Edward G. Carmines, eds. 1993. *Prejudice, Politics, and the American Dilemma.* Stanford: Stanford University Press.

Stein, Herbert. 1969. *The Fiscal Revolution in America.* Chicago: University of Chicago Press.

Sum, Andrew M., Neal Fogg, and Robert Taggart. 1996. "The Economics of Despair." *American Prospect* 27 (July–August): 83–88.

Sweeney, John J. 1996. *America Needs a Raise: Fighting for Economic Security and Social Justice.* Boston: Houghton Mifflin.

Taylor, Charles. 1992. *Multiculturalism and "The Politics of Recognition."* Princeton: Princeton University Press.

Taylor, Paul. 1991. "Plight of Children Seen but Unheeded: Even Madison Avenue Has Trouble Selling Public on Aiding Poor Youth." *Washington Post,* July 15, p. A4.

Taylor, William. 1986. "Equal Protection and the Isolation of the Poor." *Yale Law Journal* 95:1700–1735.

Teixeira, Ruy. 1996. "Who Rejoined the Democrats? Understanding the 1996 Election Results." Briefing paper. Washington, D.C.: Economic Policy Institute, November.

Teixeira, Ruy A., and Joel Rogers. 1995. "Who Deserted the Democrats in 1994?" *American Prospect* (fall).

Tierney, John T. 1992. "Organized Interests and the Nation's Capitol." In *The Politics of Interests: Interest Groups Transformed.* Boulder, Colo.: Westview Press.

Turner, Bryan. 1992. "Outline of a Theory of Citizenship." Pp. 33–62 in *Dimensions of Radical Democracy: Pluralism, Citizenship, Community,* ed. Chantal Mouffe. London: Verso.

Tyack, David, and Elisabeth Hansot. 1982. *Managers of Virtue: Public School Leadership in America, 1820–1980.* New York: Basic Books.

U.S. Bureau of the Census. 1994. *Income and Poverty.* CD-ROM.

———. 1996a. "Population Projections of the United States by Age, Sex, Race, and Hispanic Origin, 1995 to 2025." Population Division, PPL–47.

———. 1996b. "Population Projections of the United States by Age, Sex, Race, and Hispanic Origin, 1995 to 2050." Current Population Reports, Series P25–1130.

U.S. Department of Justice. 1995. "Work in American Prisons: Joint Ventures with the Private Sector." *National Institute of Justice* (November).

U.S. Senate. 1967. *Hearings Before the Committee on Finance,* 90th Cong., 1st sess., *Congressional Record,* September, p. 1739.

Verba, Sidney, Kay Lehman Schlozman, and Henry E. Brady. 1995. *Voice and Equality: Civic Voluntarism in American Politics.* Cambridge: Harvard University Press.

Voter News Service. 1996. "Portrait of the Electorate." *New York Times,* November 10.

Walker, Jack, Jr. 1991. *Mobilizing Interest Groups in America: Patrons, Professions, and Social Movements.* Ann Arbor: University of Michigan Press.

Walzer, Michael. 1992. *What It Means to Be an American: Essays on the American Experience.* New York: Marsilio.

Wattenberg, Ben J. 1996a. "Supply-Side Demographics: Other Ways to Deal with an Alleged Entitlement Crisis as the Baby Boomer Blip Busts." Paper presented at the American Enterprise Institute Policy Conference, December 4.

———. 1996b. *Values Matter Most: How Republicans or Democrats or a Third Party Can Win and Renew the American Way of Life.* New York: Free Press.

Wattenberg, Martin P. 1991. "The Building of a Republican Regional Base in the South: The Elephant Crosses the Mason-Dixon Line." *Public Opinion Quarterly* 55:424–31.

Weine, Kenneth N. 1996. "Campaigns Without a Human Face." *Washington Post,* October 27, p. C1.

Weir, Margaret. 1992. *Politics and Jobs: The Boundaries of Employment Policy in the United States.* Princeton: Princeton University Press.

———. 1997. "Politics, Money, and Power in Community Development." In *Community Development: What Do We Know, What Do We Need to Know?* ed. William Dickens and Ronald Ferguson. Washington, D.C.: Brookings Institution.

Wessel, David. 1997. "Treasury Chief Rubin: Cultivating an Atypical Image." *Wall Street Journal,* March 28, p. A18.

White, William Allen. 1910. *The Old Order Changeth.* New York: Macmillan.

Will, George S. 1996. "Newt's Rhetoric Obscures Revolution." *San Francisco Chronicle,* October 3.

Wilson, William Julius. 1980. *The Declining Significance of Race: Blacks and Changing American Institutions.* 2nd ed. Chicago: University of Chicago Press.

———. 1987. *The Truly Disadvantaged: The Inner City, the Underclass, and Public Policy.* Chicago: University of Chicago Press.

———. 1992. "The Right Message." *New York Times,* March 17, op-ed page.

———. 1996. *When Work Disappears: The World of the New Urban Poor.* New York: Knopf.

Wolff, Edward N. 1995. *Top Heavy: A Study of the Increasing Inequality of Wealth in America.* New York: Twentieth Century Fund Press.

Contributors

Alan Brinkley teaches American history at Columbia University. He is the author of *Voices of Protest: Huey Long, Father Coughlin, and the Great Depression* (Knopf, 1982), *The End of Reform: New Deal Liberalism in Recession and War* (Knopf, 1995), and *Liberalism and Its Discontents: Essays on the History of Politics and the Politics of History* (Harvard University Press, 1997). He is a member of the editorial board of the *American Prospect* and a trustee of the Twentieth Century Fund.

Marc Caplan is executive director of Northeast Action. He has twenty-five years of experience as a leader in public interest organizations in Connecticut and the Northeast. He directed the Connecticut Citizen Action Group, the state's largest citizen organization, from 1974 to 1979. From 1980 to 1985, he was the founding director of the Legislative Education Action Program, which has become a model for statewide progressive coalition building, and since then he has helped to establish similar coalitions in New England and across the country. A nationally respected consultant on coalition building and progressive political activities, Caplan has also served as campaign manager for several candidates for statewide office.

Michael C. Dawson is associate professor of political science and director of the Center for the Study of Race, Politics, and Culture at the University of Chicago. He was co–principal investigator of the 1988 National Black Election Study, and he worked with Ronald Brown on the 1993–94 National Black Politics Study. His research focuses on African-American political behavior and public opinion, the political effects of urban poverty, and the development of African-American political ideologies. Dawson is the author of *Behind the Mule: Race and Class in African-American Politics* (Princeton University Press, 1994).

Jeff Faux is president of the Economic Policy Institute (EPI), a Washington, D.C., think tank that analyzes economic issues from the perspective of Americans who work for a living. He has written, lectured, and consulted widely on the political implications of economic trends. His most recent book is *The Party's Not Over: A New Vision for the Democrats* (Basic Books, 1996). Faux practiced economic policy with the U.S. Departments of State, Commerce, and Labor and the U.S. Office of Economic Opportunity. Faux has been a manager at a large financial corporation, an executive at a small business, and a member of six labor unions, and he has held local office in Maine.

Marshall Ganz teaches organizing at the Kennedy School of Government and is a doctoral student in sociology at Harvard University. For twenty-eight years he served as an organizer—in the civil rights movement, with the United Farm Workers, and with a wide variety of electoral, union, and issue organizations. He has researched the sources of decline in union organizing and published articles on the impact of the new electoral technology and motor voter law on voter participation, and he coordinates the Civic Engagement Project, a collaborative research project on voluntary associations in American public life led by Theda Skocpol.

Stanley B. Greenberg is chairman of Greenberg Quinlan Research, a national survey and polling firm. He was polling and senior adviser to Bill Clinton's 1992 presidential campaign and pollster to President Clinton and the Democratic National Committee. He has also served as polling adviser to Nelson Mandela's presidential campaign in 1994 and Tony Blair's Labour Party campaign in 1997. Greenberg is the author of *Middle Class Dreams: The Politics and Power of the New American Majority* (Yale University Press, 1996).

Ira Katznelson is Ruggles Professor of Political Science and History at Columbia University. His books include *City Trenches: Urban Politics and the Patterning of Class in the United States* (Pantheon Books, 1981), *Schooling for All: Race, Class, and the Decline of the Democratic Ideal,* co-authored with Margaret Weir (Basic Books, 1985), and *Liberalism's Crooked Circle: Letters to Adam Michnik* (Princeton University Press, 1996). He is completing a book on the origins and character of American liberalism in the past fifty years.

Theodore R. Marmor is professor of public policy and management at the Yale School of Management and professor of political science at Yale University. His broadest book, co-authored with Jerry Mashaw, is *America's Misunderstood Welfare State* (Basic Books, 1992). Their book critically assesses the claims that America's social welfare policies are "undesirable, ungovernable, and unaffordable" and tries to set the record straight about the actual workings and accomplishments of the nation's social welfare programs. More recently, he published *Understanding Health Care Reform* (Yale University Press, 1994) and is currently at work on a second revised edition of *The Politics of Medicare* (Aldine de Gruyter, 1973). He has testified before Congress and the Senate Budget Committee on Medicare and Social Security reform, and he is frequently engaged in television and radio debates and commentaries on these issues.

Jerry L. Mashaw is Sterling Professor of Law at the Yale School of Law and a professor at the Institute for Social and Policy Studies, Yale University. His most recent book, *Greed, Chaos, and Governance: Using Public Choice to Improve Public Law* (Yale University Press, 1997), provides critical assessment and important applications of the rapidly expanding field called public choice. A board member of the National Academy of Social Insurance, Mashaw headed the organization's review of Social Security's disability program. He has testified before Congress on this subject and, with Professor Marmor, often writes editorials on social welfare issues for the *Los Angeles Times* and other newspapers.

Karen M. Paget is a political scientist and a contributing editor to the *American Prospect;* a consultant to the Twentieth Century Fund's project on the balanced budget amendment and series editor of its ten state-based reports; a consultant to the State Fiscal Analysis Initiative, a program of the Ford, Annie E. Casey, and Charles Stewart Mott Foundations; and the author of a recent report, "Building Organizational Capacity for State Budget and Tax Analysis," published by the Center on Budget and Policy Priorities. Paget is also co-author of *Running as a Woman: Gender and Power in American Politics* (Free Press, 1994).

Miles S. Rapoport was elected Connecticut's secretary of the state in 1994 and is a member of the executive board of the National Association of Secretaries of State. As secretary of the state, he has pursued a vigorous agenda promoting democracy and citizen participation, issuing Connecticut's first *Report on the State of Democracy* in 1996 and fighting for campaign finance and electoral reforms. For ten years he was a member of the Connecticut House of Representatives, where he served as assistant majority leader and house chairman of the Government Administration and Elections Committee. Before that he worked as a community organizer for fifteen years, serving as executive director of the Connecticut Citizen Action Group, the state's largest citizen organization.

Michael J. Sandel is professor of government at Harvard University, where he teaches political philosophy. His most recent book is *Democracy's Discontent: America in Search of a Public Philosophy* (Harvard University Press, 1996), from which his contribution to this volume is drawn. His writings have appeared in the *Atlantic Monthly*, the *New York Times*, the *New York Review of Books*, and the *New Republic*, to which he is a contributing columnist.

Theda Skocpol is professor of government and sociology at Harvard University, where she also serves as chair of the Faculty of Arts and Sciences Committee on Public Service. Among her books are *States and Social Revolutions* (Cambridge University Press, 1979), winner of the 1979 C. Wright Mills Award and co-winner of the 1980 American Sociological Association Award for a Distinguished Contribution to

Scholarship, and *Protecting Soldiers and Mothers: The Political Origins of Social Policy in the United States* (Harvard University Press, 1992), winner of five awards, including the 1993 Woodrow Wilson Foundation Award of the American Political Science Association. Her most recent book is *Boomerang: Health Reform and the Turn Against Government* (W. W. Norton paperback, with a new afterword, 1997). Skocpol is now completing a book on working families and the future of U.S. social policy.

Paul Starr is professor of sociology at Princeton University and co-editor and co-founder of the *American Prospect*. He is the author of *The Social Transformation of American Medicine* (Basic Books, 1984), winner of the 1984 Pulitzer Prize for Non-fiction, the C. Wright Mills Award, and the Bancroft Prize in American History. He also founded the Electronic Policy Network, a new network of policy and advocacy organizations on the World Wide Web. He is currently working on a book about the politics of information.

Margaret Weir is a senior fellow at the Brookings Institution, and in 1998 she will become professor of sociology at the University of California at Berkeley. She has written widely on social policy in the United States and Europe. Among her books are *Politics and Jobs: The Boundaries of Employment Policy in the United States* (Princeton University Press, 1992) and *The Social Divide: Party Politics and Social Policy in the 1990s* (forthcoming). Weir is now at work on a book about the political isolation of cities in the United States.

William Julius Wilson is the Malcolm Wiener Professor of Social Policy at the John F. Kennedy School of Government at Harvard University. He is a MacArthur Prize Fellow and has been elected to the National Academy of Sciences, the American Academy of Arts and Sciences, the American Philosophical Society, and the National Academy of Education. Active in civic and public affairs, Wilson is the author of numerous publications, including *The Declining Significance of Race: Blacks and Changing American Institutions* (University of Chicago Press, 1980), *The Truly Disadvantaged: The Inner City, the Underclass, and Public Policy* (University of Chicago Press, 1987), and *When Work Disappears: The World of the New Urban Poor* (Knopf, 1996).

Index